The Ultimate Business Communication Book

David Cotton,
Martin Manser,
Di McLanachan and
Matt Avery

T0286573

Martin Manser is a professional reference book editor. His major management experience has been in managing people and projects, including leading a team of nearly 100 people on one of the few twentieth-century study bibles to be originated in the UK (*The Thematic Reference Bible*, Hodder & Stoughton, 1996). He has also led teams to manage the award-winning *Collins Bible Companion* (HarperCollins, 2009) and the best-selling *Macmillan Student's Dictionary* (Macmillan, 2nd edition, 1996). Since 2001 Martin has been a Language Trainer and Consultant with national and international companies and organizations, leading courses on business communications, report writing, project management and time management. www.martinmanser.co.uk

Di McLanachan is managing director of Learning Curves Personal Development Ltd. She is an international trainer, executive coach, a master practitioner of Neuro-linguistic Programming and author of the bestselling book *NLP for Business Excellence*. She has frequently been featured on both radio and television, and has been delivering training in customer care on a regular basis since 1993. www.learningcurves.co.uk

Matt Avery trained as an actor, and speech and drama practitioner, and has trained people in public speaking for all occasions, all over the world. Matt also lectures in motivational speaking.

David Cotton is an independent leadership and management trainer, with experience of working in four continents and more than 35 countries. His client portfolio reads like a 'Who's Who' of major organizations in local and national government and nearly every industry sector. He spent more than 20 years with two of the 'Big 4' professional service firms before setting up his own training consultancy. He has written 10 books, two of which won publishers' bestseller awards, scores of journal articles and a double award-winning e-learning package on electronic marketplaces. In that time, he has spent many thousands of hours in meetings and estimates that 75 per cent of that time was wasted. He has written this book to help you to spend your time more productively.

The Ultimate Business Communication Book

Communicate Better at Work, Master Business Writing, Perfect your Presentations

David Cotton,
Martin Manser,
Di McLanachan and
Matt Avery

First published in Great Britain by Teach Yourself in 2023
An imprint of John Murray Press
A division of Hodder & Stoughton Ltd,
An Hachette UK company

4

Copyright © David Cotton, Martin Manser, Di McLanachan and Matt Avery 2023

Based on original material from *Business Communication In a Week,*
Persuasion and Influence In a Week, *Public Speaking In a Week,*
Successful Meetings In a Week

A CIP catalogue record for this title is available from the British Library

Paperback ISBN 978 1 473 68909 1
eBook ISBN 978 1 473 68906 0

Typeset by KnowledgeWorks Global Ltd.

Printed and bound in Great Britain by Clays Ltd, Elcograf S.p.A.

John Murray Press policy is to use papers that are natural, renewable and recyclable
products and made from wood grown in sustainable forests. The logging and
manufacturing processes are expected to conform to the environmental regulations of
the country of origin.

John Murray Press
Carmelite House
50 Victoria Embankment
London EC4Y 0DZ

www.teachyourself.com

Contents

PART 1
Your Business Communication Masterclass

PART 1

Introduction

We live in an age when the number of ways in which we communicate in business is constantly increasing. Years ago, we simply had face-to-face communication, phone and letter. Now we also have more, including email, websites, blogs... and yet, if we are honest, alongside this increase in the ways in which we communicate has come a decrease in the level of effective communication.

How familiar are you with the following?

Working relationships that show low levels of trust
'There's too much information and I can't "see the wood for the trees"'
Colleagues who talk only in jargon that no one understands
The minutes of a meeting are unclear
PowerPoint presentations that have too many points but are vague in their core message

Unfortunately, the list could easily go on. We are all too aware of poor communication at all levels in business. What can we do? This Part of the book will offer some positive guidelines to help *you* communicate more effectively. You may not be able to change the way your company or organization works, but you can change the way in which *you* work.

CHAPTER 1

Know your aims

In this chapter we are going to look at:

- basic aims in communicating: if we know where we are going, we are more likely to arrive at our destination than if we wander aimlessly
- different ways in which people learn: one of the key themes of this Part is to make sure that our communication is focused not on ourselves but on the person we want to communicate with. If that is so, we need to make sure that our message is expressed in the way that is most appropriate for them
- various ways in which you can communicate: another of the key themes of this Part is that there is more to business communication than just typing an email and then pressing 'send'. We will therefore explore some of these different ways of communicating here
- some barriers in communication... and how we can overcome them.

The basics of communication

I often begin my workshops on communication with the
memory prompt **AIR**:

- **A**udience
- **I**ntention
- **R**esponse.

TIP *There is more to business communication than just typing
an email and then pressing 'send'.*

Audience

'Audience' means: know who you want to communicate with.
Here the focus is not on you, but on the person/people you
are trying to communicate with. This means the question you
should ask yourself is *not* so much 'What should I say/write?'
but 'What does my audience need to hear?' To answer that
question well, you need to think about who your audience is
and what their response to your communication is likely
to be.

For example, if you are writing a document, the person
who you are writing to should affect the way in which you
write. Are you writing to your boss or to someone who has
written to your company or organization with a complaint?
In each case, how you express what you are trying to say will
be different.

If you are emailing your boss, you may simply give him or her
the information that he or she has asked for:

Hi Robert,
Sales for 2012 were 10% up on 'Introduction to Project Management'.
We have sold just over 3,000 copies and we reprinted a further 1,000
copies of that title last month.
Harry

Your boss wants the information quickly, with no extras. If you are responding to a complaint, however, your tone will be different:

> Dear Mrs Brown,
>
> Thank you for taking the trouble to write to us to express your dissatisfaction with the service you recently received at one of our restaurants. I am very sorry that you found our service unsatisfactory.
>
> I have checked the details from your letter and it appears that the member of staff you dealt with on 3 October in Grantchester was a temporary worker. He was unfamiliar with our company policy on the high levels of service we require from all our staff.
>
> I have now taken the necessary steps to ensure that such a situation will not occur again.
>
> Thank you again for writing. Please be assured that we aim to offer our customers the highest possible level of service at all times.
>
> Yours sincerely,
>
> John Duckworth

Do you see the difference? The email to your boss is short and to the point. The letter responding to the complaint is expanded and also, crucially, the *tone* is much softer.

So you need to know who your audience is. When I am preparing a talk, I will often think of one or two people I know who will be in the audience, and I gauge how they are likely to receive what I am saying, their present level of understanding and the point I want them to reach by the end of my talk.

Intention

By 'intention' I mean the message: the key point(s) you want to put over. In the above examples, the key points to your boss are stated very briefly, and the intention in replying to the person who complained was to defuse their anger and say that you had looked into the matter.

You may face some difficulties in identifying what the intention/message of your communication is.

You may not know it yourself. If this is the case, *think*. To take an example, my website was recently down and I was without one, so it made me think, 'What is the purpose of my website? Do I want people simply to find out about me and my services or to buy books from me or to contact me with questions?' Think hard until you can identify your key messages definitely and precisely. We will explore more on this crucial area of thinking and the role of mind maps or pattern notes in Chapter 3.

Is your message clear? If it isn't clear to you, then it will hardly be clear to those you are trying to communicate with. On one of my courses I discovered that the key message of one document was in a 67-word sentence in brackets near the end of the document!

Even if you do know what your key message is, you may need to explain some background to that key message before you can get to it.

TIP *If your message isn't clear to you, then it will not be clear to those you are trying to communicate with.*

Introducing change

John was hired by Denton Manufacturing Company to introduce change. There was a culture of 'we've always done it this way – why do we need to change?' in the company, but its traditional outlook meant that it was being quickly overtaken by smaller, newer firms. He gathered his fellow directors and senior staff on an awayday. His first task was to enable his colleagues to see the weaknesses in their present way of working and to create a sense of dissatisfaction that would lead them to want to change. Because John identified his primary message clearly, he could focus on that as a successful first step in introducing change.

Response

What do you want the person you are communicating with to do with your communication? Sometimes we can be so preoccupied with working out all the details of what we are trying to say that we forget what we want our readers, for example, to do with the information we give them. You may be writing to them simply to inform the people you are writing to – but it is more likely that you want them to make some decision.

Is it crystal clear how they are to respond? What are the next steps you want them to take? For example, suppose you are writing a fundraising email. You need to include in clear terms which website your readers can donate money on, giving bank account codes as necessary, and how donors can gift-aid their contributions.

Different ways of learning

Every individual is different and, if we want to communicate effectively with a range of individuals, we would be wise to try to discover their preferred learning style. There are three main learning styles:

- **visual** – those who like to see information in the written word, pictures or diagrams to take it in well
- **auditory** – those who learn by listening to information
- **kinaesthetic** – those who learn by actively doing things, for example by role play.

It can be very useful for you to discern where your own personal preference lies. I am more visual and auditory rather than kinaesthetic. The aim here is to challenge your assumption that the way in which other people learn is the same as how you learn. You need this reminder that other people's learning styles will be different from yours. To be an effective communicator, you therefore need to be alert to the styles of those you want to communicate with.

You can discern others' styles from how they respond and you can then at least use words that are appropriate to their style, for example:

- **visual** – *see, look, picture, focus*
- **auditory** – *hear* ('I hear what you're saying'), *buzz, rings a bell*
- **kinaesthetic** – *feel, concrete, get to grips with, contact*.

Different methods of communication

You can use your knowledge of the different styles in which people learn to find the best way to communicate with them. To communicate most effectively, you should send your communication in the form that is most suited to your audience. We can therefore immediately see that email will not be useful for everyone in all circumstances. For auditory learners, a phone call may well be more effective; for kinaesthetic learners, a meeting that puts suggestions into action will help.

We can also distinguish some groups further. For example, among visual learners, some will respond more to words, others to pictures or diagrams. This has significance. To give two examples: (1) If I am preparing a PowerPoint presentation, I will not simply list headings in words but I will also work hard to find a picture that encapsulates the key idea visually. This can be very time-consuming, but I am sure it is worth it. (An example: a picture of buttresses supporting a cathedral may help to communicate the concepts of strengthening and confirming.) (2) When preparing a map, don't only give directions ('After five miles on the A21, at the roundabout, turn left...') but also draw a map with lines in a diagram.

The two approaches (words and picture/diagram) in examples 1 and 2 reflect the fact that one approach (words or picture/diagram) will appeal to some but not to others. By combining two approaches I hope to reach many more people than I would have done if I had followed only one approach.

Making an informal contract

Peter had to commission several university lecturers to write a series of books for the publishing company he worked for.

As he began to email prospective authors, Peter quickly realized that some responded to emails but many did not. Later, as he met up with those he was going to commission and began to work more closely with them, he deliberately made an informal contract with them. He asked them which communication method (e.g. email or phone) they preferred and, especially if by phone, what days/times were best for them to be contacted. Having this knowledge meant that his frustration at their lack of response was significantly less than if he did not have such information and so his communication with his writers was more effective.

Email is very useful for communicating information, quick checks and seeking quick agreement. It is weak, however, in building good business relationships.

Phone calls are useful for discussions, because you can discern immediately whether or not someone has understood what you are trying to say. Unless you have a way of screening phone calls, however, they can interrupt your work. So it can be useful (1) to arrange in advance a convenient time to call or (2) to ask at the beginning of a call 'Is now a convenient time to talk?'

Be aware that your mood will often be detected by the person you are speaking to on the phone. Without being able to see the person you are speaking to, we tend to build up a mental picture of them. As far as you can, convey enthusiasm as you talk. One way that is often recommended is to smile as you speak.

Before making an important call, jot down the points you want to discuss. How often do we finish a call and then realize that we have not discussed something important?

It can also be useful to signal the scope of the call at the beginning ('Ray, I think there are three areas we need to discuss today'). Unless the matters are sensitive, aim to discuss the most important matter first, in case either party cannot continue talking and has to finish the call quickly. If one of the matters is sensitive, then you can ease yourself into tackling it by discussing less significant matters first and then proceeding to the more delicate one.

If you are trying to persuade a colleague to do something, before you begin the call list to yourself the possible objections they might raise and deal with each one. In this way, you will be prepared for what they will say.

Don't be afraid of summarizing where you have got to at a certain point in a phone call ('OK, so we've agreed quantities and delivery dates, now let's move on to prices').

Face-to-face meetings are more expensive but are indispensable in business. As we email and phone colleagues around the world we probably build up a mental picture of their appearance and manner – and when, perhaps much later, we meet them our perceptions may well be proved wrong. When two people meet face to face in such circumstances, one may well say to the other, 'It is good to put a face to a name.'

Face-to-face meetings also often provide opportunities for more informal relationship building; during a mid-morning break or lunch we can discuss our colleague's family or holiday plans, for example.

Barriers in communication

We conclude this chapter by looking at barriers to effective communication.

What is effective communication? I often present it like this:

This means that A wants to communicate content A (whatever it is), represented by a triangle. What we want B to receive and understand is a triangle, not a square, circle or a partially formed triangle.

So what prevents effective communication from taking place? What are some of the barriers to good communication and how can they be resolved?

- Your presentation is poorly focused, unclear and vague. Resolve by preparing well and being clear and precise.
- You give too little information. Resolve by getting to know your audience better and knowing the amount of information they need to make a decision.
- You give too much unnecessary detail and too much information. Resolve by getting to know your audience better and knowing the amount of information they need to make a decision.
- You use incomprehensible words and phrases. Every business has its own jargon and set of abbreviations. Resolve by using only those terms that you know your audience can understand.
- The person you are trying to communicate with is significantly less able to communicate in your language. Resolve by being far simpler in what you are trying to communicate.
- Inaccurate information undermines the credibility of the rest of what you want to communicate. Resolve by checking your facts first.
- You have negative feelings towards certain individuals; for example, someone may be perceived as too abrupt and insensitive. We devote two chapters (2 and 6) to dealing with this.
- You lack trust in a person: their words may sound right but you don't believe them. Credibility is gained and kept not only by someone's knowledge and expertise but also by the relationship you have with that person.
- The politics and/or processes of your company or organization may hinder good communication. For example, I recently heard of an organization running a conference whose management released details of the speaker and other essential details *to their own staff* only three weeks before the conference was due to take place!

- Formal channels of communication in a business setting are unclear and colleagues rely on unofficial means of communication ('the grapevine') for information, which will include rumours rather than facts. Resolve by being more decisive and, probably, more open about communicating.
- The approach is badly timed. For example, asking for an immediate decision on an important matter that requires much thought should be done at a time that is appropriate. Resolve by finding out and planning what that appropriate time is.
- Your body language is in conflict with your message. For example, you may try to sound friendly but your awkward posture and lack of eye contact with the person you are speaking to express your attitude more fully.
- In meetings, you allow the discussion to wander. On this and other deficiencies in meetings, see Chapter 4.

Summary

In this chapter we have looked at knowing the basics of communication. In particular, it is essential that you are aware of AIR: (A) your audience, who you are trying to communicate with; (I) your intention/message, what you are trying to communicate; (R) the response you are trying to gain from the person you are communicating with.

In considering who our audience is, we considered the style in which they best learn. We distinguished *visual, auditory* and *kinaesthetic* styles and can use that as a basis to determine the most appropriate way in which we can communicate with them.

1 Think of a *good* piece of communication that you have been involved in.

   A Audience: who were you communicating with?
   I Intention: what was your message? What were you trying to say?
   R Response: what response did you receive?

Why was it successful? How do you know?

2 Think of a *bad* piece of communication that you have been involved in.

   A Audience: who were you communicating with?
   I Intention: what was your message?

What were you trying to say?

   R Response: what response did you receive?

Why was it not successful? How do you know?

Fact-check (answers at the back)

1. To stop and think about what exactly you are trying to communicate is:
   a) A luxury ❑
   b) A nice to have ❑
   c) Essential ❑
   d) A waste of time ❑

2. Effective communication needs:
   a) Spontaneity ❑
   b) No planning ❑
   c) Improvisation ❑
   d) Thought and planning ❑

3. Thinking about the basics of communication, the letters AIR stand for:
   a) Abbreviations, Image, Reputation ❑
   b) Activity, Information, Reflection ❑
   c) Audience, Intention, Response ❑
   d) Attachments, Internet, Receptivity ❑

4. Clarifying who you are communicating to is:
   a) Vital ❑
   b) A waste of time ❑
   c) Unnecessary ❑
   d) Quite important ❑

5. What you are trying to communicate should be:
   a) Vague ❑
   b) Clear ❑
   c) Confusing ❑
   d) Ambiguous ❑

6. You have forgotten to think about what response you want from the information in an email you are about to send. Should you:
   a) Press 'send', knowing they can email back if they want to pursue it? ❑
   b) Rewrite the email before you press 'send'? ❑
   c) Hope that the recipient will not notice? ❑
   d) Tell your boss about it tomorrow? ❑

7. The statement 'Everyone learns in the same way as I do' is:
   a) Always false ❑
   b) Always true ❑
   c) True sometimes ❑
   d) False sometimes ❑

8. Email is the best way to communicate in business. Is this:
   a) Always true? ❑
   b) Sometimes true? ❑
   c) False? ❑
   d) True? ❑

9. Telephoning business contacts is good:
   a) For socializing ❑
   b) For finding out about your competitors ❑
   c) For developing better working relationships ❑
   d) Only when your email is down ❑

10. How would you respond to someone who says: 'There are so many barriers to effective communication that I feel like giving up now'?

a) 'Yes – leave work early and don't come back.' ❏

b) 'Sorry, what did you say?' ❏

c) 'I'll think about it and come back to you later on it.' ❏

d) 'No – that's all the more reason to listen well, develop good business relationships and work hard.' ❏

CHAPTER 2

Listen carefully

When thinking about communication, we tend immediately to think of speaking or writing. However, before we can consider those, we need to remember that our communication is not isolated from its context. We speak or write in certain situations, and listening carefully has to come before speaking or writing to enable what we say or write to be effective.

So now we consider:

- the importance of listening
- how to listen more attentively, focusing on what the other person is saying
- steps to help us listen more effectively.

In contrast to speaking and writing, which are productive skills, listening is a receptive skill. We will also look at the other receptive skill, reading, and suggest ways in which we can improve our techniques for reading texts and statistics.

Listen more attentively

In this chapter we're going to focus on listening in face-to-face relationships. As a manager, you will be expected to do a lot of listening: to your boss as he/she directs your work; to colleagues as you talk about your work; in meetings as you discuss a range of subjects and make decisions, and as you interview staff, solve problems and use the phone.

Listening is hard work

There are many reasons why listening is difficult:

- We tend to focus on what we want to say; by contrast, listening demands that our concentration is on someone else as we follow the sequence of their thoughts.
- The person we are listening to may speak unclearly, too fast or repeat himself/herself.
- The person we are listening to may be a non-native speaker and so does not speak in standard English.
- We were probably not taught to listen. I vaguely remember school lessons in which we were taught to read, write and speak but I don't think I was ever taught to listen (or maybe I wasn't listening during those lessons!).

But listening is a really valuable skill. Have you ever felt really burdened by something and opened your heart to someone else? At the end you feel relieved and can say, 'Thank you for listening.'

TIP *Listening is far more than merely hearing.*

The importance of listening

Listening:

- focuses on the other person. Often when someone else is talking, we are focusing on thinking about what we are going to say as a reply.

- values the person you are listening to as an individual in their own right, so that you understand 'where they are coming from', why they are working or speaking as they are.
- helps you understand the point at which a person is. For example, if you are trying to sell something to customers, you want to build a good relationship with them. By listening, you will discern who is interested and who is not, so you can use your time more valuably and concentrate on the likelier potential clients.
- encourages you to ask the right questions. As you focus on the other person (not yourself), you will want to know more. We can distinguish:
    - *closed* questions: ones that can be answered by a straight 'yes' or 'no': 'Was the project late?' 'Yes.' 'Will you be able to give me the figures by 5.00 p.m.?' 'No.'
    - *open* questions: ones that get people talking. Open questions begin with why, how, who, when, where, what. 'Why do you think the project is running late?' 'Because we did not plan enough time for the extra work the customer now wants.' Most of the questions you should ask as a manager should be open questions.
- means that you do not listen only to the words a colleague is speaking: you can perceive their response to what you are saying by being sensitive to their body language and tone of voice.
- allows you to 'listen between the lines', to become aware of any underlying messages – your response could be, for example, 'So I guess what you're saying is that you need someone else to help you complete this task on time.'
- allows you to distinguish between facts and opinions. You will hear both, and you can discern what is objective information and what are the subjective thoughts on such information. You are then in a position to evaluate what has been said.
- enables you to gather information so that you can solve problems and make decisions more efficiently.
- builds trust between people: you show that you are genuinely interested in them. This forms the basis to help you work well with them. Listening often improves relationships. Rather than someone keeping angry feelings to himself/herself

and becoming increasingly tense, listening – and allowing someone to speak openly about his/her difficulties – provides a release for them.

- offers an opportunity to develop more all-round relationships. For example, if a colleague says, 'I'm off on holiday tomorrow,' you can either ignore that signal (but ignoring it is possibly slightly rude) or you can use that as a hint that they want to tell you more about themselves: 'Great, where are you going to?' 'Hong Kong.' You can then remember to ask them 'How was Hong Kong?' when you next see them.
- can resolve disagreements. If colleagues are in conflict with one another, listening to, and understanding, the opinions of the other side – not necessarily agreeing with them – is an important first step in settling a disagreement.
- helps you understand people better. As you listen carefully to someone, you will discover more about that person: what is important to them, how they think and what they are feeling.

Recently a stressed-out colleague told me, 'I want to go back to Australia.' That seemed to tell me a lot about her: a desire to be released from present tensions and return to a former, more relaxed environment. Having such knowledge helps you work better with them, even if you don't like them or agree with their opinions.

Susie was angry

Susie was angry. She worked late every evening to complete her tasks in the project but she felt her work was not appreciated or valued. It was only when a new colleague, Jan, started to work alongside her that something happened. Jan was concerned less about herself and her own work (which she did well) and more about her colleague; she cared enough to stop and listen to Susie. Susie was in tears as she poured out her heart to Jan, telling her about the real pressures she was working under. At the end of their conversation Susie told Jan, 'Thanks for listening. You're the first person I've been able to talk to about these things.'

Tips on better listening

Here are some ways to help you improve your listening skills:

- Be responsible. Realize that listening is an active skill and as such is hard work. Concentrate. For example, when I meet someone for the first time, I listen particularly attentively to catch their name. If I think I have heard it accurately, I will say it back to them, for instance 'Great to meet you, Nick!' If I didn't hear their name properly, I will say, 'I'm sorry, I didn't quite catch your name' or ask (if it is unusual to me and seems difficult to spell) 'Could you spell that for me, please?' (The first time I met the girl who became my wife I spelt her name correctly and was the first person she had met to do so!)
- Focus on the other person, not yourself. Don't be tempted to interrupt the other person while he/she is talking. Stop and really listen to what the other person is saying. Make eye contact with him/her. Be interested in him/her. Rephrase what he/she has said in your own way to help you clarify the meaning in your own mind; for example, 'So what you're really saying is that we should have put in place more effective monitoring controls.' Such a rephrasing process is called 'reflective listening'.
- Be willing to accept the reasoning and opinions of others as valid. Be willing to acknowledge that you may make false assumptions and may have prejudices.
- Don't be so critical that you make an immediate decision about someone based on their appearance, their style of presentation or your first impression of their personality.
- Discern the main points of what is being said. Speakers may or may not structure their argument well. Often, in informal talks or meetings it can be difficult to distinguish between facts, opinions, examples and ideas, but try to work out the speaker's main point(s).
- Do your best to remain attentive, even if the other person is not; don't become distracted.
- Write down in note form what a speaker is saying if you need to remember what he/she is saying and you might otherwise forget it. Making notes can help you concentrate

and avoid the sense that 'things go in one ear and out of the other'.

- Don't be afraid of silence. Silence is part of a conversation. It can be:
  - a junction: which way will a conversation turn?
  - a time to catch up and digest what has been said
  - an opportunity for the other person to express their thoughts further
  - an opportunity to reflect on what has been said.

Read more effectively

So far we have thought about listening. The other receptive skill in communication is reading. As a manager you will have a lot of material to read, for example emails, reports, websites, professional literature, contracts, technical manuals.

How do you read?

It can be helpful to stop and reflect on the way in which you read. Do you:

- pronounce the words in your head as you read?
- go over every word in every sentence?
- read through a piece of writing quickly to see which parts are important and then go back to those parts again?
- stop at words you don't understand and so make very slow progress through a long piece of writing?

Here are some guidelines to help you read more effectively:

- Decide on your aims in reading a particular text. Do you want to simply check a fact, gain an overall sense of a text, grasp a detailed knowledge of a subject (for example for a report or presentation you have to prepare) or evaluate the writer's arguments and views?
- Vary the speed at which you read a text, depending on the kind of text you are reading. Spend more time on important and/or difficult parts of the text and less time on less important and/or easier parts.

- Try not to mouth words as you read them. Mouthing words in this way not only slows you down but also means that you focus on the words rather than their meaning.
- Read more widely. (At school, we were constantly encouraged to do this, but I can't remember being told why. For the reason why reading is good, see the rest of this paragraph.) Don't just read material for work. Read a newspaper or magazine (hard copy or digital). It can help if you read material on a subject that interests you, as your motivation will be higher. Choose an article. Read it once for sense, and a second time to look at the language used. Recently, I did this with some students whose use of prepositions was weak, so in the article we were reading I pointed out: *the results* **of** *the survey*; **at** *fault*; *responsible* **for**. Almost unconsciously, you will pick up new words and phrases. Consult a dictionary (again, either as hard copy or online) for certain words that you do not know.
- For some important work, take notes of what you have read (see earlier for comments on taking notes in listening). Summarizing the author's argument in your own words can be a particularly useful tool.
- If you want to undertake a more detailed read of part of a text:
  - Find out which sections of the text you want to read. Consult the table of contents/list of chapters or index. Survey or scan the text to get a wider view of it. As you do that, you will begin to see the writer's key words and phrases.
  - Look out for the signposts: the introduction and conclusions; the words *firstly*, *secondly*; the beginning of paragraphs; such expressions as *on the one hand* and *on the other hand*. These guide you to see the structure of the text and can be helpful to your understanding.
  - Focus on the key words and, even more important, key phrases. There is less need to concentrate on such functional grammatical words as *the, of, has, be* and a greater need to concentrate on significant words.

- Reword the main points in your mind, on computer or on paper. Express the author's key points in your own way. This will help increase your understanding.
- Think about the author's argument: do you agree with him/her? Does the text make assumptions that you disagree with? Ask questions of the text and see whether they are answered. Engage your mind.
- At the end of reading, check whether you can recall the main points or, even better, if you can explain the main points to someone else. You could even review what you have read later to check that you still recall it.

The following text concerns the evaluation stage at the end of a project. The key words and phrases to concentrate on in reading are in bold:

Identify what you have achieved. Specifically, **list** what you have delivered:

- The project was built on a **solid foundation.**
- You received **strong support** from your **Project Sponsor.**
- You delivered the **desired output** in terms of the **products, services**, etc.
- **Outputs achieved** the agreed **quality standards.**
- The **actual expenditure** was **on track** compared with the **original budget.**
- **Return on investment** was **good**. The **benefits** that your company received from the project are **greater** than the **costs** incurred.
- The **actual time** taken compared well with the **original schedule:** you delivered the outcomes **on time.**
- **Robust control procedures** were in place to **track** and **monitor costs** and **schedules effectively.**
- **Customers/users** and other stakeholders were **satisfied** with the project's **outcomes.**

Effective reading... and good time management

As a manager, Sarah was methodical about her reading. She checked her emails only a few times a day, dealing with essential matters as they arose. She didn't bother to check the many junk emails she received but simply deleted them.

She allocated Friday mornings, when she knew she generally received fewer emails, to important, but not urgent, reading material that enabled her to do her job more effectively.

As she was preparing to relax for the weekend on Friday afternoons, she read non-urgent but useful material that kept her up to date with other trends in the industry which were not directly related to her job but developed her wider professional knowledge.

Of course, sometimes very urgent matters arose, which meant that she could not always keep to this methodical time allocation, so in such cases she was flexible. Generally, however, Sarah was able to allot sufficient resources of time to reading what was useful and essential and to manage her time well.

Reading statistics

Here are some guidelines on reading and understanding numbers presented in tables:

- Check the basics: the dates covered, the sources used, the scale used, the context of the figures – for example, if the figures represent a sample, how large is that sample? Are the assumptions reasonable? Are certain figures omitted? Why? Check the definitions of terms used. Are they sound? If percentages are shown, percentages of what?
- Take one row or column and think through its content and implications to understand the data.

- Compare figures in columns and see whether you can discern any patterns in the data. Consider any trends: do the numbers show a consistent pattern that increases or decreases? For instance, is actual expenditure consistently higher than budgeted?
- Consider averages. Calculate the average for a particular row or column and see what variations and exceptions there are. Try to work out reasons for such differences, for example variations because of higher or lower income or differing levels of employment.
- Read the text that accompanies the data and check you agree with it; be particularly wary of such expressions as 'significant' or 'these figures of course show'.
- Be careful about putting too much confidence in extrapolations of data that assume a trend will continue.

Summary

In this chapter we have considered listening and reading, the receptive skills in communication. Improving your listening skills will mean that, when you come to speak, you will know more about who you are talking to and so you can choose your words more accurately and therefore be more effective.

Improving your reading skills will mean that you will know why you are reading a certain passage and so you can focus your energies more appropriately.

Follow-up

1 Ask colleagues whether they think you are a good listener or not. Listen (!) to their response.

2 Think about a recent business conversation. Were you too busy thinking about what to say that you did not really listen to the person you were talking to?

3 What steps can you take to improve your listening skills? Be ruthlessly practical with yourself.

4 As you have read this chapter, what struck you as new? What action will you take as a result of your reading?

Fact-check (answers at the back)

1. The key skill in listening is:
   a) Looking at a person's face ❏
   b) Thinking about what you want to say ❏
   c) Focusing on what the other person is saying ❏
   d) Looking at the floor ❏

2. Good listening:
   a) Develops worse relationships ❏
   b) Provokes arguments ❏
   c) Relaxes people ❏
   d) Develops better working relationships ❏

3. Listening is:
   a) Easy – that's why I'm the manager ❏
   b) Hard work, but rewarding ❏
   c) Not worth bothering about ❏
   d) Useful if you have the time ❏

4. When I listen well, I:
   a) Can discern the main points someone is trying to communicate ❏
   b) Am confused ❏
   c) Get easily distracted ❏
   d) Interrupt the other person ❏

5. Listening provides a basis for me to:
   a) Express my own opinion to anyone who will listen ❏
   b) Direct what I want to say more accurately ❏
   c) Decide what to eat for lunch ❏
   d) Work out who I like and who I don't ❏

6. When I read:
   a) I read everything fast ❏
   b) I read everything slowly ❏
   c) I decide why I am reading something and use that as a basis to work out my approach ❏
   d) I question why I have to read it ❏

7. To make sure I understand a difficult passage:
   a) I read it through quickly and hope for the best ❏
   b) I read it through slowly and hope for the best ❏
   c) I learn it off by heart, although I'm not sure I grasp its meaning ❏
   d) I take notes, summarizing the author's message in my own words ❏

8. In reading I focus on:
   a) Why I disagree with the author ❏
   b) The middle of paragraphs ❏
   c) The key phrases, especially at the beginning of paragraphs ❏
   d) The page numbers ❏

9. I read other material outside my subject field:
   a) Never ❏
   b) Not at all – I'm too busy to do that ❏
   c) Often ❏
   d) Very rarely. ❏

10. When I read numbers in a table:
a) I focus on what regular patterns I can see between the columns ❏
b) I get hopelessly lost ❏
c) I never read numbers ❏
d) I always extrapolate the figures to see where they lead ❏

CHAPTER 3

Write clearly

Expressing yourself clearly is essential to communicating effectively and now we are going to look at the steps you need to take to express yourself clearly in writing.

First of all, we will consider general principles of writing, which apply especially to longer documents, and then we will consider specific media of writing: emails, letters and reports.

We can break down the writing process into different steps:

- thinking
- organizing
- writing your first draft
- editing your draft.

It is important to note that there are different steps; it isn't simply a matter of typing an email with the first thing that comes into your mind and then pressing 'send'!

The writing process

Thinking

Think about what you want to write. One good way of helping you start thinking what to write is to draw a pattern diagram (also known as a mind map). Take a blank piece of A4 paper. Arrange it in landscape position and write the subject matter of the report in the middle. (Write a word or few words, but not a whole sentence.) You may find it helpful to work in pencil, so that you can rub out what you write if necessary.

Now write around your central word(s) the different key aspects that come to your mind, maybe as a result of your reading. You don't need to list ideas in order of importance; simply write them down. To begin with, you don't need to join the ideas up with lines linking connected items.

If you get stuck at any point, ask yourself the question words *why, how, what, who, when, where* and *how much*. These may well set you thinking.

When I do this, I am often amazed at: (1) How easy the task is; it doesn't feel like work! The ideas and concepts seem to flow naturally and spontaneously. (2) How valuable that piece of paper is. I have captured all (or at least some or many) of the key points. I don't want to lose that piece of paper!

An example of a pattern diagram for a report on buying new computer systems can be seen in Figure 1.

Organizing

After you have completed the thinking stages with a pattern diagram, there are two further stages before you can begin writing. It is probably better to do them in the order shown here, but if that is difficult then do **2** then **1**.

1 **Refine the key message(s) of what you are trying to communicate.** This can take some time – if you find it difficult, you can at least eliminate parts that are less important. For example, if you are analysing the disadvantages of an old computer system, then the exact technical details of the software are probably less significant

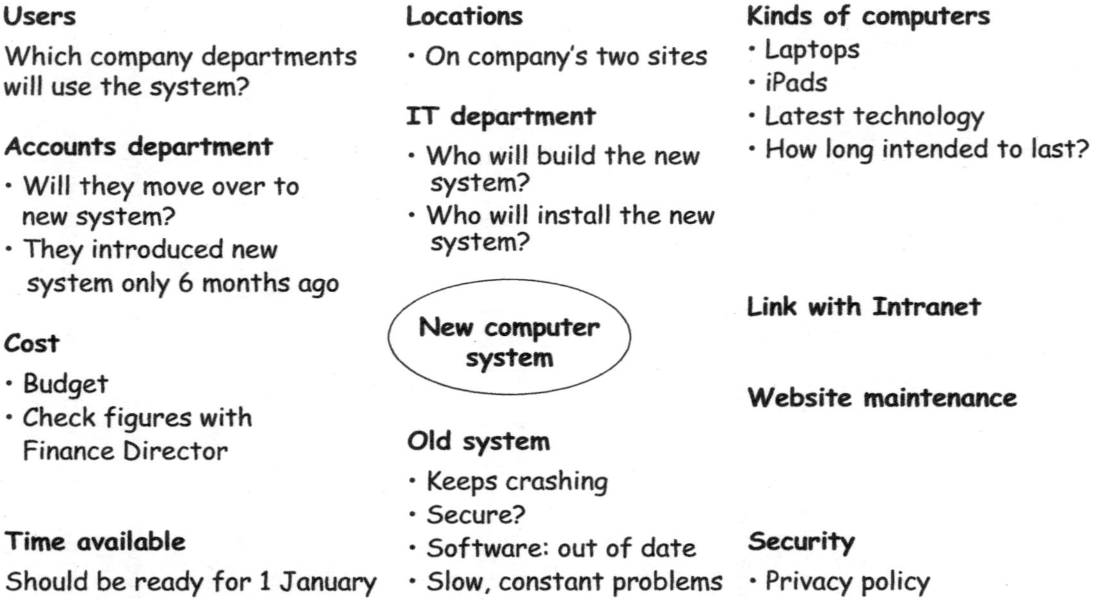

Users

Which company departments will use the system?

Accounts department

- Will they move over to new system?
- They introduced new system only 6 months ago

Cost

- Budget
- Check figures with Finance Director

Time available

Should be ready for 1 January

Locations

- On company's two sites

IT department

- Who will build the new system?
- Who will install the new system?

New computer system

Old system

- Keeps crashing
- Secure?
- Software: out of date
- Slow, constant problems

Kinds of computers

- Laptops
- iPads
- Latest technology
- How long intended to last?

Link with Intranet

Website maintenance

Security

- Privacy policy

Figure 1 Example of a pattern diagram

than the fact that it has serious drawbacks, is out of date and no longer fulfils its original purpose.

To work out what your key message is, you also need to consider your document's audience and response. If you are writing a report for your Finance Director, for example, you will want to present the financial facts (e.g. cost, return on investment) as your key message. However, if your Finance Director has already given the go-ahead to installing the new system and you are writing a report for colleagues in Research and Development who will be using the system, then your approach will be different. Your key message may then be on the usability of the new system and its advantages compared with the old one.

2 **Organize the information.** In other words, you need to arrange the information you are giving in a certain order. The aim here is to find the most appropriate logical way to present what you want to say. Ways include:

- arranging in terms of importance, probably listing the most important first
- comparing the advantages and disadvantages
- analysing different aspects of a scheme, for example under the headings *Political*, *Legal*, *Social*, *Economic*, *Financial*
- arranging in a chronological approach – considering a time sequence.

Writing the first draft

So you have prepared a pattern diagram and organized your thoughts in an appropriate order, and you now have come to the actual writing stage.

Now is the time to begin to write the following:

- an **introduction** to explain why you are writing your document
- the **main part** of your document, containing facts, explanations and other relevant information, together with your interpretation

● the **conclusion:** a summary of the key points, drawing together the issues you have raised.

Don't be tempted to ignore the preparation you have already done; build on that.

Let's now look at an example in the main part of your document. For example, you have on your pattern diagram the section:

> **Old system**
> - keeps crashing
> - secure?
> - software: out of date
> - slow, constant problems

This is fine as a basis, but you need to expand these notes into sentences.

Let's say that this is a paragraph in your report. 'Old system' isn't adequate as a heading, so you write: 'Disadvantages of the existing system'. As you consider this subject, you realize that the key thought is 'The existing system, which was installed ten years ago, has been overtaken by many new technological features', so you put that as the opening sentence in your paragraph. (This is called 'the topic sentence' – one that represents the whole paragraph in a single sentence, showing what the paragraph is about.)

You can then fill out the rest of the paragraph, expanding on the note form of your original structure to express your meaning in sentences. If you are unsure what to write, keep asking yourself, 'What am I trying to say?' It can be very helpful to discuss this with another individual in person (not by email!) to sharpen up precisely what you want to communicate.

A first draft of the paragraph might read as follows. The raised numbers discuss certain aspects of the writing process. See the notes for further explanation.

Disadvantages of the existing system

The existing system, which was installed ten years ago, has been overtaken by many new technological features. The present[1] system experiences too many failures[2], which cause colleagues a great deal of inconvenience.[3] Even when[4] the present system is functioning well[5], it is slow and often becomes locked[6]. Moreover[7], when handling large amounts of data, the existing system has been known to develop faults and some data has been lost. There are also doubts about how secure certain aspects of the system are.

Notes

1 To avoid repeating 'existing', I chose the synonym 'present'. Consult a thesaurus to help you with synonyms (words with similar meaning).
2 I thought that 'crash' was too informal for this report. I consulted a dictionary to help me find an alternative word.
3 I expanded on the effect of the computer failure.
4 'Even when' adds emphasis and a note of surprise considering the previous statement.
5 In my mind, I had 'running smoothly' but I felt that was too informal so I changed that to 'functioning well'.
6 In my mind, I thought of a computer 'freezing'; I thought that was too informal so consulted a dictionary and changed that to 'becomes locked'.
7 'Moreover' introduces a further similar line of reasoning; this additional thought occurred to me as I was writing, so I included it.

Editing

After completing a draft, go back over it and refine it. The aim here is to ensure that what you have written is clear and as you want it. When I am editing a document, I check first what is there and second what is not there. Has the first draft missed out a vital step in the argument? Alternatively, you may find that you have written too much about something that on further reflection was not very important and you have not written enough about something more important. Now is the time to redress that balance. Don't leave it as it is, thinking that it will go away or that the readers will not notice weaknesses in your argument.

Here are some tips for editing. Check that what you write:

- is accurate.
  - Check the content. We have all received emails inviting us to a meeting on Tuesday 14 September, only to discover that 14 September is a Wednesday. The result is that many colleagues spend precious time emailing requests for clarification and then having to respond to them with the exact date. It would have been better if the person who originally sent the message had checked the details before sending it.
  - Check totals of numbers, for example that percentages in a list all add up to 100.
  - Check punctuation. For example, are apostrophes and commas used correctly?
  - Check spellings. Be aware of words you often misspell. If your report contains basic errors, for example confusing *its* and *it's*, *effect* and *affect*, *of* and *off*, *principal* and *principle*, then they will undermine the overall credibility of your message.
- is brief. You may have heard of the saying, 'I wrote you a long letter because I didn't have time to write you a short one.' Sentences should be 15–20 words in length. Any longer and your readers may have difficulty following the meaning. Edit down – that is, cut out – some parts of your text that do not add anything significant to your argument.
- is clear. Is your overall message clear? If it isn't to you, it will not be to your readers.
- contains appropriate language for the medium you are using.
  - Watch the tone of your writing. There is a tendency to be too informal in more formal contexts. For example, if you are describing the role of a project manager, you could say he/she needs to be able to 'keep many balls in the air', but such language would be inappropriate in a formal report, which might instead say 'tackle a wide range of activities at the same time'. There is also a tendency to be

too formal, for example to use *necessitate* instead of *need*, or *terminate* instead of *stop* or *end*. The crucial point is to know who your audience is and write with them in mind.

- There is a tendency these days to write using a sequence of nouns but a more effective way of communicating would be to use more verbs. For example, 'an examination of the maintenance records took place' would be better expressed as 'the maintenance records were examined' (passive) or, even better, 'the manager examined the maintenance records' (active, naming who examined the records).
- Sometimes the language can be simplified: 'the repercussions regarding the effects subsequent to the explosion will be perused by the staff' can be simplified to 'the managers will consider the effects of the explosion'.
- Avoid abbreviations that are not generally known as well as jargon and slang.

● follows a logical sequence of thought.

- Often when you write a first draft, you tend to put down unrelated thoughts. At the editing stage, focus on each sentence to make sure that it fits into a logical sequence of your thoughts. In the example above, I constantly used the phrases 'existing system' or 'present system' in the paragraphs to make sure that the content of each sentence was clearly focused.
- Similarly, the progression of your paragraphs should follow a logical thought: each paragraph or series of paragraphs should deal fully with one particular idea before you move on to the next idea or thought. You can sometimes use linking words and phrases to show the connection or contrast (for example: to reinforce a point already made, *moreover, furthermore*; to introduce a contrast, *however, conversely, on the other hand*).

● expresses the meaning you want to communicate.

- Look back at the final sentence in my example: 'There are also doubts as to how secure certain aspects of the system are.' An alternative that rounds off the text better would be: 'Furthermore, faults in the present system have occasionally jeopardized (or *compromised*) the security of the overall network.'

Lists in bullet points

Consider whether the use of a list in bullet-point form is appropriate, especially for short phrases. People sometimes ask me about punctuation in bullet points: the trend these days is only to put a full stop at the end of the final point and not to have anything at the end of each point.

A more frequent mistake is that individual lines do not run on grammatically from the opening text, for example:

The successful candidate will be:

✔ skilled in numeracy and literacy

✔ able to speak at least two European languages

✘ have experience in using project-management software.

The error here is in the third bullet point, which does not follow on grammatically from the opening line, and should be changed to:

✔ experienced in using project-management software.

I have deliberately gone into some depth at this editing stage to be very practical in what to write and how to express it.

All the above applies to extended documents; we can now turn to some specific kinds of document.

Writing emails

Emails are great. We can communicate with colleagues all round the world instantly. However, emails also have their disadvantages. We can receive too many unwanted ones that stop us dealing with the tasks we are supposed to be dealing with.

Here are a few tips:

● Put a clear subject in the subject line (more than 'Hi Jane'). Being specific about your subject will help your reader know what the email is about.
● Use 'cc' ('carbon copy', from the days of paper) and 'bcc' ('blind carbon copy') sparingly. Send copies only to those

who really need to see the email. To explain 'cc' and 'bcc': if I am emailing Colin and cc Derek and bcc Ed, then Colin will see I have copied the email to Derek but Colin will not see I have copied the email to Ed. Using 'bcc' can also be useful for bulk emails when you don't want individuals to know the identity of the people on your emailing list.

- Unless you are writing to a close colleague, include some form of opening and closing greetings. The policy of your company and organization and your own personality will guide you to what is acceptable (e.g. I find 'Hi Martin' difficult to accept from someone I don't know at all).
- In a long email, put the key information at the beginning, so that it will be clear on the opening screen as your reader opens the email. Spend some time laying out your email. Group sentences that concern one subject in paragraphs. Remember that, if your message isn't clear to you, then it certainly won't be clear to your readers!
- Watch the tone of your email to make sure that it is not too abrupt. Consider adding softer opening and closing statements. Even 'Thank you' can help in this respect.
- Use only those abbreviations that are known to your readers.
- Don't type whole words in capital letters, which strongly suggest shouting.
- As part of your email 'signature', also include other contact information at the end of your email, including your job title, phone numbers (landline, mobile) and postal address. Your reader might want to phone you to clarify a point.

Writing letters

Although use of email is widespread, letters are useful for more formal statements. Business letters follow certain conventions:

- **Opening greeting.** If this is the first time you are writing to someone, use their title: Mr, Mrs, Ms and so on. If you know their first name, use that: 'Dear Freda'. You can also use the style of the person's first name and surname, especially if you are uncertain from the name (e.g. Sam, Jo, Chris) whether the recipient is male or female: 'Dear Sam Smith'. The style 'Dear Sir' or 'Dear Sir or Madam' is very formal and more impersonal.

- **Closing greeting.** If the opening greeting is 'Dear Freda', 'Dear Mrs Jones' or 'Dear Sam Smith', then the close is 'Yours sincerely' (capital 'Y' on 'Yours' and lower-case 's' on 'sincerely'). You can also add 'With best wishes' or 'Best wishes' before 'Yours sincerely'. If you have used 'Dear Sir' or 'Dear Sir or Madam', then the close is 'Yours faithfully' (capital 'Y' on 'Yours' and lower-case 'f' on 'faithfully').

Writing reports

The basics of writing reports

All the advice above on writing is important here, especially knowing why you are writing the report, who will be reading it and how you will structure it.

Kinds of report include:

- a progress report
- a health and safety report
- an investigation into the causes of an accident
- a company report
- a feasibility report
- a legal report used as evidence.

Your audience may be colleagues, shareholders, a board of directors, a project board, a team of advisers or consultants, a committee or users of a new product.

The purpose of your report may be to:

- examine whether a particular project, product or whatever is financially viable
- present a case for a decision on buying a product or service
- persuade someone to act in a certain way
- explain how a new product works
- describe the achievements, financial condition and so forth of a company
- inform colleagues of the progress of a project
- outline the cause of an accident or the nature of an incident.

Be clear about your audience, intention and response. Knowing these will determine, for example, how much information you should include in your reports. If in doubt, discuss with colleagues. In other words, do not agonize over writing ten pages when senior management want only one page. Moreover, your company or organization may already have a report template to give a structure to your report.

The content of reports

Reports normally have the following as a minimum:

- **Introduction**: this provides the report's purpose, including its scope or terms of reference.
- **Body of the report**: its main sections, outlining the procedure you have followed and findings, supported by facts and other information. Such objective evidence should be distinguished from your interpretation of those facts in your argument.
- **Conclusions**: a clear summary that draws all your arguments together, and recommends the necessary actions arising from your conclusions that must be taken to implement the report's findings.

Reports are often structured with clear numbers and headings (e.g. 1, 1.1, 1.1.1, 1.1.2, 1.2) to help readers refer to different parts easily.

Depending on the length of the report, you may also include:

- **An executive summary of the whole report.** Such a summary should be able to stand by itself and be a concise statement of all the report's significant information.
- **Appendices:** a section at the end of the report that contains technical information that is too long or too detailed to be included in the body of the text.
- **Bibliography:** a list of references and other sources of information used and/or quoted in the report.

Summary

In this chapter we have looked at writing – first of all at the general principles that apply especially to longer documents:

- thinking
- organizing
- writing your first draft
- editing.

We then looked specifically at writing different kinds of documents: emails, letters and reports.

Follow-up

1 Think which stage of writing you have most difficulty with (e.g. thinking, organizing, drafting, editing) and read again the relevant parts of this chapter.

2 Look at an email that you have just received from a colleague. Is its message clear? Is its tone appropriate? Is the action your colleague wanted you to take clear?

3 Look at an email that you have just written. Is its message clear? Is its tone appropriate? Is the action that you want the reader to take clear?

4 What practical steps will you take to improve your emails?

Fact-check (answers at the back)

1. 'I just start writing without any thinking or planning.' Do you think this way of approaching a piece of writing is:
   a) Good? ❏
   b) Bad? ❏
   c) Neither good nor bad? ❏
   d) A waste of time? ❏

2. When writing in business, what should you keep in mind?
   a) Yourself ❏
   b) The weather ❏
   c) Your readers ❏
   d) Your boss ❏

3. When I write a long document, I organize my material before I write:
   a) Never ❏
   b) Sometimes ❏
   c) Why bother? ❏
   d) Always ❏

4. Getting the tone of an email right is:
   a) Important ❏
   b) A luxury if you have the time ❏
   c) A waste of time ❏
   d) Unnecessary ❏

5. To help me write, I use a thesaurus or dictionary:
   a) Never ❏
   b) What's a thesaurus? ❏
   c) Very rarely ❏
   d) Often ❏

6. After you have drafted an email you should:
   a) Press 'send' ❏
   b) Go home ❏
   c) Keep on rewriting it ❏
   d) Check it. ❏

7. When rechecking an email before I send it:
   a) I never find anything I want to change ❏
   b) I'm a perfectionist, so I change so much that I forget to send it ❏
   c) I often change things ❏
   d) I don't bother to check them ❏

8. When I send an email, I send a copy to:
   a) Everyone in my address book ❏
   b) Only those who need to see it ❏
   c) No one: I don't know how to do that ❏
   d) My boss always, to protect myself ❏

9. When writing a report:
   a) I structure my material carefully ❏
   b) I don't bother structuring my material ❏
   c) I ask someone else to structure it ❏
   d) My structure is so elaborate even I don't understand it ❏

10. When writing a report:
    a) I put all the material down, hoping that readers will be able to make sense of it ❏
    b) I carefully distinguish facts and interpretations ❏
    c) I put everything in lists of bullet points ❏
    d) I get so lost in writing that I don't really think about what I am writing ❏

CHAPTER 4

Organize better meetings

Yesterday I met Tatiana. She started off in the company as an assistant editor. She had worked hard over the years and had now been promoted to Deputy Managing Director. She looked tired. I asked her if her life was full of meetings and she replied, 'Yes.' It was clear that many of the meetings she attended were too long and lacked focus and so had dampened her former enthusiasm.

A significant amount of your time as manager may be taken up in meetings, but they can go on too long and not achieve anything significant, and colleagues can become unenthusiastic or even cynical. How can you improve them?

In this chapter we will look at:

- the purpose of meetings
- preparing for meetings
- chairing meetings
- participating in meetings and negotiating
- following up from meetings.

We will see that the key to a successful meeting lies in its preparation.

The purpose of meetings

Meetings are useful to:

- inform colleagues, e.g. to introduce new goals or give an update on progress
- discuss with colleagues, e.g. plan together the way ahead or evaluate a solution to a problem
- reach a decision and agree on the next steps to be taken.

Team meetings are also particularly useful to develop a sense of team identity as members interact with one another. As manager and team leader, you can use team meetings to encourage better teamwork and motivate your team.

'Time is money'

We sometimes say that 'time is money', but what does that mean? Suppose you earn £20,000 per year. If we divide this figure by the number of days you work productively, that is, omitting holidays and allowing for illness, this could give, say, 46 weeks per year. £20,000 ÷ 46 = £434.78 per week or £86.96 per day, assuming five days per week. If we then divide this figure by the time per day you spend on productive work, say two-thirds of seven hours (= 4.66 hours), we come to £18.66 per hour: this is the amount that you are paid per hour gross, that is, before tax and other deductions.

That is only half the story, however. Your actual cost to your company or organization is about twice that figure. This is to allow for overheads: the general business expenses, the taxes your company pays as an employer, the rent of an office building, heating, power, water and so on. So the cost to your company or organization is £18.66 × 2 = £37.32 per hour.

So, if a business meeting lasts seven hours and is attended by six colleagues, then the cost of that meeting to the company or organization is 7 × 6 × £37.32 = £1567.44, which is probably considerably more than you thought. It literally pays, then, to run a good meeting.

> The significance of this may help you decide how many people need attend your meetings and whether everyone needs to sit through the whole meeting or whether some colleagues need come only for the part that concerns them.

Preparing for meetings

 TIP *The key to a successful meeting lies in the preparation.*

The key to a successful meeting lies in the preparation. It is essential that you:

- **Know the purpose of the meeting.** Many meetings have no clear purpose and could easily be shortened or even cancelled. You need to be crystal clear about what you are trying to achieve.
- **Plan a venue and time** (start, finish) in advance. I have arrived at the stated venue for some meetings to find the meeting is in a different place.
- **Invite the key people** to participate in advance. If you want a director with a busy diary to be present, then it is no good inviting him or her the day before; you need to have invited them a long time before. It is also useful if you can discuss with key people in private in advance any agenda items that could be controversial.
- **Circulate an agenda in advance.** This means that you will have thought about the structure and purpose of the meeting beforehand. Also, circulate important papers with the agenda, not at the meeting itself. Ideally, the length of such papers should be no more than one page each.
- **Prepare the meeting room.** Plan the seating: chairs around a table invite discussion; a chairperson at the end of a long table with ten seats either side, less so. If a PowerPoint presentation is being given, ensure that a projector and connecting lead are set up. Check that the heating or air conditioning works.
- **Read reports in advance.** If reports have been circulated before a meeting, then read them. I have been in too many meetings

where we have sat during the meeting reading material, something which should have been undertaken in advance.
- **Ensure that you come up with accurate information.** For example, if the meeting is one to monitor progress, take all your latest data on progress with you.

Chairing meetings

The chair (chairman, chairwoman or chairperson) is the one who sets the tone for the meeting and guides the participants through the discussion. His/her tasks include:

- deciding the agenda in advance
- keeping to the agenda so that the meeting starts and finishes on time
- introducing and welcoming newcomers, or asking participants to introduce themselves
- reviewing progress on action points from previous meetings
- bringing in key individuals to contribute at appropriate points
- stating key aims and objectives
- summarizing progress of the points being discussed
- drawing together the points discussed, to reach agreement and draw conclusions and to make decisions; if a point has been controversial, the chair can express exactly what is to be minuted, to avoid possible misinterpretation later
- ensuring action points are clear, particularly who is responsible for following up particular points and by when. The action points should be SMART:

SMART and SMARTER

S Specific, not vague, e.g. not 'We want to increase profits', but 'We want to increase profits by £100,000'

M Measurable and quantifiable, e.g. with milestones along the way to assess progress

A Agreed by all present at the meeting

R Realistic or resourced, i.e. 'if you want me to complete this task, you need to provide me with the resources to

> enable me to do so'
> **T** Timed: when are actions to be completed by?
> Some colleagues also add -ER to give SMARTER:
> **E** Evaluated: at a later meeting, progress is assessed
> **R** Reported: the evaluation is recorded at a future meeting.

A good chair is a diplomatic and organized leader, someone whom the colleagues trust and someone who values, motivates and involves others, checking they understand the points discussed. Ideally, he/she will be able to quieten down those who talk too much and also draw out those who talk too little but can still make valuable contributions. A good chair will also sense when the time is right to bring a discussion to an end and be able to come to clear decisions.

> *'Any committee is only as good as the most knowledgeable, determined and vigorous person on it. There must be somebody who provides the flame.'*
> Claudia ('Lady Bird') Johnson (1912–2007), widow of former US president Lyndon B. Johnson

Good team meetings

Martha was a good team leader. The meetings she led were particularly good. She kept close to the agenda, which had been circulated before the meeting, and she followed up on the action points from the previous meeting. She prepared for the meetings well, thinking in advance how she might tackle objections to her ideas that colleagues might raise. She gave out overall information about how the company was performing and led fruitful discussions on how her unit could improve their efficiency even further. On confidential matters, she was diplomatic and as open as she could be. On difficult matters, she was able to identify the core issue and lead a discussion and evaluation of possible solutions before deciding on a particular course of action.

> She was particularly good at encouraging everyone to participate and express themselves. She always summarized the discussions and came to a clear decision about the next step. She made sure minutes of the meeting were circulated promptly after meetings so that colleagues were all clear about what they should do. The result was that colleagues in her team all felt inspired and wellmotivated.

Participating in meetings

Everyone has a part to play in a successful meeting. I have never understood how people can come out of a meeting asking 'What was the point of that?' when they themselves have not contributed anything. Each of us has a role to play by:

- listening well and concentrating. Switch phones and other electronic gadgets off; avoid sending text messages; don't interrupt when someone else is talking.
- asking for clarification if you are unsure about a point that has been made. It is highly likely that other colleagues will also want clarification but have been afraid to ask, perhaps for fear of looking ignorant.
- being constructive: having a positive attitude. Even if you disagree with what has been said, there are positive ways of expressing a difference of opinion by challenging an idea without angrily criticizing the person expressing it or publicly blaming an individual for a wrong action.
- confronting issues. Focus on the real issues; don't get sidetracked. Too many of our meetings avoid discussing 'the elephant in the room', the subject everyone is aware of but doesn't mention because it is too uncomfortable.
- being willing to change your mind. If you are listening and persuasive arguments have been offered then allow yourself to be convinced by them and change your opinion about an issue.

Negotiating: win-win situations

In negotiating, we are aiming for a win-win situation. A win-win situation can perhaps be well illustrated by an example. My son Ben has just moved to Asia and he wanted to sell his camera. His friend Rob wanted a camera to take photographs on his travels. Ben sold Rob his camera – both won. Both gained what they wanted: Ben money, Rob a camera.

In his book *The 7 Habits of Highly Effective People*, Stephen R. Covey points out that the basis for a win-win situation is our character:

> *'If you're high on courage and low on consideration, how will you think? Win–Lose. You'll be strong and ego-bound. You'll have the courage of your convictions, but you won't be very considerate of others. ... If you're high on consideration and low on courage, you'll think Lose–Win. You'll be so considerate of others' feelings that you won't have the courage to express your own. ... High courage and consideration are both essential to Win–Win. It's the balance of the two that is the mark of real maturity. If you have it, you can listen and you can empathically understand, but you can also courageously confront.'*

The 7 Habits of Highly Effective People Personal Workbook, Stephen R. Covey (Simon & Schuster, 2005), p. 91

A good negotiator of contracts

Danielle was respected as a good negotiator in contracts. The secret of her success lay in good planning. She spent a long time thinking through different business models and pricing levels so that, when it came to the negotiations, she knew exactly what approach to take. After both sides had presented their initial case, she was sometimes able to detect the weak points in the arguments of the other side and exploit them according to her own personality. When they came to the final bargaining she had clarified the critical issue (the price) in her mind and knew the less significant matters she could be flexible on; she didn't mind bringing delivery of the products forward by six weeks. She was assertive and firm on what was non-negotiable, however: the price. So she was able to settle and close deals well and arrange the next steps in business relationships between the two sides.

Videoconferencing

Videoconferencing means that you avoid spending travel costs and that you can link colleagues over the Internet. Here are some tips to help you plan a videoconference session:

● Make sure that the room in which the meeting takes place has good acoustics and also is tidy.
● Agree and circulate the agenda in advance to all participants. Appoint a chair who can introduce the participants. Email any special presentations (e.g. PowerPoint) in advance.
● Identify individuals using cards in front of them with their name on.
● Remind participants to look at the camera while they are talking. Ask other participants to listen while one person is speaking.

Follow-up from meetings

A meeting where decisions are made but after which no one acts on these decisions is a waste of time. If colleagues have action points to pursue, those colleagues should follow them up.

The minutes of a meeting are a record of what happened in a meeting, including its action points. The person taking the minutes does not need to write down everything that goes on, but significant decisions, especially the action points concerning dates, schedules and financial matters, must be noted specifically.

The sooner the minutes of a meeting are circulated to those present at the meeting and other key colleagues, the more likely it is that colleagues will follow up the action points asked of them.

A good manager will also follow through between meetings on the progress of the key action items; he/she will not leave it to the next meeting only to discover that action has not been taken and so valuable time has been lost.

Summary

In this chapter we have considered how to make your meetings more effective. I have particularly emphasized the need for careful preparation: think *why* you are holding the meeting (the reason needs to be something more than 'It's our normal monthly meeting'), *who* needs to be there, *what* you will consider, *when* it will start and finish and *where* it will take place. Plan and circulate the agenda in advance, together with any key documents. Make sure that proper minutes are circulated promptly and then also reviewed at the next meeting, to ensure that all the action points have been dealt with well.

Follow-up

1 Think about a meeting that you have attended recently. What were its good points? What were its bad points? What practical steps can you take to ensure that the bad points are not repeated in future?

2 If you are chairing meetings, what practical steps can you take to improve your leading of meetings?

3 If you are not chairing meetings, what practical steps can you take to improve your participation?

Fact-check (answers at the back)

1. My attitude to meetings is that:
   a) Occasionally they are productive ❏
   b) They are boring ❏
   c) They are a necessary evil ❏
   d) I want to make sure that they are better ❏

2. The key to a successful meeting lies in the:
   a) Room ❏
   b) Participants ❏
   c) Length of time it lasts ❏
   d) Preparation ❏

3. 'Every business meeting should have an agenda':
   a) False ❏
   b) True ❏
   c) Sometimes true ❏
   d) If you say so ❏

4. A good chairperson will:
   a) Summarize progress and make clear decisions ❏
   b) Wander away from the agenda ❏
   c) Let everyone have their say but never reach a decision ❏
   d) Expect all meetings to run smoothly ❏

5. When a decision is made, ensuring that someone is responsible for implementing that decision is:
   a) Nice to have ❏
   b) A luxury ❏
   c) Essential ❏
   d) We never make decisions ❏

6. In setting SMART action points, the S stands for:
   a) Silly ❏
   b) Specific ❏
   c) Special ❏
   d) Standard ❏

7. In setting SMART action points, the T stands for:
   a) Timed ❏
   b) Tough ❏
   c) Thought-through ❏
   d) Technical ❏

8. If I am not chairing the meeting:
   a) I can send text messages to friends ❏
   b) I can distract the colleagues sitting opposite ❏
   c) I am negative about my colleagues ❏
   d) I know I still have an important part to play ❏

9. If I am in a meeting and don't understand what is being discussed:
   a) I am silent ❏
   b) I want to go home ❏
   c) I ask, even though it may make me look ignorant ❏
   d) I wait for the chairman to explain it ❏

10. After a meeting, minutes should be circulated:
    a) What are 'minutes'? ❏
    b) Never ❏
    c) Promptly ❏
    d) If we are lucky ❏

CHAPTER 5

Give
successful
presentations

So far, we have looked at our aims, the importance of listening, writing documents and running better meetings. Now we come to another key aspect of your work as a manager that takes in all of the above: speaking, as you give a presentation.

You may never have given a presentation before and understandably you may be nervous, but you can relax, because the skills you need are the ones that you have been reading about and practising:

- Knowing your aims – who you are speaking to; what you know about them (you gather that from listening); what your key messages are and what response you want from your audience
- Planning what you want to say – you can build on the techniques you read about in Chapter 3 (for example, using a mind map to get your creativity going)
- Knowing your own special unique contribution to the meeting at which you are to speak.

As well as these key skills, we also discuss the use of visual aids, including PowerPoint, body language and feedback.

Lay a strong foundation

Look back at Chapter 1 and AIR (Audience, Intention, Response). Who is your audience: senior managers? colleagues? colleagues from outside your company, some of whom might be critical?

How many will be in your audience: five, 50, 500? How much do they already know about what you are going to say? Will you need to sketch in some background? What are their thoughts and feelings towards you, as speaker, likely to be? Discover as much as you can about your audience before you plan your presentation.

Sometimes, when I give a presentation, I actually think of one or two real individuals in the audience and, on the basis of my knowledge of them, prepare as if I am speaking only to them.

Think why you are giving the presentation. What is the background context in which you have been asked to give it? Is there a hidden agenda?

Try to summarize your message in 12 words. For example, if I were speaking about the context of this chapter in a presentation, the key message would be 'Prepare your presentation well'.

Remember practical points:

● Know how long you will speak for: 15 minutes? an hour? People will be grateful if you finish early (but not too early!) but will not appreciate it if you go on too long.
● Consider the layout of the seating. At one workshop I led with 15 delegates I complained that the suggested seating looked too much like that of a classroom, so we adjusted it to a 'horseshoe' or 'U' layout, which helped interaction between the participants. Don't forget the room's lighting, heating or air conditioning.
● Think about what you are going to say. Look back at Chapter 3 on using a mind map and answering the question words *why, how, what, who, when, where* and *how much*. You may think it unnecessary to do this but doing so is often fruitful, because you are putting down your key thoughts before you begin to organize and order them.

Before you organize your thoughts, I am going to add an additional stage to the ones I have already given. The keywords in your mind map are probably nouns (names of things); the aim here is to add a verb (doing word) to make a more powerful combination. For example, a draft for this chapter was:

Foundation		Yourself
Message	Presentation	Body language
Visual aids		Feedback

I then added verbs:

Lay a foundation		**Prepare** yourself
Refine your message	**Give** a presentation	**Be aware of** body language
Prepare visual aids		**Expect** feedback

And I even went on to a third stage and began to add adjectives (describing words):

Lay a **strong** foundation		Prepare yourself
Refine your message	Give an **effective** presentation	Be aware of body language
Prepare **useful** visual aids		Expect **positive and negative** feedback

Do you see? What I am trying to do is spread the load of the core meaning: rather than simply 'visual aids' I ended up with 'prepare useful visual aids'.

Use a thesaurus and/or a dictionary of collocations (word partners) to develop your words and phrases. Work on them, hone them, sculpture them so they clearly express what you want (*expect positive and negative* feedback; *refine* your message).

Organize your thoughts. You are now in a position to put your thoughts and basic messages in a certain order. You have worked out your key message 'Prepare your presentation well' and you can put the material in a certain order. Note that:

- you need to add an introduction and a conclusion; they are separate
- you should put your most important point first in the main part of your presentation.

The order of your draft may be different from the one you end up with. That is OK. It is only a draft. It is better to work on some order. For example, I know that 'Prepare useful visual aids' and 'Expect feedback' are important but they are not the basic, primary aspects of what I am trying to say, so they can go later in the presentation. So the final order of my draft is as follows (you can compare this with the final text):

1 Lay a strong foundation 2 Refine your message 3 Prepare useful visual aids	Give an effective presentation	6 Prepare yourself 4 Be aware of body language 5 Expect positive and negative feedback

In the end, I put '6 Prepare yourself' as a short paragraph – not as a main point – under '4 Be aware of body language'.

Refine your message

- **Work out your key messages.** Be crystal clear on what you are trying to say. Keep your 'headlines' simple. Don't try to cram too much in – 'less is more'.
- **Break down your key points into subpoints.** Work on your words. Use short everyday words rather than longer ones. So use *try* rather than *endeavour*; *need*, not *necessitate*; *stop* or *end* rather than *terminate*; *harmful* rather than *detrimental*.
- **Say the same thing more than once.** If your key point is 'Prepare well' then say that and add something like 'You need to work hard at the planning to make your presentation effective'. This is *expanding* on 'Prepare well', saying it again in different

words. This is something you do more in speaking than in writing. You also do it in speaking when you see that your audience doesn't really understand what you are saying. This means that you should look at them when you are speaking, not at your notes. Hopefully, you are so familiar with what you want to say that you do not need to follow your script word for word.

- **Think about how you will communicate.** Ask questions. Give a specific case study (example) or tell a story to back up the point you are making. Include some well-chosen quotations or statistics. Be creative. Find a picture that will illustrate the key point of your talk (but make sure that you are not in breach of copyright if you use it).
- **Work on different parts of your presentation.** Work especially hard on the *beginning*, to capture your audience's attention with your introduction ('Did you know... ? I was reading in today's newspaper...') and the *end* ('So the next step is...') to round off your presentation, drawing together and reinforcing application of your key points.
- **Structure your main points in a logical sequence.** If you can structure them by making them all start with the same letter of the alphabet, or by 'ABC' (e.g. one of the talks I give on writing encourages writers to be *accurate, brief* and *concise*), then your points will be more memorable.
- **Check your message.** This is one of the key points for you to remember. Check facts and dates to make sure that they are accurate.
- **In your preparation, continue to think what the response of your audience is likely to be.** Interested? Bored? In need of persuasion? Sceptical? Anticipate likely reactions by dealing with them in your preparation and preparing answers to questions.
- **Write your presentation down.** Either write down (1) every word you plan to say or (2) notes that you can follow. If you do (1), then don't read it out word for word from your paper. Hopefully, your thoughts will have become part of your way of thinking. As you gain more experience, you will probably find you can work from notes. When I started giving presentations I wrote everything in pencil (so I could rub words out), then I typed them up (and enlarged the

printout so that I could read it). Now, with more experience, I write out the key points with important phrases or words highlighted. Do what you are comfortable with.

- **Be enthusiastic; be positive.** You have a message to declare. Go for it! Think about your own approach to your talk. You have your own unique personality, skills and experiences. Be natural; be yourself. It took me years to discover and work out my own style for giving presentations. I was amazed when a colleague contacted me after a space of five years to ask me to lead a workshop at his company and he said, 'I remember your style.'
- **Plan in a break.** If your presentation is going to last longer than 45 minutes, then schedule a break so that your audience can relax for a few minutes.

Unseen, but important, preparation

Hasheeb was wise. He had given a few presentations and was beginning to enjoy them, even though he was always nervous before he gave one. He realized that he would probably be giving presentations for a few years into the future, so he began to read more widely round the subject. He kept a hard-copy notebook and a computer file of useful ideas, stories, quotes and notes he came across. In this way, when he was asked to speak, he had a resource he could refer to, so that his interest and passion remained fresh. This unseen, but important, preparation work was one of the secrets of his effectiveness as a speaker.

Prepare useful visual aids

Will you give handouts of your presentation? How many will you need? Work out when you will give them out: before or at the end of the presentation? My personal preference is before, so that the audience knows where I am going. The disadvantage of that is that they do know where I am going, so always make sure that your notes are a skeleton (not the full text) of your presentation. Make enough copies of your handouts and some spare.

I made the mistake in one of my early presentations of preparing handouts that were in effect my full notes; so when a colleague said, 'We didn't really need to come, we could have just read your paper', I didn't have an answer.

Use tables and charts to support your points – but don't be so complex or technical that your audience can't understand what you are trying to say. Be as simple as you can be.

Use a flipchart if appropriate; I personally prefer a flipchart to a PowerPoint presentation as I find a flipchart more flexible than the rigidly ordered PowerPoint.

If you are using PowerPoint, then:

- Allow plenty of time to prepare the presentation, particularly if you are not familiar with the presentation software. To begin with, it is likely to take far longer than you think.
- Don't try to put too much information on the slides. Keep to your headings, not the complete outline of your talk.
- Keep to one main font. Use a large font size, ideally at least 28 points. Aim to have no more than six lines per slide (do you remember peering over people's heads trying to read tiny print on a slide?). In PowerPoint, a sans-serif font is easier to read than a serif one. Headings arranged left (not centre) are easier to read; capitals and lower-case letters are also easier to read than text in all capitals.
- Check the spelling of words on your slides.
- Work out which colours work well, for example red on grey, yellow on blue.
- Use tables and charts to support your message; bar charts, pie charts and flow charts that give the key information visually work well.
- Use illustrations that support your message, not ones that show off your (lack of!) design or animation skills.
- Don't put the key information at the bottom of slides; colleagues far away from the screen may not be able to see over other colleagues' heads.
- Rehearse the presentation with your notes/text in advance.
- Check whether you or a colleague will supply the projector, leads to connect the projector to your laptop and a screen. Arrive early to set everything up.

- Put your presentation on a memory stick (saved in earlier versions of PowerPoint for good measure) in case your laptop fails and you have to view it from someone else's laptop.
- Make sure that when you give your presentation your eye contact is with your audience, not with your laptop or the screen.
- Organize the room so that everyone can see the screen.

TIP *Prepare your message so thoroughly that it becomes part of you.*

A picture is worth a thousand words

Jason was looking for suitable illustrations to accompany a talk he was giving on encouragement. He was emphasizing the 'tough but tender' aspect of encouragement and had a picture of a father and son to illustrate tenderness. He found it more difficult to find one for the tough aspect, however, until he remembered one of the tableaux in the Bayeux Tapestry in which Bishop Odo was said to 'comfort' his troops by prodding them with a club. In modern colloquial English he was 'giving them a kick up the backside' to goad them into action. The picture Jason found was a good illustration of the point he was trying to make.

Be aware of body language

A friend once told me, 'They are not listening to a message; they are listening to a messenger', so be yourself. Look smart and then you are more likely to feel smart and more confident. Dress professionally. A colleague and I once met a publisher to try to persuade them to take up the idea of a book we were working on. I was appalled when my colleague turned up in a sweatshirt and jeans – that wasn't the professional image I was trying to express!

When giving your presentation, stand up straight and relax your shoulders. Don't hide behind the lectern (although I am aware that positioning yourself there can hide your nervousness); you could even move around the room a little.

Maintain good eye contact with your audience – for me that is the critical point. If you are using a flipchart or PowerPoint, don't look at that while you are speaking; look at your audience. But look across your whole audience, not just at those you like. Remember too that your whole posture will reveal a lot about yourself.

Use your voice well: speak sometimes loudly, sometimes softly; sometimes faster, sometimes more slowly. Don't mumble; speak out your words clearly. Be expressive: vary the tone in which you speak. Use hand gestures, according to your personality. Smile (in my early days of giving presentations I went so far as to write the word 'Smile' on every page of my notes). Pauses can be useful to help your audience digest what you have just said.

Prepare your message so thoroughly that it becomes part of you. Practise it by speaking it out loud. This will also help you time it.

Prepare your *self* as well as your *message*. The important point here is to be positive: you have been asked to give a presentation, so others have confidence in you. Be as enthusiastic as possible. Control your nerves. Take deep breaths. Drink water.

In your actual presentation, be authentic. Sometimes at the beginning of the workshops I lead, when I sense that participants and I are all nervous, I will say, 'How are you feeling about today?', adding 'I'm as nervous as you.' Such genuine self-deprecating comments can help defuse their tension.

A difficult but good experience

Harry was keen to improve his presentation skills, so his colleagues recorded a presentation that Harry gave. Harry realized that watching himself on video was a difficult but useful experience. He noticed what mannerisms he was unaware of (jangling his keys), words he kept on repeating (his recurrent one was 'OK?'). But it was worth it. The awkwardness and embarrassment he felt were a necessary part of his own learning experience. Becoming aware of

> his faults as others saw them was an important first step
> to his correcting them, as part of fulfilling his overall
> desire to become an even more effective presenter.

Expect positive and negative feedback

'Feedback' means questions from your audience – and you would be wise to prepare for them. These days I think a trend is to say at the beginning of a talk something like, 'I'll take any questions for clarification during the talk but please keep any more significant questions to the end.' If you say that, allow time, both for questions to aid your audience's understanding during the talk but also for the more significant questions at the end.

Here, as with so much of what you have read, the key lies in good preparation. Expect feedback. Expect a particular colleague to raise objections because that's what he/she always does. Expect them – and plan for them. Deal with their objections, and where possible return to the key messages you want to communicate. (I learned a trick here: when replying to an objector, don't keep eye contact only with that person, but let your eyes roam more widely through the room. If, while you give your answer, you look only at the person raising the objection, then he/she may take that as an opportunity to respond even further.)

If you don't know the answer to a question, be honest enough to say so. Often other colleagues in the room may be able to help you out. Conclude a question-and-answer session by again positively highlighting the key message(s) you want to communicate to round off the whole presentation.

After your presentation, evaluate it. You could also ask trusted colleagues to give their realistic assessment of your performance. What was the content like? Was your delivery/presentation too slow or too fast? Was it directed at the right level? Did the handouts/visual aids/PowerPoint detract from or add to your presentation? Recognize what worked well but don't be afraid to acknowledge what didn't work so well, so that you can learn lessons for the future. Remember, 'the person who never made mistakes never made anything'.

Summary

In this chapter we have looked at giving presentations. We have seen that to give an effective presentation means that you need to prepare well. You will:

- know who you are speaking to
- know what you are trying to achieve by your talk
- think about what you want to communicate
- plan and organize your thoughts
- work hard at the logical order and structure of your presentation
- work hard at your words
- work hard at your introduction and conclusion
- prepare any visual aids or PowerPoint slides but be as simple as possible; don't try to be too clever
- be aware of your body language as you deliver your talk. Be especially aware of keeping good eye contact with your whole audience.

Follow-up

Think about a presentation you have to give in the next few weeks. Write out your key message in 12 words.

Fact-check (answers at the back)

1. You have got to give a presentation in a week's time. Do you:
   a) Prepare well? ❏
   b) Panic? ❏
   c) Get so nervous that you don't prepare at all? ❏
   d) Not bother preparing, knowing you are good at improvising? ❏

2. What is the most important aspect about giving a presentation?
   a) Working out what PowerPoint slides you can use ❏
   b) Knowing how long you are to speak ❏
   c) Knowing what the weather is like ❏
   d) Knowing what your key message is ❏

3. When preparing what I am going to say:
   a) I jot down the first thing that comes into my mind ❏
   b) I take it slowly, thinking about my key message ❏
   c) I don't prepare; I just improvise on the day ❏
   d) I spend all my time thinking but never writing anything ❏

4. When giving a presentation, repeating what you say using different words is:
   a) Useless repetition ❏
   b) Useful to reinforce your message ❏
   c) Nice if you have a thesaurus ❏
   d) A waste of time ❏

5. When constructing my argument:
   a) I carefully order the points I want to make ❏
   b) I don't bother organizing my points ❏
   c) I improvise ❏
   d) I lose the train of thought in my whole talk ❏

6. When I think about my conclusion:
   a) I just repeat my six main points ❏
   b) conclusion – what's that? ❏
   c) I round off my presentation with the next steps I want my audience to take ❏
   d) I add two new points to liven up my talk ❏

7. I use PowerPoint:
   a) Always, as I want to show off my technical skills ❏
   b) Never; I hate technology ❏
   c) Usually, and put nearly all of my presentation on it ❏
   d) Wisely, to support the points I want to make ❏

8. When giving my presentation:
   a) I keep my eyes on my notes ❏
   b) I look only at my colleagues ❏
   c) I look at the attractive men/women in the room ❏
   d) I look around widely at the audience ❏

9. When speaking:
a) I vary the speed and volume
   of what I say ❏
b) I always speak in one tone ❏
c) I think I am as bored as my
   audience ❏
d) I often use such words
   as *um* and *so* ❏

10. I expect feedback from my
    presentation:
a) Rarely ❏
b) Never ❏
c) Often ❏
d) If I am lucky ❏

CHAPTER 6

Build strong working relationships

In a section on business communication, you could assume that it would all be about finding the right formula to include in an email and choosing your words carefully in a presentation, but there is something underlying and deeper going on: developing good working relationships. Good working relationships are the glue that holds a company or organization together.

We can also express that positive idea negatively: bad working relationships – or the absence of good (or any) working relationships – will mean that the company or organization will not function well.

I chose the words in the title of this chapter very carefully. *Build*: we can take active steps to cultivate and work at relationships; *strong* working relationships are ones that are firmly established – which takes time – and are not easily broken.

So now we consider how we can cultivate such strong working relationships, and how they are seen in practice, including working in teams, in delegating work and in resolving conflict.

Develop better working relationships

I want this chapter to be practical. Establishing good rapport – a sense of mutual respect, trust and understanding – seems to come naturally and easily to some people, but not to others. My wife is much more naturally confident with people than I am, but she has taught me some skills that have helped me.

Here are some tips. I hesitate to call them 'techniques' because that can make them seem artificial and, if you try them, that could make them appear awkward.

- **See things from another person's point of view.** Listen to them – *really* listen to them (look back at Chapter 2 for more hints on listening).
- **Pay attention; be genuinely interested in other people.** I hesitate to write 'look interested' because that is all it could be – an appearance without a genuine interest. Smile; look at them; make eye contact with them.
- **Notice colleagues' body language.** Do you sense that they are awkward or relaxed? What expression do they have on their face? Does their tone of voice reveal their insecurity? However, be aware that you can misinterpret people's body language. A speaker was giving a talk and a colleague in the audience had her eyes closed. The speaker interpreted the closed eyes as a sign of lack of interest whereas in fact they helped the colleague concentrate on the speaker's message.
- **Adapt what you want to say to colleagues to suit them.** This, for me, is vital. For example, when I lead a two-day course on communications, I am aware that the time before the mid-morning break on the first day will be spent mainly *listening* to the participants – for example, how they are fed up with the politics of their company; how their bosses do not listen to them or value them. Once these colleagues have got these feelings off their chest, they are ready to

listen to what I have to say. If I were to start off with great enthusiasm and energy with *my* presentation and ignore the context of their frustration, they would not be ready to listen to me. I have to 'get on to their wavelength' – understand them first – and then adapt what I want to say to the reality of their situation as I have discovered it to be. In fact, I often explicitly say at the beginning of my courses, 'I am more interested in helping you than in getting through my material.'

- **Be flexible in your response.** If you are truly focused on the person you are talking to rather than on yourself, you will have a variety of responses available to you, for example 'One solution to this is...', 'Only you can decide' or even 'I'm not sure we're answering the right question. Isn't it more about...?'

- **Notice what colleagues are saying.** Pick up on their key thoughts and words. For example, I recall a meeting some years ago to discuss different departments' allocations of income in their budget. One head of department said he was 'firing a warning shot across the bows', that he was prepared to strongly oppose any attempts to reduce his department's budget. Knowing looks were exchanged by other colleagues and the chair of the meeting immediately withdrew his suggestion that his colleague's department should suffer a reduction in funding.

- **Engage in 'small talk',** conversation about ordinary things that are relatively unimportant from a strictly business point of view. When you meet someone for the first time, it's all right to talk about their travel to the venue, the weather, their family, the previous night's football results, holiday plans, and so on. Engaging in such conversation helps the actual business run more smoothly than if you did not have such conversation. Share a little of how you see life; ask questions, especially closed questions (ones that can be answered with a straight 'yes' or 'no') to begin with and then move on to some open questions (ones that may begin with *why, how, who, when, where, what* and get people talking), but don't make it seem as if you are interrogating the other person.

- **Be aware of roles.** When you meet someone for the first time and they tell you that they are, for example, a dentist, doctor, police officer or accountant, be aware that you will probably then put them into a category of that profession and that you will trust them accordingly.
- **Be aware of colleagues' status and power, but treat each person as a unique individual.** If you meet a headteacher for the first time, you may assume that he or she has a lot of authority and you may feel insecure because you have a lower status than they do. However, the problem may be more in your perception than in reality. If the headteacher genuinely says to you, 'I'm interested in what you can tell me about...', you may feel honoured that a person in such a position of authority has asked for your opinion. For me, what is important is valuing each person as unique. I recall a comment on a teacher friend years ago: 'He even talks to the cleaners.' Realize that you can crush someone's sense of identity by belittling them, constantly interrupting them or ignoring them. Treat each person as a unique individual.
- **Communicate what you are doing clearly and consistently and also why you are doing it.** This is particularly important in introducing change management; you will constantly need to state why you are doing things to counter the 'we've always done it this way' approach.
- Ensure, as far as it is up to you, that **the messages expressed by different departments in your company or organization are consistent,** that is, that they don't contradict one another.
- **Put the aims of your company or organization first** and make sure that you fulfil your own work to the best of your capabilities. In most organizations there will be office politics and you will find people you like and people you don't like. Part of doing your job professionally is rising above, as far as you can, any different outlooks that colleagues have and their diverse personalities. Always be polite; don't engage in gossip. You may need to stop complaining about your colleagues and make sure that you do your own work as professionally as possible.

Introducing changes gradually

Martha was promoted to team leader and had many good ideas on changing things, for example by introducing team statistics, rotas, new personal targets. However, her colleagues reacted badly to the speed of changes and her mentor had a quiet word with her ('Go for "evolution", not "revolution"'). So Martha slowed down and introduced the changes at a more measured pace, explaining to each colleague in informal one-to-ones why changes were necessary. The result was that her colleagues felt more valued and their self-confidence increased as they successfully navigated the changes.

A close working relationship

I have worked with Tony for over 30 years. We have worked on many long-term projects together: he as designer, I as writer/editor. We trust and respect each other for our different skills and experience. We have talked things through when we have had opposing views, to reach a positive solution. I phone him regularly when he is slightly behind schedule. We ask each other's opinion when we are unsure how to proceed. In 2011 we were awarded a prize for the work we and others had undertaken on *Collins Bible Companion* in a 'Reference Book of the Year' competition. When other colleagues have joined us in meetings, they have noted how we tend to think each other's thoughts and express them. Over our long period of collaboration, we have built up a close working relationship.

Develop stronger teamwork

A team is a group of diverse people who are working together towards a common goal. Team members bring a wide range of roles, which should *complement one another*: one person's weakness is balanced out by another person's strengths.

How can you build stronger working relationships in a team? One way is to be aware of different roles. A widely known set of roles was developed by Dr Meredith Belbin as he looked at how team members behaved. He distinguishes nine different team roles:

- **Plant**: creative, good at coming up with fresh ideas and solving difficult problems in unconventional ways
- **Resource investigator**: outgoing; good at communicating with outside agencies
- **Co-ordinator**: good as chairperson, focusing team members on the goals; a good delegator
- **Shaper**: dynamic action person who can drive a project forward through difficulties
- **Monitor/evaluator**: able to stand back and bring objective discernment
- **Team worker**: bringing harmony and diplomacy for good team spirit
- **Implementer**: dependable, efficient practical organizer
- **Completer/finisher**: able to follow through on details meticulously to complete a project
- **Specialist**: giving expert technical knowledge.

For further details and how to identify colleagues' different roles, see www.belbin.com.

This analysis is useful since it can reveal possible gaps – that is, your team may be lacking certain skills, which you can then seek to cover. For example, discussing these roles on one committee I was part of revealed we had no monitor/evaluator, someone who could stand back and objectively assess ideas. Identifying someone with those skills was therefore one of our aims.

Encourage better teamwork

As team leader, you are responsible for encouraging your team to work together successfully. To do that, you need to do the following:

- Communicate a vision. Where is the team going? What is its purpose? As leader, you need to present a strong and inspiring vision of your goals.

- Set your goals clearly. There is nothing like an abstract statement which is not earthed in reality to turn people off. It is hardly surprising that colleagues come out of a team meeting feeling cynical when only a vision has been cast but no practical implications have been drawn from that vision. A vision must be turned into practical steps.
- Ensure that your team values are agreed. Do team members trust and respect one another? Do individuals feel important and part of something bigger than themselves? Encourage team members to remain positive, to believe in the strength and unity of the team.
- Clarify responsibilities of each member of the team so that not only each individual knows their responsibilities but also the whole team knows what each member does. Different members of the team will bring different skills, so play to colleagues' strengths. For example, don't give the chairmanship of a meeting to someone who is unclear or indecisive.
- Ensure that lines of authority and responsibility are clear. Be clear about whether individual team members have authority to spend sums of money up to a certain amount or should direct all requests for purchases through you as team leader.
- Show that you value team members. Listen to them; provide opportunities for members of your team to approach you if they need help. You should not be aloof; be available for them to bring their concerns to you. Understand them. Try to find out 'what makes them tick'. Talk to them (not *at* them). Find out what interests them outside work.
- Show that you value their work. One worker worked in a factory for years producing a small part in a large machine without knowing what the large machine was for. He was amazed, and felt more fulfilled, when he knew the function of the large machine and where his work fitted into the overall picture.
- Ensure that their work is interesting and challenging. No one likes boring repetitive tasks. Make sure that your colleagues' work contains at least some interesting tasks that will stretch them.
- Be flexible about what is negotiable and different styles of working. Listen to suggestions from your colleagues. Be prepared to 'think outside the box' to find solutions to difficulties.

- Be fair and treat all your colleagues equally, even though you may like some more than others.
- Make sure that all team members work as hard as one other; everyone has to 'pull their weight'. You can't afford to carry 'passengers': those team members who work significantly less than others.
- Show enthusiasm in your work. Enthusiasm is infectious, and so is the lack of it. If you are half-hearted in your commitment, that will show in your tone of voice and body language, and colleagues will be aware that you may be saying all the right words but not believing them yourself.
- Encourage openness. As far as you can, involve members of the team in making decisions. Bring out those who are shy and use your skills of diplomacy to quieten those who talk too much.
- Encourage team members to use their initiative. They do not always need to come back to you to solve small difficulties but can be enterprising and resolve issues themselves.
- Encourage colleagues to look out for one another, so that, for example, when one colleague is struggling, a fellow team member can step in and help.
- Encourage uncooperative colleagues to try a new system if they are reluctant to follow it, or even ask them if they could suggest new ways of solving a problem.
- Focus on specific, measurable, agreed, realistic/resourced and timed goals (look back at Chapter 4 for SMART goals), not on vague ideas.
- Give feedback. You as team leader should give informal feedback to team members on whether they are doing well... or not so well. Be specific (e.g. 'I thought the tone of your email in response to the complaint was excellent') as far as possible.

Back to the shop floor

As Managing Director, Joe felt he needed to 'get back to the shop floor' and find out what his staff really thought of his organization. So he sat alongside members of staff for several days, listening to their concerns. They didn't feel their work was valued, and communications from 'them' (senior management) were thought to be very poor. At

the end of the week, Joe was able to take these valuable
lessons back to his role as MD and begin to change the
company's practices.

Delegate well

Delegate more rather than less. There are a few matters you
cannot delegate (e.g. managing the overall team, allocating
financial resources, dealing with confidential matters of
performance management and promotion), but you can and
should both delegate many of your actual work tasks and
some routine administrative activities. Here are some further
guidelines for good delegation:

- Be clear about the tasks you want to delegate. Don't give
  vague instructions (e.g. 'Could you write a short report on
  failings in security?') but be specific: 'I'd like a ten-page
  report giving examples of major security breaches together
  with possible reasons behind them and recommendations
  on how to avoid them in future.'
- Check that the person has understood the task you want
  him/her to undertake. Do this not by just asking, 'Have
  you understood what I want you to do?' but something
  like 'Could you summarize what you will be doing?' Their
  response will show how much they have understood your
  explanation.
- Give background details, so that the colleague knows why
  he/she is doing the task and how his/her task or activity fits
  into the overall scheme of things.
- Where necessary, follow up any spoken instructions in
  writing with a full brief, outlining the work.
- State the time by which you want your colleagues to complete
  the work. Remember that what may take you (with all your
  experience) a short time will probably take much longer for
  the colleague you are delegating to.
- Supervise their work properly: provide the necessary
  equipment and other resources that the colleague needs.

- Let the person to whom you are delegating the work decide the details of how he/she will undertake the work.
- Where problems arise, encourage the person to whom you are delegating to come to you not only with the difficulty, but also with thoughts on possible solutions.
- When your colleague has completed the task, thank the person, expressing your appreciation. Recognize him/her and the achievement.

Learning to trust

Oliver was usually fine at delegating tasks. He explained tasks well and let his team members get on with it, checking both informally – 'How's it going?'– as well as, less often, formally. However, with one colleague, Janet, he used to continually come and stand by her desk, moving about nervously, and constantly ask how she was getting on. This annoyed Janet so much that one day she lost her temper with Oliver and burst out, 'Why don't you trust me just to get on with the job?' Oliver had to learn to back off and gradually was able to trust Janet, enabling her to continue her work with less supervision.

A good salesman

Andy was a good salesman. Over the years, he had networked widely, earning his clients' trust and the right to be listened to... and to sell his products. He was known for his commitment, thoroughness and integrity.

He was also persuasive. He was an astute listener, empathizing with and respecting his clients, and so was aware of their needs, helping his customers to make an informed choice. He was able to match his products to his clients' requirements because he genuinely wanted to provide products that were of real value to them. He knew his subject well and was very passionate about it. He really did believe in his products. So no wonder he was the country's best salesman.

Resolve conflict

At times, you are bound to meet conflict. Trust breaks down. Personalities clash. Departments each want a bigger slice of the budget or to avoid the biggest cutbacks.

Deal with conflict quickly; tackle the issues. Don't be cautious and fearful about speaking directly and clearly about difficulties.

I have found the books *Difficult Conversations: How to Discuss What Matters Most* by Douglas Stone, Bruce Patton and Sheila Heen (Michael Joseph, 1999) and *The Peacemaker: A Biblical Guide to Resolving Personal Conflict* by Ken Sande (Baker, 1991) very useful. The following is based on what those authors helpfully suggest:

- **Distinguish the incident – what is happening/happened – from feelings about the incident.** Consider separately:
  - the incident – someone said something; someone is to blame. Try to focus on the real issue. Remain calm. Listen closely. Ask open questions. Understand other people's interests as well as your own.
  - feelings about the incident, for example anger, hurt
  - the identity of the person. Sometimes a person's identity, including their own self-worth, will feel threatened. Calmly affirm your respect for them.
- **Do what you can to resolve the issue and maintain the relationship if possible:** prepare and evaluate possible solutions to agree on the way forward.

Summary

In this chapter we have been concerned with cultivating stronger working relationships: establishing a better rapport between colleagues. Key to this is taking the time to understand your colleagues and develop even greater respect and trust and stronger teamwork.

Follow-up

1 Think about the colleagues in your company or organization. Think about the ones you like. Why do you enjoy working with them? Now think about the ones you don't get on so well with. What practical steps can you take to improve your working relationships with them?

2 Think about what you can do to rise above the petty aspects of office politics. What can you do (and what can you not do) to be even more professional in your work?

3 Think about an area of conflict at work. What can you do to listen to people's different viewpoints and distinguish the incident from feelings about the incident? What are the next steps for you to undertake?

Fact-check (answers at the back)

1. Having strong working relationships in an organization is:
   a) A luxury ❑
   b) Essential ❑
   c) A waste of time ❑
   d) Unimportant ❑

2. In trying to build better relationships, think more about:
   a) Yourself ❑
   b) Your boss ❑
   c) Your colleagues ❑
   d) Your holidays ❑

3. When you are in a discussion with colleagues:
   a) Make sure you that say what you have to, not thinking about your colleagues ❑
   b) Look at your notes and never make eye contact with them ❑
   c) Be embarrassed because you like them a lot ❑
   d) Listen and respond to what they are saying. ❑

4. I am aware of colleagues' body language, posture and tone of voice:
   a) Never ❑
   b) Always ❑
   c) Rarely ❑
   d) Often ❑

5. 'Small talk' is:
   a) A useful tool to establish rapport ❑
   b) A complete waste of time ❑
   c) More important than the actual business ❑
   d) Just about adequate ❑

6. When thinking about others' roles:
   a) I am awed by those with higher status ❑
   b) I am very bossy towards those with lower status ❑
   c) I have this at the back of my mind but don't let it control me ❑
   d) I don't think about others ❑

7. In our team, we are clear about having:
   a) Strictly defined roles that we discuss whenever we meet ❑
   b) Different roles that we use as a basis to help us ❑
   c) No set roles at all ❑
   d) All the same roles ❑

8. I would like to improve teamwork in my team:
   a) But it is already as good as it can be; I don't need to do anything more ❑
   b) And I am keen to take practical action to do so ❑
   c) But I am so aware of my failings as team leader ❑
   d) But I am too lazy to do anything about it ❑

9. When I delegate work, I do so:
   a) Clearly ❑
   b) What is delegation? ❑
   c) In a vague way, hoping the colleague will work out what I mean ❑
   d) In so much detail that I confuse everyone ❑

10. When resolving conflict, first of all I:

a) Go straight to the solution ❑
b) Put off dealing with it ❑
c) Ignore everyone ❑
d) Listen closely to what both sides have to say ❑

CHAPTER 7

Engage effectively online

We conclude this Part by looking at how you can develop an online presence and engage in business online, from the point of view of communication. Much of what we discuss builds on what you have read earlier: this chapter pulls together a number of themes that we have already discussed, such as writing with a particular audience in mind, writing clearly and developing effective business relationships.

Websites have become an essential part of business life and it is difficult to imagine how we ever managed without them. Yet we are also aware that some websites are easier to navigate than others and information is more accessible on some than on others. So now we will consider:

- knowing your aims and planning your website carefully, so that the information is organized in a way that is accessible to the users you want to target
- writing text for your website, with tips on design and layout of your words
- exploiting the importance of social media in business.

Your company website

Know your aims

As for all forms of communication, it is essential that you clarify the exact aims of your website.

You may say that your company's or organization's website is your 'shop window', but what exactly do you mean by that? Your website will show the location of your office or store, and your opening hours. The website may show your goods or services, but do you want customers to buy direct from you or through a retailer or other intermediary? How do you want interested users of your website to respond to you? If you are offering a service, and if users want to complain, do you want to make it easy or more difficult for them to do so? You may want to promote an author or a rock band. You may want to inspire users by your choice of photographs, stories or poems. You may want to inform or educate users about a particular need or hobby and maybe ask them to give money towards your cause.

Plan your website

Work out your users' needs. We are back to AIR (Audience; Intention; Response), which we looked at in Chapter 1.

What are your users' needs? To know the aims of your company or organization? To be persuaded that they need to buy your product or service or ought to donate money? One way of beginning to think about this is to write a brief mission statement. You can fill this out with longer explanatory paragraphs and case studies (real-life examples) of your company or organization at work.

Think hard about how and when your users will use your website and what information they want. For example, we are currently renovating our bathroom and have accessed different companies' websites for details of the tiles, baths, basins, and so on they offer. Some companies give prices on the website, some in a separate downloadable brochure; some don't give prices at all!

Some users will view your website for only a few moments; others want to read what you have to say and respond positively, for example by buying a product or finding the information they want. Do you want users to download further files (e.g. in PDF)? How do you want users to contact you? Think all this through practically and realistically.

Organize your website

Here are some tips:

- Plan a hierarchy of information, that is, how you want users to go from one page to the next.
- Remember that people will navigate your site in a variety of ways.
- Separate your information into major – but manageable – parts. Group such parts into categories.
- Plan from 'the bottom up'; start with your most detailed pages and work backwards to your home page.
- Allow for flexibility. For example, if you are selling ebooks in various formats, allow for further tabs on your website alongside your existing ones to anticipate future changes in technology.
- Imagine a user accessing your website and work through how he/she will navigate your site. Make sure that the choices you are offering are the ones you want to offer. Some websites are built on the 'three-click' principle: give users the information they want within three clicks from the home page or they will go elsewhere. But the truth is, in reality, if users are interested – and determined – enough, they will explore your website more deeply.
- Have a balanced combination of words and images. Some websites seem to contain only words; some only images. I think an effective website will contain both.
- Plan how you will maintain your website. It is fine to work very hard on your website now, making it live by a certain date, but you also need to plan how you will keep it up to date. Too many websites have a section with 'latest news' that give stories that happened a year ago or more. Having out-of-date information does not communicate an image

that your company or organization is successful now. So the rule is: plan to keep your website fresh.
- Consider specifically search engine optimization (SEO): how you will reach your target audience most effectively through the use of keywords, tags and so on.

A new concept

Ray, one of the directors of the plumbers Smithson & Son, asked Jo, a website consultant, to design and build their company's website. When Jo first met Ray, she explained that a website was different from the normal printed pages of a book, in that a website does not really have a finishing point; it is much more flexible than the traditional printed page. Pages are more like photographs: they provide a visual snapshot for users. This interactive nature of the website was an entirely new concept to Ray. Previously, he thought that he could just put his company's existing leaflets on the website and that was it. Jo helped Ray see that the company's website could open up a whole new world, enabling customers to see what the company offered.

Write your website

Here are some useful tips:

- Keep in mind your users' needs. You are writing for them, not for yourself. Writing for a website is like having a conversation, except you cannot see the person you are talking to.
- Make sure that your home page says:
  - who you are and your basic aims
  - the goods and/or services you offer
  - how users may obtain your goods and/or services.
- Make your text easy to read. The following points are good practice:
  - Don't put text right across the whole width of the screen; if you do so, the text will not be legible. It is better to use up to half the width of the screen.

- The best position for text is towards the top of the screen and towards the left.
- Text that is centred on the page is difficult to read, so align your text – including headings – to the left, but keep the right-hand side 'ragged' (unjustified).
- A sans-serif font is more legible than a serif one on a computer screen.
- You should keep the colours of your text and background different, but don't use too many colours.

- Give each page its own title.
- Divide your text into paragraphs and write a clear heading above the paragraph. Keep paragraphs to no more than 100 words.
- Have white space around your text; this creates an impression of openness.
- Put the most important information first in each paragraph.
- Use everyday words that you would say in a normal conversation, e.g. *explain*, not *elucidate*; *more* or *extra*, not *supplementary*.
- Keep your sentences short: a maximum of 15–20 words.
- Make sure that your text is clear. Draft the text and then revise it, asking yourself what the paragraph is about. For example, some friends were writing about fishing for their website but had assumed that their readers knew all about that particular kind of fishing. When we discussed this, it became clear that what was missing was an opening definition of the particular kind of fishing they were writing about.
- Add hyperlinks to other pages on your website and/or back to your home page, for example: 'Click here to find out more or contact us.' (When users click on the underlined words they will be taken to a new page or a form.) Excessive use of hyperlinks can, however, make the page look too detailed.
- Make sure that your spelling is correct. 'Stephenson' or 'Stevenson'? 'Philips' or 'Phillips'? Be consistent (e.g. use *-ise* or *-ize* throughout).
- Keep punctuation to a minimum; full stops at the ends of bullet points can make a website look fussy.
- Avoid abbreviations that are not generally known and jargon and slang.

- Put information in lists, which work well on websites.
- Make sure that your text is accurate. Check dates and financial information so that they are correct.

Look back at editing documents in Chapter 2 for further guidelines.

Business and social media

In recent years, as the pace of innovation in the Internet age has quickened, use of social media sites such as Facebook has become an important part of many people's lives. The impact of these sites is still being assessed but undoubtedly digital formats will remain immensely significant for the foreseeable future.

- Professional networking sites such as LinkedIn allow you to keep informed about trends in your area of business, network with colleagues around the world, discuss matters of common interest and see what business opportunities may arise.
- Blogs and Twitter help you to develop an online community by connecting with potential and existing clients, sharing links to interesting articles, exchanging pictures, information and specific insights, discussing ideas and asking – and responding to – questions.

Summary

In this chapter we have looked at engaging effectively online by first of all considering your website: how to know your aims and move on from those to planning and organizing your website so that it fulfils those aims. We then looked at different aspects of writing for your website to make sure that your message is communicated successfully.

As an effective manager, you will also want to engage with your potential and existing customers using online social media. It can be very useful to think which online media networks will be most profitable both in the short term (spreading the message now) and also in the medium and long terms (maintaining good business relationships).

Follow-up

1 Summarize the aim of your website in 12 words.

2 Now think about your website and think how much it fulfils that aim.

3 How will you change and maintain your website to make sure it stays up to date?

4 How effective to your business are the social media sites that you use?

Fact-check (answers at the back)

1. Your website is:
   a) A luxury ❏
   b) A waste of time and money ❏
   c) Essential ❏
   d) Nice to have when you can afford it ❏

2. Your website is your organization's:
   a) Shop window ❏
   b) Rubbish tip ❏
   c) Set of printed leaflets ❏
   d) IT department's responsibility ❏

3. The first thing to do when planning a website is:
   a) Start writing as soon as possible ❏
   b) Organize the pages ❏
   c) Be flexible ❏
   d) Know your aims ❏

4. When designing web pages, put text in:
   a) Whatever the committee we will set up decides ❏
   b) Less than half the width of the screen ❏
   c) The whole width of the screen ❏
   d) More than the width of the screen ❏

5. Working out how users will navigate the website is:
   a) A luxury ❏
   b) Essential ❏
   c) A waste of time ❏
   d) Important if you have the money ❏

6. When designing web pages:
   a) Use a sans-serif font and lots of headings ❏
   b) Use a serif font and lots of headings ❏
   c) Use a serif font and no headings ❏
   d) Use a sans-serif font and no headings ❏

7. Giving each page a title is:
   a) Unnecessary; users can see what it's about ❏
   b) A nice idea if you are creative ❏
   c) Important – do it! ❏
   d) Extravagant – it takes up too much space ❏

8. You need to update your website:
   a) Regularly ❏
   b) Never ❏
   c) We haven't got a website to update ❏
   d) I will have to ask, as I'm not sure ❏

9. After writing text for the website:
   a) The website goes live immediately ❏
   b) If I have time, a colleague may check it ❏
   c) The website goes down; what did I do wrong? ❏
   d) Check the text to make sure that it is clear and accurate ❏

10. I use social media in my work:
    a) For a laugh ❏
    b) Never ❏
    c) To interact with potential and existing clients ❏
    d) As the only means of business communication ❏

7 × 7

1 Seven steps to sharpen your writing

- Plan! Think about what you want to write, why you are writing, what you hope to achieve and what response you want from your audience. Drawing a pattern diagram is a great first step.
- Identify your key messages and your audience – what will be the most effective way to impart this information?
- Structure your text; consider presenting arguments in order of importance (most important first), as a comparison of advantages and disadvantages, chronologically, or broken down by theme.
- Write a first draft; the blank page won't write itself! Focus on providing an introduction, the key data and a conclusion.
- Edit your draft; check accuracy of facts, spelling and punctuation, length (whether you are aiming for short and snappy or lengthy and detailed), and whether your overall message is clear.
- Reread your text after editing. Check it against your original plan – have you achieved what you wanted to achieve? If so, move to the next step; if not, loop back to another round of editing.
- Press 'send'! All too often, people use just two of these steps: 'Write a first draft' and 'Press "send"'; follow all seven steps to make your writing stand out.

2 Seven reasons to listen up

- Listening helps you to understand where the other person is coming from, and what they are trying to communicate.
- Listening encourages you to ask the right questions; as you focus on the other person, you will want to know more.

- Listening allows you to read between the lines; or, more correctly, hear between the lines – what's the underlying message?
- Listening helps you to understand your colleagues better: what's important to them, what concerns them, how they think, and how they are feeling.
- Listening gives you the opportunity to distinguish between fact and opinion.
- Listening builds trust between colleagues: value them and they will value you.
- Listening can resolve conflict: hearing and understanding – if not agreeing – are the first steps to resolution.

3 Seven ways to improve your business reading

- Decide what your aim is before starting to read: what do you want to get out of this?
- Vary your speed: spend more time on the important parts of the text, and be prepared to skim the waffle.
- Focus on key words and key phrases to identify the most significant sections of the text.
- Read more widely: reading is good! The more you read – whether relating to business or not – the more you will learn new words, phrases and ideas, and be better placed to apply them to your work.
- Try not to mouth words as you read them – this slows you down and also forces you to focus on the words rather than the sentiment.
- Think about the author's argument – do you agree with him/her, and, if not, why?
- If you find it helpful, take notes as you read. Summarizing the author's argument in your own words can be a powerful learning tool.

4 Seven tips for organizing meetings

- Know the purpose of the meeting.
- Plan a venue and time.
- Invite the key people.
- Circulate an agenda in advance.
- Prepare the meeting room.
- Read reports in advance.
- Ensure that you come up with accurate information.

5 Seven tips for chairing meetings

- Stick to the agenda and ensure that the meeting starts and ends on time.
- Introduce and welcome newcomers, or ask people to introduce themselves.
- State the meeting's key aims and objectives.
- Review progress on action points from previous meetings.
- Bring in key speakers to contribute at appropriate points.
- Summarize the points being discussed.
- Draw conclusions and make decisions: ensure that action points are clear and state who is responsible for following up on particular points (and by when).

6 Seven ways to polish presentations

- Try to summarize your message in 12 words or fewer. This is your key message to deliver: keep your headline simple.
- Know how long you will speak for. It's fine to finish a little early, but people start to fidget when they realize that you are overrunning.

- Think about what you are going to say! Check out the 'Seven steps to sharpen your writing'.
- Write your presentation down: either write word-for-word what you're going to say, or create a list of key points to guide you – whichever method works best for you.
- Deploy useful visual aids: yes, you cut a fine figure of a gentleman or lady, but give your audience something else to look at from time to time!
- If your presentation lasts for more than 45 minutes, plan a short comfort break for the audience.
- Be enthusiastic! Be positive and sell your message; your audience wants to hear your views, so share them gladly.

7 Seven things to avoid

- Confusing jargon and unknown terminology. Industry-specific language is fine, but avoid buzzwords and over-complication.
- Poor timing: whether asking for an immediate response or delivering bad news last thing on a Friday afternoon, timing is an incredibly important communication tool. Think about when will achieve the greatest impact.
- Voice says one thing, body says another: ensure that your body language is sending the same message as your wording.
- Unfocused, vague presentation: instead, be clear, precise and prepared.
- Wandering off the point.
- Providing too little information: everyone likes snappy communication, but assess your audience to better decide the best information to give.
- Providing too much information: see above, but in reverse! Once again, know your audience to judge exactly what to communicate.

PART 2

Your Persuasion and Influence Masterclass

Introduction

As social animals, we human beings cannot *not* communicate. Even if we are not speaking, our visual appearance and body language will 'speak' for us. It is therefore not surprising that people who have learned to be influential and persuasive communicators enjoy great success in life. This Part will teach you how to master a range of practical and proven techniques for influencing and persuading others, which will work in all aspects of your personal and business life.

This section is more than just a collection of theories on how to persuade and influence others. Spread throughout are real-life examples of people who have been acknowledged globally as highly successful influencers, together with insights into how they achieved this. And if they can do it, you can too!

CHAPTER 8

What is influence?

According to dictionary definitions, 'influence' can mean:

- to affect how others see a certain point or action, and react upon it
- to leave a mark on someone (not literally)
- to have someone or something start acting a bit like you.

Influencing others is one of the prime objectives of communication and is particularly important in the business world. In his 1936 book *How to Win Friends and Influence People*, Dale Carnegie wrote that dealing with people is probably the biggest problem we face, especially in business. He went on to say, 'There is only one way under high heaven to get anybody to do anything and that is by making the other person want to do it. There is no other way.'

In this chapter we will be examining some of the factors that have been proven to be effective and powerful influencers, delivered by personalities as diverse as Sir Winston Churchill and Sir Bob Geldof. We will also explore what influences you – whether you make 'head' or 'heart' decisions, and how you 'sell' yourself when you want to promote yourself to others.

What influences your decisions?

Think about the last time you bought something that was a 'want' rather than a 'need'. Perhaps you were out and about, and you just saw something that caught your eye. You liked the look of it and you decided you wanted it, even though you knew you didn't need it. You might have been aware that, at that point, a voice inside your head went into 'justification mode'. It started generating 'reasons' why you really should have this object of your desire. Before you knew it, you had made your purchasing decision, handed over some money and it was yours.

Perhaps you remained pleased with that purchasing decision, or perhaps, in the cold light of a day or two later, you wondered what on earth possessed you to hand over good money for this 'thing'. Whatever your feelings about that decision, your personality type will have influenced it.

The following is a list of different personality types related to buying decisions. Notice whether you identify with any of them.

The gadget geek

If it's the latest technology, cutting-edge design and it's considered cool to possess one of these, then the gadget geeks want it. They have an image to sustain, after all. If Apple brings out a new iPhone, then they have to be first in the queue to get one. They may even be prepared to pay someone to stand in the queue all night on their behalf so that they get pole position. They don't even need to know what new features this iPhone has: if it's new, it must be a better, improved version of the last model and it's essential for them to be bang up to date.

When the Apple iPhone5 first went on sale in London, among the people in the queue eager to part with £599 was a man who justified his purchase by telling a journalist that he had just bought an Audi A6 and it was 'only compatible with a phone that has a milled aluminium finish'! These people make justified, 'from-the-head' decisions.

The connoisseur collector

These people don't buy; they invest. They seek 'elite purchases', which they refer to as 'investment pieces'. They attend fine-art auctions or – if the item they want has a particular rarity value – they stay away and become a telephone bidder, in case their presence inflates the price. Although they love beautiful things, connoisseur collectors are also prepared to invest in items that are acknowledged as desirable and therefore valuable, even if they are not to their personal taste. These could include fine wines, which they 'put down' in a temperature-controlled wine cellar, never to be consumed.

Admiration is everything and the quality of their possessions reflects their personal aspirations. They want to be seen as discerning buyers with impeccable taste. Although image is important to this group, their purchasing decisions tend to be led by the head rather than the heart because of the investment factor.

The memorabilia collector

These people consider themselves to be similar to the connoisseur collectors but dedicated to a particular theme. The theme might be *Star Wars* merchandise, royal family memorabilia or Barbie dolls through the ages. Because there tends to be no limit to the size of their collections, they are constantly adding to them, sometimes to the extent that their collected 'treasures' take over all the space in their homes. Charity shops, car boot sales, eBay and sci-fi fairs are all happy hunting grounds for these 'from-the-heart' buyers.

The trend follower

Trend followers are celebrity spotters. They avidly read the celebrity gossip magazines and, if they see that someone they admire has just started a new trend – perhaps with a hairstyle, tattoo, beauty/health treatment, fashion accessory or clothes – they have to follow it. Their hope is that, if they emulate their idol, some of their 'stardust' may rub off on them. Plus they will be seen to be 'on trend' with the latest 'in thing'. The higher the profile their adored one has, the more the trend follower will want to replicate them. A prime example of this kind of idol is the Duchess of Cambridge. If she wears an outfit from a high-street retailer, it will instantly sell out, both in store and online.

These people are 'heart buyers', who may not necessarily think through their real reasons for making a purchase. For example, one serious downside of this behaviour has been the fallout from copying the 'handbag dog' accessory trend, i.e. carrying around a small dog in a handbag. First seen in the film *Legally Blonde* and then picked up by celebrities such as Paris Hilton, this treatment of small dogs as fashion accessories rather than as pets often results in the animals developing significant behavioural issues. Battersea Dogs Home has reported that they are increasingly being asked to rehome these disturbed small dogs.

The impulse buyer

Impulse buyers are easily influenced by other people's persuasiveness and by 'bargain' purchases, and they are often great fans of television shopping channels. Their emotional states often drive their spending habits. For example, if they feel sad, they will buy something to cheer themselves up. If they feel happy, they will splash out on a treat of some kind in order to celebrate. If they are out shopping with a friend who is buying, they join in because they tell themselves that it would be unsociable not to and, in any case, they deserve it (whatever 'it' happens to be).

Unfortunately, impulse buys are often not wise buys. The impulse buyer can easily end up with wardrobes full of clothes they never wear. Their 'spend, spend, spend' habit can even take them hurtling towards financial ruin. A famous example of this was the football pools winner Viv Nicholson, who won £152,319 in 1961 (£5 million in today's money), but who became penniless within a few years. These people are definitely 'from-the-heart' buyers.

The self-help junkie

On a permanent quest for personal growth, material success or spiritual enlightenment, the self-help junkie buys a huge number of books, ebooks, training programmes, CD sets and DVD sets on their chosen subject. They are often prepared to travel anywhere in the world to attend their favourite teacher or guru's seminars or retreats, where they hang on their every word. They consider their purchases to be investments, and it has to be said that some of these devotees do indeed utilize what they learn and go on to achieve all they desire in life. However, the majority of followers just accumulate a wealth of books that any library would be proud of, along with an extensive CD/DVD collection.

Until they feel that 'something' in their quest has made a difference to them, the self-help junkie will keep searching and buying because the answer has to be 'out there' somewhere; it's just a matter of time before they find it. They make intuitive, heart-based purchasing decisions in their search for fulfilment and happiness.

In order to influence others, especially in the context of selling them something, we must offer them something to which they will attribute value. This is why it's important to understand their personality type and what drives them to make purchasing decisions.

Personality and perceived value

You may have noticed that only the first two personality types described make 'head' decisions and that only one of those invests in purchases with the potential to increase in value. And yet 'value' is the common denominator for all six types. What converts a 'want' to a 'need' is its perceived value. Every one of the personality types listed has perceived a value of some kind in their potential purchases, and a 'need' has evolved that can only be satisfied by possessing it.

Let's revisit these personality types to understand the different values they attribute to their 'objects of desire'.

- **The gadget geek** is vulnerable to peer pressure and has an innate need to be 'leader of the pack'. This desire is so strong that it is programmed into their mental DNA and thus their purchasing decisions become logical, next-step actions. Possessing the most up-to-date, superior, shiny gadget has the value of fulfilling this non-negotiable need.

- **The connoisseur collector** is always focused on the financial value of a potential purchase and evaluates it in terms of future return on investment. He or she may invest in a Picasso that is not to their personal taste because they know that, whether it is hung on the wall or not, it is an asset that can only appreciate in value.

- **The memorabilia collector** has huge affection for their chosen theme. When they see a new 'desirable', especially if it is something they don't yet have in their collection, their heart starts racing and an 'inner smile' just takes them over. They take great care of their treasured objects and attach much value to their activity because of the happiness they gain from it. They find it hard to part with any of the objects they have collected, even when the size of their collection becomes excessive.

- **The trend follower** is searching for an identity. Lacking the courage to be original, they prefer to emulate others who they perceive to be setting new, desirable trends. Because their idols tend to be well known and publicly admired, the trend follower believes that they, too, will become popular if they dress the same way or do the same things. They have a strong need to feel admired and greatly value anything that might facilitate this.

- **The impulse buyer** readily responds to their emotions. He or she will 'invest' in something that will either change an undesirable emotional state or enhance an enjoyable one to make it last. For example, they are on holiday in Spain, having a marvellous time. On the last day they experience a burning desire to take something home with them that will capture this sense of happiness. They browse the tourist shops and there it is – a straw donkey the size of a small child, wearing a sun hat. They have to have it! It's a challenge carrying it home on the plane but now it sits, in pride of place, in the hallway at home. It's in the way, of course, but every time our impulse buyer pats it on the head, happy memories of that holiday in Spain come flooding back.

- **The self-help junkie**, in search of personal fulfilment and meaning in life, attributes value to anything that appears to aid them in their quest. They see their chosen gurus as having successfully completed a journey upon which they are keen to embark. They are eager to learn and to replicate everything that their chosen one did along the way. If their guru is happy to impart this knowledge in a book, on a CD or DVD, or in person at a seminar, then the self-help junkie is a willing follower, valuing every morsel of advice they can glean.

The role of the champion

Another situation in which people place great value on their needs being met is during a time of crisis. People look for someone to become their 'champion', someone who will take control and lead them forward to happier times. Great value will be attributed to the person who fulfils this role and, in this position, he or she becomes extremely influential. Two examples of such champions are Winston Churchill and Bob Geldof.

The influence of Churchill

During the Second World War, Great Britain's 'champion' was Winston Churchill. An outstanding orator, his inspirational speeches provided a psychological boost to British morale exactly when it was needed. Two of his most memorable speeches – delivered in a tone of voice that resonated with unshakeable confidence and determination – were made during the dark days of 1940.

The first one came on 4 June, just hours after the evacuation of Dunkirk, in which 338,226 British and French soldiers, cut off by the German army, were rescued from the Dunkirk beaches by a hastily assembled fleet of 850 boats. Many of these boats were just small pleasure craft – the smallest was only 14 ft 7 in (4.45 m) long – but they all played an essential role in saving lives. The 'miracle of the little ships' has remained a prominent legend in Britain. Some of the surviving boats took part in the Queen's Diamond Jubilee river pageant in 2012, 72 years on from their finest hour.

The following is an extract from Churchill's post-Dunkirk speech:

> We shall not flag or fail; we shall go on to the end. We shall fight in France; we shall fight on the seas and oceans. We shall fight with growing confidence and growing strength in the air. We shall defend our island whatever the cost may be. We shall fight on the beaches; we shall fight on the landing grounds. We shall fight in the fields and in the streets, we shall fight in the hills; we shall never surrender.

Churchill referred to the outcome of the evacuation as a 'miracle' and the British press termed it a 'disaster turned into triumph'. To this day, the phrase 'Dunkirk spirit' is still used in Britain to describe people who pull together to overcome times of adversity.

Churchill made a second memorable speech on 20 August, when the crisis of the Battle of Britain was imminent. German air attacks were being directed against the RAF airfields in the south of England, and Churchill used the phrase 'so few' to describe the RAF fighter pilots:

> The gratitude of every home in our Island, in our Empire, and indeed throughout the world, except in the abodes of the guilty, goes out to the British airmen who, undaunted by odds, unwearied in their constant challenge and mortal danger, are turning the tide of the world war by their prowess and by their devotion. Never in the field of human conflict was so much owed by so many to so few.

The power of the pause

One technique that Churchill deployed in order to add impact to his speeches was the use of pauses. Read the following extract out loud, exactly as it is written:

'Never in the field of human conflict was so much owed by so many to so few.'

Now read it out loud again, pausing where there are dots, and notice the difference:

'Never ... in the field of human conflict ... was so much ... owed by so many ... to so few.'

Suddenly, it now has a deeper level of meaning, a gravitas that truly 'moved' people emotionally. Churchill knew about the power of the pause and he used it to great effect.

The influence of Bob Geldof

Another, more unlikely, champion emerged in 1984. On the evening of 23 October, rock singer Bob Geldof, like many thousands of others in Britain, was watching the 9 o'clock news on BBC television. Like thousands of others, he was appalled by a graphic report on the human suffering and huge loss of life occurring in Ethiopia as a result of drought, disease and famine.

In his view, '30 million people are dying; meanwhile, in Europe, we're spending tax to grow food we don't need, we spend more tax to store it and we pay further tax, most disgracefully, to destroy it.' He saw this as a crime; it made him angry and this galvanized him into action.

He *needed* to make a difference; the British public *wanted* to make a difference but didn't know how. Geldof had the answer. Within weeks, he had assembled a group of high-profile singers, and composed and recorded with them the Band Aid single, 'Do they know it's Christmas?' with the chorus of 'Feed the World'. It was released on 7 December, became the fastest-selling single ever and raised £8 million.

The following summer, Geldof initiated the satellite-linked UK and USA Live Aid concerts. By now he had support from the highest in the land, with Prince Charles and Princess Diana attending the Wembley concert alongside an audience of 72,000 people. TV pictures were beamed to over 1.5 billion people in 160 countries in the biggest broadcast ever known.

Between music sets, Geldof made frequent passionate appeals to viewers to 'Give us your money – there are people dying right now.' He shouted, he swore, and it worked. Across the UK, 200 phone lines were set up and manned to receive credit-card donations. Geldof personally took the call from the ruling family in Dubai when they made the biggest single donation of £1 million. In the USA, 22,000 pledges of money were received within five minutes of the Beach Boys taking to the stage in the simultaneous concert at JFK Stadium, Philadelphia.

Live Aid eventually raised a total of £40 million; in 1986 Bob Geldof was awarded an honorary knighthood. The success of Live Aid came about because Geldof had shown people a tangible way to make a difference to those who couldn't help themselves. Through our donations we could save lives and at the same time ease any feelings of guilt we may have been experiencing. And we placed *great value* on that.

TIP *You need to convey passion and conviction when you are aiming to influence others, and remember that part of what you are fulfilling is an emotional need.*

Summary

In this chapter we have explored what influence is and how it manifests itself in our lives. We have looked at this in the context of how a 'want' can be transformed into a 'need' if sufficient value is added. This is apparent in our purchasing decisions, for a variety of different reasons, as demonstrated by the six 'buying personality' types.

We are also influenced and even inspired by 'champions' – people who step up into the leadership limelight just when we have an emotional need for someone to fill that role. Winston Churchill and Bob Geldof couldn't be more different and yet they both took on this role to great effect.

Value is thus the essential ingredient if we are thinking about influencing others. In order to influence others, we must offer them something to which they will attribute value. Whether it is a product or a well-reasoned argument that persuades people to do something or feel something, value is what makes the difference.

Fact-check (answers at the back)

1. What is influence?
a) Leaving a visible mark on someone ❑
b) The power someone has to affect other people's thinking or actions ❑
c) Preventing people doing what they want ❑
d) Forcing people to agree with you ❑

2. Which personality types buy 'from the head'?
a) The gadget geek and the connoisseur collector ❑
b) The memorabilia collector and the trend follower ❑
c) The impulse buyer and the self-help junkie ❑
d) The gadget geek and the trend follower ❑

3. How do people justify making a purchase?
a) By being influenced by other people's persuasiveness ❑
b) By copying other people's purchases ❑
c) They need to be bang up to date ❑
d) They convert their 'wants' into needs ❑

4. Which personality type focuses on particular themes?
a) The trend follower ❑
b) The memorabilia collector ❑
c) The gadget geek ❑
d) The impulse buyer ❑

5. What does every personality type need when buying?
a) To perceive a value in their potential purchases ❑
b) To follow their peer group rather than be leaders ❑
c) A potential return on their investment ❑
d) Admiration of their purchases by others ❑

6. Which personality type focuses on the potential return on their investment?
a) The self-help junkie ❑
b) The connoisseur collector ❑
c) The impulse buyer ❑
d) The trend follower ❑

7. Which personality type is in search of personal fulfilment?
a) The self-help junkie ❑
b) The connoisseur collector ❑
c) The impulse buyer ❑
d) The memorabilia collector ❑

8. What was Churchill's value as champion?
a) Supporting RAF fighter pilots ❑
b) Winning the Battle of Britain ❑
c) Inspiring people during a time of crisis ❑
d) Helping people to overcome adversity ❑

9. Prior to Live Aid, what was Bob Geldof famous for?
a) Being a TV chef ❑
b) Being a rock singer ❑
c) Making a difference ❑
d) Raising taxes to relieve suffering ❑

10. What was Bob Geldof's value as champion?

a) Enabling people to help save lives and at the same time ease any feelings of guilt ❑

b) Organizing a great rock concert ❑

c) Allowing credit-card donations ❑

d) Being awarded an honorary knighthood ❑

CHAPTER 9

Conveying the right image

Influencing effectively and powerfully is about more than just being a good speaker. We are most influenced by the type of person who 'walks their talk' – in other words, we look for congruence between the message and the person delivering it.

Even though Bob Geldof seemed initially an unlikely candidate for the role of global fundraiser and humanitarian, in his appearance, behaviour and communication style he remained true to his primary role of 'rock star'. We could label him 'the angry rock star, passionate about a good cause'. The pieces fitted together, we shared his mission and the whole package worked.

In this chapter we shall explore the consequences of being both totally congruent – when image, message and behaviour are all in alignment – and incongruent – where these elements are in conflict with each other. You will learn how and why people stereotype others, and how you can use this phenomenon to your advantage when influencing.

We shall also look at two individuals who have each in their own way been profoundly influential on a global scale. One overturned a stereotyped response and the other 'walked the talk'.

What is stereotyping?

As human beings, we have an innate desire to make sense of things. We need to know what's going on around us and how it affects us so that we can decide how to behave in response. This gives us a sense of comfort and the phrase 'comfort zone' is often used to describe this state of wellbeing. As part of this process, we like to draw rapid conclusions about our environment. For example, within four seconds of seeing someone for the first time, we start to make assumptions and judgements about them.

We may assume that at first glance we can tell the person's:

- age
- occupation
- financial worth
- lifestyle
- level of education
- ethnic origin
- marital status.

In addition, once the person starts to speak, we make further assumptions about their background, where they are from and even their level of intelligence, based on their accent or dialect, the type of vocabulary they use and their style of speech. At this point, our ego gets involved. We start to make comparisons between them and us, to determine how this person 'measures up'. Are they superior or inferior to us in some way? How should we behave towards them?

There is a danger here that we then act out an ego-driven behaviour based on false assumptions. If this happens, we may not be behaving in the most appropriate and best way possible, and in so doing we will not be able to influence effectively.

The positive purpose of stereotyping

However, this instant stereotyping can have a positive purpose, which is that it can protect us from danger. If we detect potential danger, our brain's fight-or-flight response allows us to take action against it. For example, imagine you are walking along a street at night and a figure steps out of the shadows in front of you. Your eyes scan him or her for signs of whether they are a friend or foe and, judging this stranger to have a 'menacing' appearance, your mind concludes that you could be in danger. This instantly triggers your fight-or-flight response, adrenaline is released into your body and you are now equipped either to stand your ground and defend yourself or to run away.

Because you have in your mind your own 'templates' of friend and foe, and you needed to make sense of the situation, you compared the appearance of the stranger before you to these images and found that he or she matched the 'foe template'. At that point, you stereotyped this person as some kind of troublemaker. You allowed yourself to be influenced by appearance and made an assumption that had at least a 50 per cent chance of being correct.

The first impression we form of someone tends to be a lasting one unless we receive some powerful and convincing evidence to the contrary. Moreover, our mind has a 'thinker' and a 'prover'. Whatever the thinker is thinking about, it is the prover's job to provide supporting evidence that says, 'Yes, you're right.' Once the thinker forms a first impression, the prover will only notice corroborative evidence; anything else will be dismissed as incorrect. This will continue until the thinker adopts a different viewpoint, but it usually takes something quite dramatic to bring about this 180° shift.

Overturning the stereotype: Susan Boyle

Susan Boyle is a Scottish singer who attracted worldwide public attention after appearing on the television show *Britain's Got Talent* in April 2009. Born in 1961 with a mild learning difficulty, Susan was bullied as a child and left school with few qualifications. However, her passion was singing and having taken part in, and won, several local amateur singing competitions, her mother urged her to enter the show in order to develop her confidence for singing in front of a large audience. Sadly, Susan's mother died before the audition took place and Susan nearly withdrew her application. However, her voice coach persuaded her to go ahead. Susan's performance on *BGT* was the first time she had sung in public since her mother's death.

When Susan walked out on the stage, a plain, slightly overweight, nearly 48-year-old, and said that her aspiration was to become a professional singer as successful as Elaine Paige, the audience laughed. They had stereotyped her in those first four seconds as delusional and decided that there was no way she could possibly be a talented singer. The judges clearly shared their scepticism, as this unlikely-looking candidate prepared to sing 'I dreamed a dream' from *Les Misérables*.

When Susan's clear, note-perfect mezzo-soprano voice filled the theatre, jaws dropped and eyes widened in astonishment at the clarity and beauty of her voice. The applause started just four seconds after Susan's first note and became a standing ovation that continued long after she'd finished singing, with the judges also on their feet. Judge Amanda Holden remarked on how the initially cynical attitude of the audience (and the judges) had been completely overturned by Susan's performance, calling it the 'biggest wake-up call ever'.

After that edition of *Britain's Got Talent* was televised, Susan appeared on the Oprah Winfrey show in the USA via satellite link. The final of that year's *BGT* commanded a record UK television audience of 17.3 million. Although favourite to win, Susan came second to dance troupe Diversity, but it didn't matter. She became a highly successful, internationally acclaimed professional singer, setting new records in both the UK and the USA for the fastest-selling album of a debut artist in decades.

Susan Boyle's story offers a profound example of how initial stereotyping based on appearance not only can be completely wrong but also *can* be overturned by overwhelming evidence to the contrary. However, she is the exception that proves the rule that 'You only get one chance to make a first impression'. It is far better to make the first impression the one you desire than to have to prove people wrong and force them to change their minds about you.

TIP *Tens of millions of people worldwide have already viewed the YouTube video of Susan Boyle's* **Britain's Got Talent** *audition. Watch it if you haven't already done so: it is an inspiring and even emotional experience to see it.*

What is congruence?

An example of someone who very much 'walked her talk', whose appearance and behaviour were 100 per cent congruent with everything that she stood for – enabling her to exert her influence on a worldwide scale – was Anita Roddick, founder of The Body Shop. Although technically an international corporate executive, Anita never presented herself in a way that would have supported such a stereotype, for example dressing in a designer 'power suit' and high heels and carrying a smart leather briefcase. Such an image would have been at odds with The Body Shop 'brand' and seen as inauthentic.

The following case study about Anita Roddick shows the consequences of congruence. Anita believed that businesses have the power to do good in the world and The Body Shop mission statement reflects this sentiment and incorporates her own values, opening with the words, 'To dedicate our business to the pursuit of social and environmental change'. The Body Shop's mission had a global effect: it raised awareness of global issues, promoting third-world trade and discouraging the testing of products on animals. Because she lived her beliefs and values, both personally and in her business life, Anita Roddick will always remain synonymous with The Body Shop.

Walking the talk:
Anita Roddick

Anita Roddick was born in a bomb shelter in 1942 in Littlehampton, Sussex, England, her Italian immigrant family having fled Naples just before the outbreak of the Second World War. Growing up in an English seaside town, Anita always felt she was a natural outsider, drawn to other outsiders and rebels such as her teenage idol James Dean. She also developed a strong sense of moral outrage at the age of ten when she read a book about the Holocaust.

Having trained as a teacher, she worked on a kibbutz in Israel, which led to an extended working trip around the world, during which she spent time in primitive farming and fishing communities, exposed to and learning about the body-care rituals of the women she encountered there. Influenced by her mother's wartime thriftiness of refilling, re-using and recycling, combined with a passion for environmental activism, Anita created a small range of body-care products and opened the first branch of The Body Shop in Brighton in 1976. Within six months, she had opened a second shop and eventually The Body Shop went global through the growth of a franchise network, serving some 77 million customers worldwide.

Anita always retained the appearance and demeanour of a 'wild child', her natural attractiveness the perfect advertisement for her beauty products. The issues she cared passionately about, such as social responsibility, respect for human rights, the environment, animal protection and community trade, became absorbed into The Body Shop's values. The company was at the forefront of using ingredients that had not been tested on animals and of actively trading with developing countries. For example, a moisturizing oil used in some of its products is extracted from Brazil nuts gathered sustainably by Amazonian Indian tribes.

During her lifetime, Anita was awarded many accolades, including the OBE in 1988 and the DBE in 2003, but perhaps one of the most significant and meaningful awards was presented to her in 1999 when she was made the 'Chief Wiper-Away of Ogoni Tears' for her involvement in the movement for the survival of the Ogoni people in Nigeria. Anita died in 2007, having fulfilled her promise to leave her estate to charities on moral grounds.

Presentation: the four-second rule

The way you present yourself sets the scene for how well you can influence others. The following table lists aspects of your appearance that people *will* notice within four seconds of meeting you. Although they might sound like common sense, neglecting any of these can result in the projection of a negative first impression, which can then undermine your ability to influence.

Aspect	Impression
Hair	Messy, unwashed hair or, worse, flakes of dandruff on your shoulders projects an extremely unprofessional image.
Nails	Bitten-down or dirty nails or chipped varnish indicate low personal standards.
Personal hygiene	A strong body odour makes it unpleasant to be around you. Ensure that you wash and use deodorant daily.
Perfume and aftershave	Use sparingly. An overwhelming 'vapour trail' can be almost as offensive as a strong body odour.
Breath	If you have been eating garlic or spicy food such as curry or drinking alcohol within the past 12 hours or so, your breath may still reflect this. Consider carrying mints and/or breath freshener with you at all times.
Dress code	Always dress appropriately for your audience and take cultural norms into account. For men, this could mean a smart suit, collar and tie, and for women a skirt length on or below the knee and tights rather than bare legs. Whatever you are wearing, it must be clean and pressed. If you are a smoker, check for the smell of stale cigarette smoke on your clothes, as this will be particularly noticeable to non-smokers.

(Continued)

Aspect	Impression
Shoes	Footwear must be clean and in good repair. Dirty, scuffed shoes with worn-down heels can let down the smartest outfit.
Tie	You may love the brightly coloured, cartoon-character tie your child gave you and it may reflect your quirky personality, but unless you know your audience really well, err on the side of formality and choose something more sober. Ensure that your tie has no marks or stains on it; because it is immediately below your face, it will always be noticed.
Neckline	Wearing a top with a low neckline is not acceptable in a business environment as it sends out the wrong message. Keep clothes like this for your personal life.
Frayed collars/ hanging threads/loose buttons	All indicate an attitude of neglect. Missing buttons, tears and holes are even worse. Make it a habit to carry out occasional wardrobe checks and repairs so that problems such as these can be avoided.
Jewellery	The principle of 'less is more' works well in the workplace, particularly for men. Wearing an excessive amount of jewellery distracts your audience from you and your message.
Make-up	As with jewellery and perfume, it is important not to wear too much. However, it should be noted that in a corporate environment, a woman wearing no make-up at all may be perceived as not professional enough. Cosmetics need to be well applied with subtlety so as to enhance rather than dramatically change the appearance of the wearer.
Handshake	A firm handshake, but not a bone-crusher, inspires confidence. A limp or damp handshake may be interpreted as a 'weak' personality trait.

TIP

Something as apparently insignificant as a stain on a tie or bitten-down fingernails can make the difference between your ability to be an effective influencer and a mediocre one. The little things really do make a big difference; take them seriously.

Consulting the professionals

To enhance aspects of your visual and vocal impact, which will in turn improve your ability to persuade and influence, think about consulting the following professionals.

Image consultant

An image consultant will carry out a colour and style analysis for you, enabling you to select clothes and colours that significantly enhance your appearance and improve your confidence levels. The intention is that you 'dress to impress', which will also strengthen your ability to influence others. A reputable image consultant can make all the difference to your 'visual charisma' and I cannot recommend this service highly enough.

Voice coach

If you feel that your voice lets you down in some way, consider consulting a voice coach. Many people in the public eye do this. Margaret Thatcher, in preparation for her bid to become leader of the Conservative Party, worked with such a coach, who enabled her to lower the pitch of her voice and slow down the speed of her vocal delivery. The result was that her voice gained an authority and gravitas that ultimately helped her to become the first female British prime minister.

Summary

In this chapter we discovered that, in order to influence and persuade effectively, it is essential to convey the right image. We explored the phenomenon of stereotyping and how this occurs naturally within the first four seconds of seeing someone for the first time. The example of Susan Boyle demonstrates this well, but it also shows that a negative stereotype *can* be turned around. However, it does require something extraordinary to make this happen.

For most situations it's important to make sure that you and your message are in complete alignment. Failure to do this results in an inauthentic impression of 'Do as I say', rather than 'Do as I do' and reduces your powers of persuasion. You may have noticed that politicians often fall foul of this principle!

To generate the most positive stereotype you can in those crucial first four seconds, you learned the importance of thinking about your personal presentation. The elements to consider may seem obvious, but they are easily overlooked. Consulting professionals can also help you to enhance your impact.

Fact-check (answers at the back)

1. What does 'congruent' mean?
   a) Your image, message and behaviour are out of alignment ❑
   b) You won't be stereotyped ❑
   c) Your image, message and behaviour are in alignment ❑
   d) We like people who look like us ❑

2. How quickly do we make assumptions about others?
   a) Within the first four seconds of seeing them ❑
   b) Within five minutes of seeing them ❑
   c) After we have talked to them at length ❑
   d) As soon as they start to speak ❑

3. What are stereotypes based on?
   a) Assumptions about others' financial worth ❑
   b) The attractiveness of someone ❑
   c) Comparisons with ourselves ❑
   d) What someone looks and sounds like ❑

4. What's the role of the ego when making assumptions?
   a) The ego never makes assumptions ❑
   b) Determining whether someone is superior or inferior to us ❑
   c) Making sure our assumptions are correct ❑
   d) Assumptions play no part in determining our behaviour ❑

5. What is the positive purpose of stereotyping?
   a) To protect us from potential danger ❑
   b) To release fight-or-flight hormones into the body ❑
   c) To make instant assumptions about others ❑
   d) To enhance our powers of persuasion ❑

6. How can we overcome initial stereotyping based on appearance?
   a) Through overwhelming evidence to the contrary ❑
   b) It's impossible ❑
   c) By ignoring our initial view ❑
   d) By forgetting what we first thought ❑

7. How does congruence enhance our ability to influence?
   a) By reflecting and incorporating our values into all our actions ❑
   b) By showing the world we mean business ❑
   c) By giving a good impression in a meeting ❑
   d) By making sure we dress smartly ❑

8. Why is the way you present yourself important?
   a) It helps us relax ❑
   b) It sets the scene for how well we can influence others ❑
   c) It keeps us one step ahead of the competition ❑
   d) It stops us feeling like a 'natural outsider' ❑

9. What's the best way to make a good impression?
a) Telling others to 'do as we say' rather than 'do as we do' ❑
b) Cultivating a 'lived-in' look to show we are 'hands-on' ❑
c) Paying attention to aspects of our appearance that people will notice ❑
d) Splashing out on perfume, aftershave or cologne ❑

10. What's a useful rule of presentation to remember?
a) Dress appropriately for your audience ❑
b) Scuffed shoes don't matter, as nobody will notice them ❑
c) Wear as much gold jewellery as possible, to impress others with your wealth ❑
d) A limp handshake is good, as it demonstrates your sensitive nature ❑

CHAPTER 10

Becoming a voice of authority

So far, we have looked at what influence is, the factors that affect it, both positively and negatively, and the importance of conveying the right image so that, when others construct a stereotype impression of you, it is exactly the one you intended. In this chapter we will explore how and why a voice of authority influences people.

The 'authority research' originally carried out by Stanley Milgram in the 1960s, and successfully replicated on television by Derren Brown in 2006, showed the extent to which people were willing to follow an authoritative voice, even to the point of them obeying that voice without question. Being aware of the conclusions from these experiments will enhance your ability to be authoritative, while remaining approachable and respected.

You'll also discover one of the reasons why Martin Luther King's famous 'I have a dream' speech had such a memorable impact and how you can adopt his tactic for yourself when making a presentation. You will also learn a technique for sounding assertive, reasonable and in control in even the most confrontational situations, as well as some other proven strategies for becoming a confident, effective and influential figure of authority.

Who are your authority figures?

Let's start by examining examples of authority figures. Think back to your childhood and specifically to the people who represented figures of authority to you. These are the people who impressed and inspired you, people you admired and respected. If one of these people asked you to do something, you would have done it willingly and without question. You listened to their advice and took it on board. They may have been your parents or other family members, a teacher, a friend or someone else in your peer group, a neighbour or some other member of your community.

Identify three of these authority figures and write down their names in a table like the one below. Then, for each one, define exactly what characteristic(s) it was about them that generated your respect and prompted you to call them to mind.

Name	Characteristic(s)
1	
2	
3	

Now repeat the exercise, this time identifying the authority figures you feel you have in your life now. Choose three people whom you did not select before, and include any public figures who fulfil the criteria for you, even if you have never met them. The following are typically some of the characteristics that you may have identified:

Good listener
Very understanding
Showed compassion and empathy
Championed my cause
Took a genuine interest in me
Always had time for me, even when busy
Believed in me and my ideas
Led by example
Gave support and encouragement
Brave, courageous
Light-hearted, always positive and smiling
Never made unreasonable or unfair demands
Generous spirit
Decisive
Knowledgeable and competent

Reassuring	Took complete responsibility
Optimistic in the face of uncertainty	for him/herself and his/her actions
An achiever, but never arrogant about it	Always embraced a challenge
Happy to share their ideas/ solutions with me	Constantly strove to be their 'best self' and to make a difference to others
Prepared to step up and lead when someone was needed	Good problem solver with innovative ideas

You may have identified some additional ones. However, the common theme here is that all of these are qualities we tend to admire and respect so, if we attribute any of them to another person, we are more likely to accept them as a figure of authority, deserving our respect and co-operation.

In identifying significant authority figures from your childhood, you were recalling people who were important to you when you were at an impressionable age. You may have found that, when you then identified more recent authority figures, the characteristics you sought in them were different from the childhood ones.

Now take some time to review the list above and the characteristics you identified in this exercise. How many of these attributes do *you* have? The more of these that you possess, the easier it will be for you to become a figure of authority.

 TIP *Select a characteristic from the list that you feel you don't currently have and set yourself an action plan to develop it.*

The Milgram experiments

During the early 1960s the Yale University social psychologist Stanley Milgram conducted some experiments. His intention was to measure the willingness of participants to obey an authority figure – one who would instruct them to perform actions that conflicted with their personal conscience and deepest moral beliefs.

The experiment involved three roles:

- The experimenter – this was an authoritative role of 'experimental scientist'
- The teacher – this role was fulfilled by a volunteer, intended to obey the orders of the experimenter
- The learner – this was a role fulfilled by an actor who pretended to be another volunteer, and who would be the recipient of the actions carried out by the teacher

Although the volunteer and the actor drew slips of paper to determine their roles, both slips would say 'teacher' and the actor would always claim that his slip read 'learner'. They were then separated into different rooms where they could communicate but not see each other. In some instances, the learner would make a point of mentioning to the teacher that he had a heart condition.

The teacher was then told that he/she would be teaching a list of word pairs to the learner. Having read through the entire list to the learner, the teacher would then read the first word of each pair together with a list of four possible answers. The learner would press a button to indicate his response. If the answer was correct, the teacher would read the next word pair. However, if the answer was incorrect, the teacher would administer an electric shock to the learner, with the voltage increasing in 15-volt increments for each wrong answer. Before commencing, the teacher was given a mild electric shock as a sample of the initial shock they would be administering to the learner.

In fact, the learner in the next room received no electric shocks whatsoever. The actor playing this role would deliberately get some answers wrong and then react to the 'shock' administered by the teacher by crying out, apparently in pain. With each increase in voltage, the actor would also ramp up his performance so that it would sound as if he was in significant distress, at times even begging for the exercise to stop.

Meanwhile, the teacher was being instructed by the experimenter – as the voice of authority – to continue administering the increasingly powerful 'shocks' despite the apparent cries of pain from the learner. Throughout the experiment, the volunteer 'teachers' displayed varying degrees of tension and stress. Every one of them at some point paused and questioned the experiment but, nevertheless, more than 60 per cent of them continued up to the point where they were inflicting 'fatal voltages'.

Milgram and obedience to authority

The conclusions drawn from the Milgram experiments were as follows:

1 Somebody who has neither the ability nor the expertise to make decisions, especially in a crisis, will leave decision making to someone they consider to be more authoritative.
2 If a person comes to view themselves as the instrument for carrying out another person's wishes, they will no longer see themselves as responsible for their actions.
3 When experts tell people something is all right, they think it probably is, even if it does not seem to be.

Derren Brown's *The Heist*

In 2006, as part of a UK Channel 4 TV special called *The Heist*, Derren Brown re-enacted the Milgram experiments as part of a selection process to determine which of his volunteers would be prepared to stage an armed robbery, if instructed to do so. The results were almost identical to those of the original experiments, with over 50 per cent of participants continuing to administer 'shocks' up to the fatal voltage of 450V. From his final selection of four candidates, three did in fact carry out an 'armed' robbery of a security van, albeit with toy guns.

After filming, all four participants were 'deprogrammed' of any temporary criminal inclinations, spending time with Brown and an independent psychologist. *The Heist* faced some controversy after it was aired, but the four final participants reported that they were all pleased with the programme and, indeed, they are shown stating that it was a positive experience. A 2011 viewer poll revealed that *The Heist* was the viewers' favourite of all of Derren Brown's specials.

Similarly, 84 per cent of Milgram's participants surveyed after his experiments said that they had been 'glad' or 'very glad' to have taken part. Many of them wrote to Milgram later to express their thanks and some offered further assistance or asked to join his staff.

Authority and leadership

While it is unlikely that you would want to influence people to administer electric shocks to others or carry out an armed robbery, the following learning points are also relevant to a leadership or other influential role in a business environment:

1 If people are in a situation of uncertainty, they not only look to be led but *like* to be led and to be told what to do.
2 The views of someone who appears to be knowledgeable, confident, assured and an expert in their field are unlikely to be challenged.
3 Because of the previous two learning points, it is vital that the person fulfilling the role of authority figure conducts him- or herself with the utmost personal integrity.

Influencing with the 'power of three'

Although this book is not primarily about selling techniques or presentation skills, it is worth examining a principle that works effectively as a 'convincer' and is therefore a good tactic to use in a situation where you need to be influential.

Research has shown that people need repetition in order to feel 'convinced'. Further, it has been found that the 'magic' number of repetitions is three. In a sales context, this is often used as a closing technique where the sales person will ask the potential customer three questions, to which the answers will most likely be yes. The fourth question will then be the 'closing-the-deal' question and, because the customer has just replied positively three times, there is a strong chance that they will say yes again.

The power of three in action

Q1. 'So have I covered everything you need to know about this product?'

A. 'Yes.'

Q2. 'And you're happy with our free delivery service?'

A. 'Yes.'

Q3. 'And it's this particular model that you're interested in, isn't it?'

A. 'Yes.'

Q4. 'Good. So shall we process the paperwork and get it all sorted for you now?'

A. 'Yes.'

The same principle, of the power of three, also works well as a convincer when we are making a presentation. For example, a commonly used presentation structure is:

1 Tell them what you're going to tell them (introduction).
2 Tell them (content).
3 Tell them what you've told them (conclusion).

This structure means that your content is, in fact, delivered three times and thus gains more impact and becomes more memorable. There are many ways of using the power of three in a presentation or speech.

Martin Luther King and the power of three

An American Baptist minister, Martin Luther King Jr was best known for his role as a leader in the African-American civil rights movement. An advocate of non-violent civil disobedience, in 1964 he received the Nobel Peace Prize for combating racial inequality through non-violence and, over the next few years, until his assassination in 1968, he was also an activist in the fight against poverty and the Vietnam War.

In 1963, during a march on Washington, he established a reputation as one of the greatest orators in American history when he delivered his 'I have a dream' speech. Although it was just one of many speeches he delivered during his career, this is the one that people tend to remember him for, and the power of three played a very important part in it.

King not only used the power of three with the phrase 'I have a dream' but he also used it *to* the power of three – in other words, three times three times, in a total of nine iterations. The following is an extract from that speech with the key phrase shown in bold a total of nine times:

And so even though we face the difficulties of today and tomorrow, *I* still ***have a dream.*** *It is a dream deeply rooted in the American dream.*

I have a dream *that one day this nation will rise up and live out the true meaning of its creed, 'We hold these truths to be self-evident, that all men are created equal.'*

I have a dream *that one day on the red hills of Georgia, the sons of former slaves and the sons of former slave owners will be able to sit down together at the table of brotherhood.*

I have a dream *that one day even the state of Mississippi, a state sweltering with the heat of injustice, sweltering with the heat of oppression, will be transformed into an oasis of freedom and justice.*

I have a dream *that my four little children will one day live in a nation where they will not be judged by the colour of their skin but by the content of their character.*

I have a dream *today!*

I have a dream *that one day, down in Alabama, with its vicious racists, with its governor having his lips dripping with the words of 'interposition' and 'nullification' – one day right there in Alabama, little black boys and black girls will be able to join hands with little white boys and white girls as sisters and brothers.*

I have a dream *today!*

I have a dream *that one day every valley shall be exalted and every hill and mountain shall be made low, the rough places will be made plain, and the crooked places will be made straight; 'and the glory of the Lord shall be revealed and all flesh shall see it together.'*

This is our hope, and this is the faith that I go back to the South with.

After using the phrase for the first time, King repeated it *at the beginning* of each of the next eight statements, which was another good tactic for making it memorable and for positioning himself as a voice of authority.

Authority and tone of voice

In order to project a voice of authority, it is important that you consistently speak with a confident, firm (but not arrogant) tone. As already mentioned, Margaret Thatcher worked with a voice coach to lower her voice pitch and slow down her pace of speaking in order to give gravitas and authority to her voice. King George VI famously worked with Australian speech therapist Lionel Logue in order to overcome a stammer that was proving to be a major vocal impediment for his many public-speaking duties. (The story is captured in the film *The King's Speech*, which won Colin Firth an Oscar for his excellent portrayal of the king.)

Bad habits

When presenting, beware of the following (very common) habits that can undermine your voice of authority:

- Making very little eye contact with your audience
- Saying 'um' or 'err' a lot
- Speaking too quietly for people at the back to be able to hear you
- Rocking on your feet
- Turning your back to your audience to read from the PowerPoint slide displayed behind you
- Repeatedly clicking the top of a ballpoint pen
- Fiddling with cufflinks
- Fiddling with jewellery
- Repeatedly scratching the top of your head
- Clapping your hands together at the end of every sentence
- Hands in pockets

Sounding firm, fair and assertive

Maintaining a voice of authority when faced with an aggressive person or some other confrontational situation can be a challenge. However, the following structure, known as the **assertive sentence**, works extremely well. The results you get will greatly increase your confidence and generate a perception of you as someone who sounds like a voice of authority, to be respected. The assertive sentence is a valuable 'tool' to have in your mental toolbox, to use whenever an opportunity arises.

The assertive sentence has four parts, as follows:

1 **Acknowledge the other person's situation** – this demonstrates that you have listened to them and that you understand their position.
2 **Next, say 'However...'** – never use the word 'but', which will set up a barrier to what you are going to say next.
3 **State your position** – this might be quite different from theirs and needs to be out in the open.
4 **Suggest a mutually acceptable outcome** – you are looking for a workable compromise, a 'win/win' that will accommodate both their needs and yours.

An example of this is:

> *'I appreciate that you currently have a very high workload; however, your input at today's meeting is vital so that important decisions can be made, and therefore I'd be grateful if you could attend for the first 20 minutes to provide us with your data.'*

The end result always sounds very reasonable and, because the other person's situation has been acknowledged right at the beginning of the sentence, it is hard for them to refuse to co-operate. However, if you don't get the desired result the first time, and particularly if the other person says, 'Yes, but...' and puts forward another line of argument, then run through it again, this time using their new situation at the beginning.

Summary

In this chapter we explored how you can become a 'voice of authority' by looking at the characteristics of someone acknowledged as an authority figure.

The research by Stanley Milgram, later replicated by Derren Brown, proves that, in certain circumstances, people will do whatever they are told to do if they believe that the request is initiated by someone who is knowledgeable and in a position of authority. If you relate this to the business environment, you may observe that effective leaders tend to be those who are perceived as having expertise combined with confidence.

The power of three is a 'convincer strategy' that works well in a variety of situations, including that of making an influential presentation. The analysis of Martin Luther King's famous 'I have a dream' speech shows that that key phrase was used three times multiplied by another three times, for maximum effect.

You also learned about the importance of tone of voice, the bad habits to avoid and a technique for sounding firm, fair and assertive.

Fact-check (answers at the back)

1. What's an 'authority figure'?
a) Someone older than you are ❑
b) Someone not generally respected ❑
c) Someone who impresses and inspires others ❑
d) Someone who, if they asked you to do something, you would refuse ❑

2. What is a key skill of an authority figure?
a) The ability to listen ❑
b) Seeming to be too busy to have time for others ❑
c) The ability to sound like an expert ❑
d) The ability to enforce obedience ❑

3. What characterizes authority figures?
a) Arrogance ❑
b) A habit of making unreasonable demands on others ❑
c) A willingness to keep secrets ❑
d) The ability to embrace a challenge ❑

4. What were the Milgram experiments designed to measure?
a) Obedience to an authority figure ❑
b) Disobedience to a teacher ❑
c) How people learn ❑
d) How people react to electric shocks ❑

5. What roles did participants play in the Milgram experiments?
a) Experimenter, teacher and learner ❑
b) Questioner, teacher, onlooker ❑
c) Interrogator, victim, onlooker ❑
d) Evaluator, learner, convincer ❑

6. What were the conclusions of the Milgram experiments?
a) People will let an authority figure make decisions for them ❑
b) If people see themselves as the instrument for carrying out another person's wishes, they won't feel responsible for their actions ❑
c) People learn that, when experts tell them something is all right, it probably is, even if it does not seem so ❑
d) All of the above ❑

7. How many 'teachers' in the Milgram experiment continued to increase the voltage up to fatal levels?
a) Fewer than 20 per cent ❑
b) 35 per cent ❑
c) More than 60 per cent ❑
d) 100 per cent ❑

8. What was the purpose of The Heist TV special?
a) To stage an armed robbery of a bank ❑
b) To show that people can be influenced to behave out of character ❑
c) To show people receiving electric shocks ❑
d) To show that people like to be told what to do ❑

9. What is an effective method of convincing people of something?
   a) Clapping the hands together loudly ❑
   b) To use the 'power of three' technique ❑
   c) Mentioning it once is enough ❑
   d) To speak in a soft tone of voice ❑

10. What's the best way to project a voice of authority during a confrontation?
   a) To speak quietly and hesitantly ❑
   b) To use the assertive sentence technique ❑
   c) To avoid making eye contact in case they turn hostile ❑
   d) Keeping your hands in your pockets ❑

CHAPTER 11

Speaking the language of influence

The best influencers are superb communicators – this is the *key* skill that will deliver the best results for you.

Whether you're communicating with others face to face, over the telephone or in writing, you need to be clear, positive and persuasive. Your message does not have to be verbal: even the way you dress delivers a message about you that may enhance or damage your ability to influence others.

In this chapter we will explore how to improve your communication using proven, effective techniques. You will learn about rapport, why it's essential to have it in order to influence others, and how to build it effortlessly and rapidly. You will understand what makes everyone unique, and why it's so important to have a flexible communication style in order to influence the maximum number of people.

You will also learn how to calm down an angry person easily and assertively, without taking on board their emotional state. You will discover the language to use and the actions to take to get people on board with your way of thinking. You will even learn how to 'read' people's eye movements and understand what they *really* mean.

There is only one version of you

Each one of us is as individual as a fingerprint. Although we might be similar to others, there will always be differences that contribute to our uniqueness. The way we make sense of the world around us – and how we think, feel and behave as a result of that – has an effect on how we communicate with others and how we like others to communicate with us. By understanding how this process works, you can start to develop flexibility in your communication style, which will enable you to become far more persuasive.

The following diagram represents the 'core model' of neuro-linguistic programming (NLP) and illustrates how we take in information from around us (external events), pass it through our own individual set of 'filters', make sense of it, react to it emotionally and physically, and finally behave in a way that feels appropriate to us.

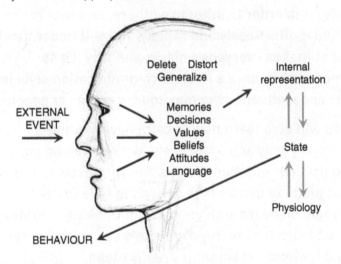

The NLP model of what we do with external information

We take in what is going on around us through our five senses. However, if we tried to process all this information, it would be more than our conscious mind, with its limited capacity, could handle. By contrast, the unconscious mind has a virtually unlimited capacity: it contains thoughts, memories and desires as well as automatic skills that are under the surface of our conscious awareness but which still have a great impact on our behaviour.

Filters and our 'map of the world'

To protect our conscious mind from overload, we all have a set of 'filters', made up of such things as memories, decisions, values, beliefs, attitudes, language and a lot more. We create and amend these filters as we progress through life, based on our ongoing experiences. Because everyone's experiences of life are different, everyone's set of filters is unique to them.

The role of the filters is to delete, distort or generalize information coming in, in order to make sense of it. The information then becomes an 'internal representation' of what is going on outside us – in other words, it becomes a thought. Attached to the thought is a state of mind, or emotion, so the thought could, for example, be happy, sad or angry. Aligned to the emotional state of mind is the physiology, or body language.

As a result of this whole process, we create an internal 'map of the world', which we use to find our way around the 'territory' out there. The output from this core model is our behaviour, which will always make perfect sense to us but may not be perceived in that way by other people.

Given, then, that everyone is unique, it is a challenge to influence other people and gain their co-operation. To achieve this, we need to find a way to 'build a bridge' across to their personal map of the world. We do this by building rapport.

What is rapport?

The word rapport stems from the French verb *rapporter*, which literally means to carry something back. In 'building our bridge' across to someone else, they connect with us and a feeling of mutual understanding flows right back. If you experience resistance or negativity in someone you wish to influence, this may indicate that rapport is missing.

Rapport builds naturally and can often be witnessed when the body language of two people who are getting on well together becomes 'matched' or 'mirrored'. Matching means that their body language is identical – for example, each person has their right leg crossed over their left and is leaning to their left. Mirroring means that one person is the mirror image of the other, so if one of them has their right leg crossed over their left and is leaning to their left, the other person will have their left leg crossed over their right and be leaning to their right. You are more likely to be *matched* with someone you are sitting or standing next to and *mirrored* with someone opposite you. Both are external indicators that rapport has been built.

This natural matching and mirroring process is also referred to as 'entrainment'.

Entrainment

A Dutch scientist named Christian Huygens discovered the phenomenon of entrainment in about 1665. Huygens had a room with a number of pendulum-driven clocks in it, and he observed that, over time, the pendulums of all the clocks fell into synchronization with each other. Even if he deliberately started them swinging at different times, he would inevitably return to find they had all become synchronized. He named this synchronization tendency 'entrainment'.

Building rapport

It is, of course, possible to speed up this process of rapport building through entrainment by deliberately matching or mirroring the other person. If you choose to do this, subtlety is essential because, if what you are doing is too obvious, it may cause offence.

The following pie chart shows the three elements of communication – physiology (body language), tone of voice and words – and their relative proportions. Much research has been conducted on these figures, principally by Albert Mehrabian, Professor Emeritus of Psychology at UCLA.

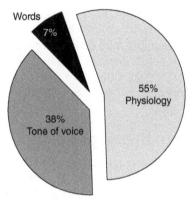

Segments of communication

The largest slice of the pie is physiology, or body language, at 55 per cent. Even if you are not speaking, your body language 'speaks' for you. However, on the telephone, you have lost this element because your body language cannot be seen. However, a smile can be heard: if you change the shape of your mouth into a smile, your voice will sound different. It will sound happier and more positive, so it's always a good idea to answer the phone with a smile on your face.

Let's explore how you can utilize each of these three elements to build rapport.

Physiology – the 55 per cent

Start by matching or mirroring the other person's posture, gestures and movements. Be careful to avoid mimicry. For example, if someone is sitting opposite you and they suddenly cross their legs, lean forward, put one elbow on the table and rest their chin on their hand, do not immediately do the same thing. This would be too obvious and could well cause offence.

Instead, make gradual movements of your own until you have created a similarity to their body language.

Matching another person's breathing rate is a far more subtle and yet powerful way to build rapport. Watch for the slight rise and fall of their shoulders and adjust your breathing into the same rhythm.

The final thing that you can match on body language is your blink rate. Again, don't be obvious, and if the other person has an eye defect such as a squint, don't hurt their feelings by mirroring this. Otherwise this is another very effective way of creating a similarity and building rapport at an unconscious level.

Tone of voice – the 38 per cent

Have you ever spoken with someone who had a strong accent or dialect and become aware that you were unintentionally starting to speak in that same accent or dialect? This is a guaranteed way of offending through mimicry, caused by your unconscious mind's desire to create a similarity and build rapport. Although this can happen when you are speaking face to face, it is more likely to happen during a telephone conversation, when physiology plays very little part and tone of voice becomes approximately 80 per cent of the communication.

Instead, you can safely match the following characteristics of the other person's voice:

- volume
- speed
- tone
- pitch
- energy
- intonation
- phrasing

Imagine for a moment that you have an angry person in front of you. What has happened to their voice? It has probably speeded up, got louder and become higher pitched. Perhaps you've been in this situation and you chose to stay really calm, but the other person, instead of calming down, got even angrier. The reason for this is that rapport was lacking; the gap between you was too wide for you to be able to be a calming influence on them. The other person's unconscious mind was telling him or her that, because you were so different from them, you just didn't understand the gravity of the situation and so they would have to 'ramp up' their own behaviour in order to make their point more clearly.

In this scenario, you can use a technique called *pacing and leading*. If you listen to the vocal characteristics of this angry person and reply using those same characteristics, you are expressing empathy and building a bridge across to their map of the world. This is called *pacing*. After a short time of doing this, start to slow down your voice, turn down the volume and lower the pitch. If sufficient rapport has been built, the other person will now start to follow you and calm down. You are now *leading*. This is a very effective strategy and, because the other person is responding at an unconscious level, it will feel completely natural to them and not manipulative at all.

Words – the 7 per cent

Words form the smallest element of communication. If ever you have spent many hours writing a speech or a presentation, you will be pleased to know that this constituted just 7 per cent of your total message. The other 93 per cent was conveyed in how you stood up and delivered it! Over the telephone, words play a greater part in rapport building, increasing in value to about 20 per cent.

In order to match someone else on their vocabulary, listen for the following:

● **Key words** – these are either individual words or short phrases that we like and use a lot. They vary from individual to individual, depending on their preferences, and may include words such as:
  - basically
  - actually
  - cool
  - like

- you know
- OK
- at the end of the day
- the bottom line is...

If you detect that someone is using a particular word or short phrase repeatedly, then you are hearing their key words. When you respond to them, incorporate those same words into your reply, and you are then 'speaking their language'. A word of caution – do not reflect back their key words in every sentence you speak as it will be too obvious that this is what you are doing.

● **VHF words** – when we speak, we tend to use words that fit into our preferred 'channel' of communication. These can be:
  - **visual**
    'I see what you mean', 'Looks good to me', 'Show me more'
  - **hearing**
    'I hear what you're saying', 'That rings a bell', 'Sounds familiar'
  - **feeling**
    'I want to get a grip on this idea', 'I'm going with my gut feeling', 'That really touched me', etc.

If you can hear someone using vocabulary that falls predominantly into one of these three channels, then adjust your language so that you are using the same type of words. When you do this, you have 'tuned into their wavelength' and can begin to 'speak their language'.

What's your preference?

Because we naturally communicate in the channel that is our predominant one, you may not be aware of whether your preference is visual, hearing or feeling. Complete the following questionnaire by reading each question in turn and circling the answer a, b or c that is most appropriate for you.

Question	Answer
1 What would make you think that someone might be lying to you?	a) The way they look – or avoid looking – at you b) Their tone of voice c) A feeling you get about their sincerity
2 How do you know that you have had a good day at work?	b) A productive meeting or good news over the telephone a) A clear desk or a 'to do' list with everything ticked off c) An inner glow, a smile and a feeling of deep satisfaction
3 What kind of activity do you prefer on holiday?	c) Lazing on a sun-drenched beach, swimming to cool off b) Attending a concert or a lecture on local culture and history a) Seeing the sights and local colour, visiting a museum or art gallery
4 Which of the following groups of hobbies/ interests appeals most to you?	a) Cinema, photography, art, interior design c) Sport, sculpture, cookery, gardening b) Playing a musical instrument, listening to music or an audio book, singing.
5 What types of television programme do you prefer to watch?	c) Wildlife and animals a) An artist at work b) Musical concert
6 Which of the following would you prefer as a 'special' treat?	b) A personal dedication on the radio by a celebrity you admire a) A weekend break away somewhere you have never visited before c) Your favourite meal with good wine and good company
7 Which would be the best way for you to unwind at the end of a hard day?	a) Gazing at something relaxing such as a candle flame c) An aromatherapy massage b) Talking to a friend
8 If you want to thank or reward someone for doing you a favour, what would you do?	b) Telephone them to tell them how grateful you are c) Give them a bottle of their favourite drink/bottle of perfume a) Write them a thank-you note

(Continued)

Question	Answer
9 Which of the following groups of careers most appeals?	a) An artist or designer in television b) Lecturer, telesales or professional speaker c) Gardener, nurse or counsellor
10 Which accessories do you like to have in your home?	b) Wind chimes, background music, ticking clock a) Lots of pictures, accented lighting, a focal point, e.g. a fireplace c) Pot-pourri, soft cushions, comfortable, squashy chairs
11 Which type of magazine would you be most likely to pick up and read?	c) Home decorating, sports or creative crafts b) Music or current affairs a) Art, photography or fashion
12 How would you discipline a naughty child?	a) With a severe look or frown c) With punishment by deprivation, e.g. no pocket money b) By shouting or using a stern tone of voice

Add up your scores by letter and make a note of them.

a) .... (visual)
b) .... (hearing)
c) .... (feeling)

Your preferred 'channel' is the one with your highest score.

The VHF types

The following are descriptions of the three types. Notice whether the description of your preferred 'channel' is a good match for you.

● **Visual**

Typically, people who are in a visual mode stand or sit with their heads erect and their eyes up and will be breathing from the top of their lungs. They often sit forward in their chair or on the edge of the chair. They tend to be quite organized, neat, well groomed and orderly. They are appearance-oriented, and may sometimes be quieter than other people. They are generally good spellers, memorize by seeing pictures and are not easily distracted by noise. They may have trouble remembering verbal instructions and are bored by long verbal explanations because their mind tends to wander. They would rather read than be read to and, ideally, like to have information presented to them using pictures, charts and diagrams.

A visual person will be interested in how someone looks at them, and will notice details of others' appearance such as their dress style. They will tend to use visual imagery in phrases like 'See you later', 'Looking good', 'In my mind's eye', 'I get the picture', etc.

● Hearing

Someone who has a 'hearing' preference will move their eyes sideways and may tilt their head to one side when they are listening. They breathe from the middle of the chest. They often move their lips when they are mentally saying words and may even talk to themselves when thinking something through. They are easily distracted by noise but can generally repeat things back to you easily. They may find spoken language easier than maths and writing. They like music and learn by listening; they memorize by using steps, procedures and sequences.

A 'hearing' person is often interested in being told how they're doing and is more likely to notice tone of voice and other vocal characteristics. They tend to use hearing imagery in words and phrases like 'Tell me more', 'That rings a bell', 'Sounds familiar', etc.

● Feeling

There are two types of 'feeling' people. The first type has a posture that tends to slump over and they may move and talk slowly. They are laid back, with a calm demeanour, and fond of relaxing. The second type is more active and 'talks with their hands', i.e. they gesticulate when speaking and may fidget when sitting still. Both types will typically access their feelings and emotions to 'get a feel' for what they're doing, so they may be naturally intuitive.

Feeling people can be quite tactile and they like to learn by doing – the 'hands-on' approach. These people will really notice a limp handshake and be thoroughly unimpressed by it! They use feeling words and phrases like 'I've got a gut feeling', 'Get in touch', 'I'm going with my instincts', 'Let's make contact', etc.

Eye movements and thinking styles

Imagine that you're having a face-to-face conversation with someone. You're listening for the VHF words but the language seems neutral. There is another way of telling whether someone is thinking in pictures, sounds or feelings and that is by the way their eyes move when they are thinking of what they are going to say next or when they are processing the answer to a question.

Carry out the following exercise with the participation of someone else. You will see that there are a series of questions, five for 'A' and five for 'B'. Take it in turns to ask each other the questions, one of you as 'A' and the other as 'B'. Use a grid for each question like the one shown below and, for each one, position your pen or pencil in the middle of the grid and trace the other person's eye movements on the grid as they mentally process the answer to that question. Draw exactly what you see. If their eyes move upwards and to the right, draw that, even though this would be to their left. The eyes may move to several different places before the answer has been processed and this is fine – just track every movement you observe on to the grid.

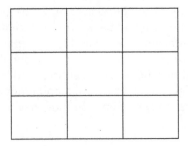

Questions for 'A'

1 What does your favourite actor sound like?
2 What would a pink giraffe look like if it were wearing sunglasses and open-toed sandals?
3 Can you spell your full name backwards?
4 What was the front-page headline in your newspaper yesterday?
5 What would the national anthem sound like if it were sung backwards, under water?

Questions for 'B'

1 What would a whale singing 'Happy birthday to you' sound like?
2 How many doors are there in your home?
3 Who was the first person you spoke to on the telephone yesterday?
4 What clothes were you wearing last Saturday?
5 How much is 1,296 divided by 4?

When we are thinking about what we are going to say next, or we are processing the answer to a question, our eyes move in particular directions, depending on whether we are mentally processing in pictures, sounds or feelings.

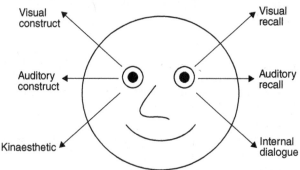

How people think – eye-accessing cues

V: visual thinkers
If the eyes go up, we are visualizing:

● Up and to our right (left if you are observing someone else's eyes) means that we are visually constructing an image of something we haven't seen before.

- Up and to our left (right if you are observing someone else) means that we are visually recalling something that we have seen before.
- We are also visually processing if our eyes are looking straight ahead into the distance, or if they are closed, as if we are getting images on the backs of our eyelids.

H: hearing thinkers

- If our eyes move sideways and to our right (left in someone you are observing), we are imagining what something could sound like that we haven't heard before.
- If our eyes move sideways and to our left (right in someone you are observing), then we are remembering what something sounds like that we have heard before.

F: feeling thinkers

- If our eyes move down and to our right (left in someone you are observing), then we are processing in feelings, or kinaesthetically. These could be emotions or we could be imagining the physical feel of touching something.
- If our eyes move down and to our left (right in someone you are observing), then we are listening to our internal dialogue – that voice inside our head that lets us know what we are thinking and feeling.

You can use this eye movement information as an aid to influencing. Let's say that you are having a discussion with someone and you have made some kind of proposal to them. As they are silently considering it, their eyes look upwards. You now know that they are processing in pictures, so you could match your language to their thought patterns. You could, for example, say, 'I can *see* that you are giving this a lot of thought. Is there anything else I can *show* you that might make it *clearer*?'

TIP *You cannot not communicate. Even if you are not speaking, your body language and overall appearance will speak for you. Make sure the message that you're sending out is the one you want to convey.*

Rapport in writing

If you are writing to someone and you don't know their preferred VHF channel, or if you are writing something that will be read by many people – so that there will be a mix of all three channels – then balance the number of visual, hearing and feeling words you use. This will ensure that at least a third of your text will be 'speaking their language'. For example, 'We love to keep *in touch* with our customers, to *show* them that we are really interested in *hearing* how they are getting on.'

One author who does this very effectively and successfully is J. K. Rowling. If you open any of her Harry Potter books anywhere, you will see that she has skilfully balanced the visual, hearing and feeling words on every page. If you are an aspiring author, this could be a good technique to emulate.

Summary

In this chapter we explored how to communicate influentially and build rapport with others, at both a conscious and an unconscious level.

The NLP 'core' model illustrates how everyone is unique, constructing their own personal 'map of the world' determined by internal 'filters'. Building rapport with someone creates a bridge to their world which enables a two-way spirit of co-operation to develop. The three elements of communication – body language (physiology), tone of voice and words – provide opportunities for matching and mirroring face to face, over the phone and in writing.

You now know whether you are predominantly a visual, hearing or feeling person and how to detect these different ways of thinking in others by observing their eye movements. By matching your vocabulary to the 'channel' in which the other person is thinking, you'll be able to 'speak their language' and thereby become more influential.

Fact-check (answers at the back)

1. How do we protect our conscious mind from overload?
   a) Through a set of 'filters' that are unique to each of us ❏
   b) By ignoring our memories ❏
   c) By using our unconscious mind with its unlimited capacity ❏
   d) By processing input from three senses only ❏

2. What do our filters do?
   a) Exclude painful thoughts ❏
   b) Separate us from others ❏
   c) Cause the conscious mind to become overloaded ❏
   d) Make sense of incoming information ❏

3. What's the fastest way to change our state of mind?
   a) Change our environment ❏
   b) Talk to someone with a different point of view ❏
   c) Change our physiology, or body language ❏
   d) We can't – our thoughts and emotions are fixed ❏

4. What is our 'map of the world'?
   a) Our unique way of seeing the world ❏
   b) What we make of others' memories ❏
   c) A three-dimensional map of our neighbourhood ❏
   d) How we visualize our thoughts ❏

5. Why is rapport important in communication?
   a) It's not important ❏
   b) People like to see others copying their movements ❏
   c) It makes us more aware of others' eye movements ❏
   d) It enables us to build a bridge to someone else's map of the world ❏

6. What are the three elements of communication?
   a) Physiology, tone of voice, words ❏
   b) Eye contact, handshake, written word ❏
   c) Dress code, smiling, gestures ❏
   d) Telephone, face to face, emails ❏

7. What makes up the smallest element of communication?
   a) Physiology ❏
   b) Words ❏
   c) Tone of voice ❏
   d) Pacing and leading ❏

8. When should you use pacing and leading?
   a) When you want to experiment with a new way of communicating ❏
   b) To mimic the other person's accent ❏
   c) To help calm down an angry person ❏
   d) When you can't match somebody's blink rate ❏

9. What is 'speaking somebody's language'?
a) Matching their key words ❑
b) Mimicking the other person's breathing rate ❑
c) Speaking more loudly if someone is quietly spoken ❑
d) Using the same tone of voice over the telephone ❑

10. What does VHF stand for?
a) Virtual, hearing, feeling ❑
b) Visual, hearsay, feedback loop ❑
c) Visual, hearing, feeling ❑
d) Viral, healing, falling ❑

CHAPTER 12

Flexible influencing

You can use several further NLP techniques to enable you to develop more flexibility in your influencing and persuasion methods.

In this chapter we shall look at some of the 'presuppositions' or 'excellence beliefs' upon which NLP has been built and see how operating within these beliefs can improve your success. We'll also explore some of the NLP language techniques that work particularly well when influencing. We will review the importance of having empowering beliefs in place when you are aiming to increase your ability to influence well, and how your own language may be undermining your belief in yourself.

Finally, you will learn how to create a 'future history' through a specific visualization technique. This technique allows you to visualize a future event unfolding in exactly the way you want it to, in order to help you generate a good outcome in reality. You can use the technique in advance of any situation in which you need to be at your influential best.

The power of 'excellence beliefs'

NLP was first developed in the 1970s as a study of excellence, with top achievers such as Walt Disney being researched and 'modelled' so that their tried-and-tested techniques for success could be learned and used by others. It is now accepted globally as one of the most powerful and effective personal development methodologies available. Working within its 'principles of excellence' or presuppositions, listed below, can strengthen your communications and in turn improve your power to persuade and influence others.

'The person with the most flexible behaviour can have the most influence on an outcome.'

This 'excellence belief' means that, if your strategy is to have a number of different approaches planned in advance, then you can easily switch between them to achieve a desired outcome. By contrast, if you have planned only one route to your goal and an obstacle occurs that blocks this route, you will not achieve your goal. This attitude is typical in people who say things like, 'It's my way or the highway.' In other words, if others do not 'buy into' their views, they have no fallback option as an alternative.

'The meaning of communication is the response it elicits.'

In any communication, whether one to one or one to many, the only way you can know how you are doing is by noticing the feedback you are getting. You will probably have experienced this, perhaps if you were explaining something a little complicated to another person and you noticed a puzzled expression on their face. You instinctively realized that they did not understand what you just said, so you might have continued with, 'In other words...' and then explained it again in a different way. When their response changed to one of comprehension, indicated perhaps with a slight smile and nod of the head, this told you that your message was understood.

During any kind of influencing scenario, it is essential that you are continually noticing the feedback you are getting from your audience.

TIP *The fastest way to change your state of mind is to change your body language. If you are feeling nervous before a presentation or meeting, choose to adopt upright, open, confident-looking body language and it will have a positive effect on how you feel. You could say that this is 'fake it 'til you make it', but if it works, why not?*

'If you always do what you've always done, you will always get what you've always got. So if what you're doing isn't working, do something different.'

Einstein's definition of insanity was 'doing the same thing over and over and expecting to get different results'. If, for example, your presentation that you hoped would influence and persuade didn't work the first time, there is a strong chance that it will fall short next time also. Revisit it, review it, revise it – do whatever it takes, but make sure you do something differently in order to generate a different result.

'There is no such thing as failure; there is only feedback.'

Imagine that you have an important meeting with a senior director in your organization. Your objective is to present your ideas for a radical new product or service that you are passionate about and which you would like your organization to adopt. You think it goes well but the director rejects your proposal. You leave the meeting feeling that you have failed.

You didn't fail. In fact, all that happened was that you got a result that wasn't the one you wanted. Instead, what you actually got was a valuable learning opportunity. Use it well and then do something different next time. When things go the way we expect them to, we learn nothing. When things *don't* go the way we want them to, they present fabulous opportunities to learn and grow. Allow your mind to formulate an answer to this question: 'What would you do if you *knew* you couldn't fail?'

'If one person can do it, others can too.'

This presupposition reflects the fundamental principle of NLP, that of modelling excellence in others. Think of someone you know who has influencing abilities that you admire. What exactly are they doing to be so persuasive, and how could you adopt their techniques for yourself? And then think of others whom you admire, and do the same thing. Model their excellence and you will be able to replicate their success.

Modelling excellence: the four-minute mile

Before 1954, when Roger Bannister became the first person to run a mile in under four minutes, many 'experts', including doctors, had confidently stated that it was impossible for a human being to achieve this feat. They said that their heart would explode, their lungs would collapse and their shinbones would shatter. Perhaps not surprisingly, the previous record of four minutes 1.4 seconds had stood for nine years, because who would want to have all these awful things happen to them? However, Bannister, himself a junior doctor as well as an athlete, decided not only that it was possible but that he was the man to do it.

The record he set, of three minutes 59.4 seconds, stood for just 46 days until it was broken and it has since been broken by many more athletes. In the last 50 years the record has been lowered by almost 17 seconds, and it is now estimated that well in excess of 1,000 athletes have run a mile in under four minutes.

Memory and imagination

'Memory and imagination use the same neurological circuits and can potentially have the same impact on the individual.'

Because memory and imagination use the same neurological circuits, your mind cannot tell the difference between a remembered activity and an imagined one, which means that if you visualize something vividly enough, your mind thinks it is looking at a memory. And your mind believes that if you've already carried out this activity in the past, then you can do it again.

Visualization: Linford Christie

In 1992, British sprinter Linford Christie won the 100m gold medal at the Barcelona Olympic Games, becoming at 32 years of age the oldest athlete to have achieved this feat. As part of his training, he had worked with a visualization of running down an imaginary tunnel on the stimulus of the sound of the starting gun. The purpose of the tunnel in the visualization was to eliminate all other visual distractions such as the other competitors and the crowd. The auditory stimulus was the 'B' of the 'bang' from the gun.

In his mind, Christie had run this race hundreds of times and, of course, he had won it every time, so when he lined up on the starting blocks that day, there was no doubt in his mind that he was about to replicate his imagined, gold-medal-winning performance. And so he did.

This is the reason why so many outstanding performers, whether in sport, business or other arenas, attribute their success to visualization. Roger Bannister visualized himself running the four-minute mile. Boxer Muhammad Ali would create what he called 'future history' by visualizing every round of a forthcoming boxing match in minute detail and then predicting the round in which he would knock out his opponent. He would then take great delight in announcing this to his opponent prior to the fight commencing, along with his affirmation, 'I am the greatest.'

How to create a winning visualization

If you have a meeting or presentation coming up at which you need to be at your influential best, then create a visualization of the event unfolding exactly the way you want it to and keep running through it as a mental rehearsal. For the best results, incorporate the following points:

1 You need to be fully 'associated' with it, so imagine that you are seeing the event through your own eyes, as if it is going on around you.
2 Break the event down into stages and build a checkpoint into each one. For example, when you enter the room where the event is to take place, who is the first person to greet you and what exactly will they say? What would be the next stage and what checkpoint could you create for that? And so on.
3 The more sensory information you can incorporate, the better. What do you see? What does the room look like? What are you wearing? What do you hear? Include specific words that the other people there would say, such as 'impressive' or 'this sounds really good'. How are you feeling? Confident? Relaxed? Include whatever feelings are appropriate. Even include smell and taste if you can – perhaps you would be drinking a cup of coffee or a glass of water. If so, include these.
4 Imagine that the final part is the successful outcome that you want to achieve. Build in exactly how that will feel and imagine how you will congratulate yourself on a job well done.

Influencing through language

When we speak, we are usually conveying a shortened, simplified and generalized version of what we are thinking. In so doing, we often leave out or even distort some of the information, which leads to misunderstandings and to some important facts being withheld.

Much of the language adopted in NLP was modelled from well-known psychiatrist and hypnotherapist Milton Erickson, who was able to facilitate phenomenal changes in his clients conversationally. The NLP 'meta model' uses language to clarify meaning and thus ensure that you gain a clear understanding of the words used by others. The benefit of using the meta model is that it helps you to gain a better understanding of what somebody is *really* saying. Because a person will always be speaking through the filters of their own personal map of the world, we may often be unsure about what they really mean. However, we can clarify what they mean by asking specific questions. This will then enable us to be far more effective as an influencer.

The following are elements of the NLP meta model.

Unspecified nouns

This is where we replace the noun in a sentence with words such as 'they' or 'it', or where the noun is implied rather than specified. To gain a more accurate understanding, ask questions such as 'Who or what, specifically?' For example:

- 'They are making a decision today.' 'Who are?'
- 'It's always been done this way.' 'What, specifically?'

Unspecified verbs

This follows the same principle as unspecified nouns, but here it is the verbs used that fail to convey enough information to get across the full message. In this case, ask, 'How, specifically?' For example:

- 'I was helped to do this.' 'How, specifically?'
- 'Just get on and do it.' 'How, specifically?'

Comparisons

Comparisons are often used in advertisements, for example when a product is described as 'better' without the ad saying what it is being compared with. Clarify by asking, 'Compared with what?' For example:

- 'This one is better.' 'Better than what?'
- 'He was at his worst today.' 'Compared with what?'

Judgements

These are similar to comparisons, in that a view is expressed without specifying whose view it is. Clarify by asking questions to establish whose judgement it is and/or on what basis the judgement has been made. For example:

- 'This is the best one on the market.' 'By what criteria is it the best?'
- 'This does the best job.' 'In whose opinion?'

Nominalizations

Also called abstract nouns, nominalizations are nouns that started off as verbs. As nouns they are vaguer and more intangible than the original active verb. A verb such as 'educate' becomes a static noun ('education'). To clarify its meaning, turn the nominalization back into a verb and ask for qualifying information. For example:

- 'I received a good education at home.' 'Who educated you? How did they do that?'
- 'We had lengthy discussions.' 'What did you discuss?'

Modal operators of possibility

These are words that reflect our beliefs around what is and is not possible for us. They may well reflect limiting beliefs and can be explored by asking, 'What would happen if you did?' or 'What stops you?' For example:

- 'I can't present in public.' 'What would happen if you did?'
- 'I can't speak to him.' 'What stops you?'

Modal operators of necessity

These are similar to the possibility words but they reflect needs rather than beliefs. They can be explored using similar questions as for modal operators of possibility. For example:

- 'I must be the last to leave the office.' 'What would happen if you weren't?'
- 'I ought to learn how to do that.' 'What would happen if you didn't?'

Universal quantifiers

These are sweeping generalizations that allow for no exceptions. They utilize words such as 'all', 'every', 'always' and 'never' and can be challenged by reflecting them back or by asking about any possible exceptions. For example:

- 'I never remember people's names.' 'Never? Has there ever been a time when you did remember a name?'
- 'I always make bad decisions.' 'Always? Have you ever made a decision that wasn't bad?'

Complex equivalence

This is when two statements are linked to imply that they mean the same thing, but they may well be based on an incorrect assumption. Clarify the statements by asking how one statement 'means' the other one. For example:

- 'He doesn't attend our weekly meetings any more ... he must be too busy.' 'How does his lack of attendance necessarily mean that he is too busy?'
- 'She never rings me any more ... I must have offended her.' 'How does her not ringing you mean you've offended her?'

Presuppositions

Presuppositions – a term also used to mean beliefs that underpin NLP – imply, in the context of language, assumptions that may or may not be correct. Clarify such an assumption by asking, 'What leads you to believe that...?' For example:

- 'Would you like the blue one or the red one?' 'What leads you to believe that I wish to purchase either of them?'
- 'When you go to the meeting, what will you say?' 'What makes you think I'm going? How do you know I'm going to speak?'

Cause and effect

Although similar to complex equivalence, in cause and effect one statement is taken to have caused the other one. This can reflect an inappropriate 'blame' being allocated, especially if emotions are involved. For example, 'You make me so angry when you do that' implies that one person has complete control over another person's emotions, whereas the reality is that we all choose our own emotions. Clarify the statement by asking exactly how one element has caused the other one. For example:

- 'I'd like to exercise more but I don't have the time.' 'What would have to happen for you to have the time to exercise?'
- 'I was going to say something but I knew he'd take it the wrong way.' 'How do you know he'd take what you said the wrong way?'

Mind reading

This is where one person presumes that they know what another person is thinking. We often base our presumptions on how we ourselves would be thinking or feeling in the same situation and we project it on to the other person. Alternatively, it could be the result of a misinterpretation of the other person's body language. We can ask for clarification by saying, 'How exactly do you know...?' For example:

- 'I know you don't like my idea.' 'How exactly do you know that?'
- 'She's ignoring me.' 'How can you be sure?'

Summary

In this chapter we have drawn on some of the key principles of NLP in order to incorporate flexibility into your influencing style. The more flexible you can be, the better equipped you will be to 'think on your feet' during any interaction in which you need to influence others.

The quality of your language will determine the quality of your results. You discovered how the elimination of words such as 'try' and 'don't' can make profound positive differences to your outcomes, and you saw how you can filter language not only to influence others but also to influence yourself.

You also discovered how to create and use an effective visualization, a technique used by highly successful people as a mental rehearsal for their achievements.

We also explored the meta model of language, which employs questioning to clarify what others are saying, avoid misunderstandings and open up opportunities for influential conversation.

Fact-check (answers at the back)

1. What does NLP stand for?
a) Neuro-linguistic procedures ❏
b) New language perception ❏
c) Neuro-linguistic programming ❏
d) Neurotic language principles ❏

2. What's the best way to ensure that your message is understood?
a) By ignoring the feedback – it's unnecessary when you are communicating with someone ❏
b) By repeating it more loudly until it is understood ❏
c) By noticing the feedback you are getting and adjusting your message accordingly ❏
d) Trying again later by going over it again in the same way ❏

3. What is the best way to achieve a goal?
a) By having several possible routes to that goal ❏
b) With one good, well-thought-out route ❏
c) By keeping on with what you are doing, even if it doesn't work first time ❏
d) By being content with any result, even if it isn't the one you wanted ❏

4. What's the best way to think about a problem?
a) Some problems have no solution ❏
b) There is a solution to every problem, although it may not be the ideal one ❏
c) Holding on to a problem is a stress-free option ❏
d) Solutions must be ideal, or they are no solution at all ❏

5. How did athletes break Roger Bannister's four-minute mile record?
a) By modelling excellence ❏
b) By ignoring the naysayers ❏
c) By competing with one another ❏
d) By improving their fitness ❏

6. How can you tell whether you have achieved rapport with someone?
a) They show resistance to your ideas ❏
b) They start to match and mirror your body language ❏
c) You have made physical contact with them ❏
d) You feel that you can read their mind ❏

7. What's the fastest way to change your state of mind?
a) Ask your mind to process a negative command ❏
b) Change your body language ❏
c) Leave the room and do something else for a few minutes ❏
d) Say what you don't want in order to get what you do want ❏

8. Why should you never have the word 'try' in your influencing vocabulary?
a) It makes you look weak ❏
b) The mind can't process it ❏
c) It's too vague ❏
d) The mind interprets 'try' as 'try and fail' ❏

9. What's the NLP meta model?
a) A way of disguising your feelings ❏
b) A method of getting along with people ❏
c) A way of using language to clarify language ❏
d) A modelling technique ❏

10. What is visualization?
a) A mental rehearsal of a future situation ❏
b) Seeing yourself running down a tunnel ❏
c) Sensory overload ❏
d) Daydreaming ❏

CHAPTER 13

Proven persuasion techniques

In this chapter we will explore a range of proven persuasion techniques that will further enhance everything you have learned so far.

Listening is an essential communication skill and a key skill in influencing. A good listener will easily detect all the cues (which could be buying signals) in the other person and then just match their proposal to their needs. You will discover the three levels of listening and which one never to use if you want to influence someone.

You'll also learn about two tried and tested persuasion formulae – FAB and AIDA – and how to incorporate them into marketing and sales activities, including conversations.

Significant research has been conducted on which words are the most influential and are therefore used most often in 'persuasive literature'. Now you'll learn why each of these top 15 words works so well. Some of them will be obvious but others may surprise you.

In Chapter 11 we looked at 'convincers' and the power of three. We will explore some additional convincers and other 'emotional triggers' here that have been proven to work well in situations such as networking events.

The three levels of listening

While hearing is a function (you have ears and they detect sounds), listening is a skill. The more you develop this skill, the better a communicator and an influencer you will become. There are three different levels of listening, as follows:

● **Level 1 – internal listening**
At this level, the listener is focused on him/herself. They are interpreting whatever is being said in terms of what it means to them. If it brings something to mind, they will interrupt the speaker in order to share that thought. This is a very selfish type of listening; continually interrupting someone else is extremely disrespectful. *Never* use level 1 if you want to influence someone.

● **Level 2 – focused listening**
This is attentive listening, with the focus on the speaker. The listener may be leaning forward, engrossed in the conversation. They will notice the speaker's body language, tone of voice and words, as well as elements such as energy, expression, what is being not just said but also implied, and so on. This is a good type of listening to use if you are in a one-to-one situation.

● **Level 3 – global listening**
Also known as 360° listening, the speaker is being listened to as if part of a wider environment. The listener is using their intuition to sense 'signals' and to take in all information available. (The best stand-up comedians use this type of listening to interact with their audience and to know the exact moment to drop in their punchline for the greatest effect.) This is the best level to use if you are making a presentation to a group of people that you want to influence.

 TIP *As with any skill, the more you practise effective listening, the more competent – and influential – you will become.*

FAB statements

Everyone's favourite radio station is WIIFM, or 'What's in it for me?' This means that, whatever it is that you want to convey in your influencing conversation, the other party must be able to see some benefit, and be able to sense that benefit quite quickly in order to stay interested. One technique that achieves this very effectively is the FAB statement.

FAB stands for Feature, Advantage and Benefit. The statement is structured as follows:

- **Feature** – here you say what a product or service is or focus on a specific aspect of it: 'Because…'
- **Advantage** – this describes what that product/service/aspect does: 'It can/you can…'
- **Benefit** – this explains why the advantage is a really good thing to have: 'which means that…'

An example is: '*Because* this mobile phone has a camera function, *it can* take photographs and even short video clips, *which means that* you will never miss a photo opportunity again.'

FAB statements incorporate the conventional 'features and benefits' format but, with the addition of the 'advantage' element, two levels of benefits are being presented, which makes it even more persuasive. It is always a good idea to have several FAB statements prepared in advance of any situation in which you may need to influence others. Use a table like the one below to create three examples for yourself. For each one, think of a particular aspect of your product or service, ideally one that is unique to you or your organization.

Feature	Advantage	Benefit
1 Because…	it can/you can…	which means that…
2 Because…	it can/you can…	which means that…
3 Because…	it can/you can…	which means that…

Having a variety of FAB statements prepared will give you flexibility. Depending on the cues you pick up from the other person by listening attentively to them, you will be able to choose the appropriate statement to use. It may be that they have outlined a problem they have; if you can phrase your FAB statement so that it sounds exactly like the solution they need, they are likely to be very interested in what you have to offer.

AIDA

Another formula with a proven track record in terms of influencing people to respond to marketing communications is AIDA. (This has nothing to do with Verdi's opera of the same name, although that connection does help to make the acronym more memorable.) The letters stand for Attention, Interest, Desire and Action:

- **Attention**
  Attract the attention of the reader by making a bold statement that is relevant to them and that will generate awareness of your product or service, or of a problem that they may not have realized they have.
- **Interest**
  Raise interest by focusing on and demonstrating advantages and benefits (rather than promoting features, as in traditional advertising).
- **Desire**
  Convince the reader that they really want your product/service and that it will satisfy their needs or solve their problem.
- **Action**
  Tell the reader what to do next; what action must they take now in order to buy your product or take you up on your offer?

For example:

- **Attention**
  Do you have any old mobile phones lying around that you no longer use?
- **Interest**
  Did you know that they could be worth a significant amount of money?
- **Desire**
  We buy old mobiles and will pay you a good price for yours.

- **Action**
  Go to our website now and check out how much yours is worth. Then simply post it to us and you will receive a cheque by return.

This formula also works well in letter format, in which case each letter of AIDA would comprise one paragraph, building up to the call to action.

The 15 most influential words in marketing

Research has shown that certain words are extremely effective for influencing people, especially if they communicate at both the conscious and unconscious levels of the mind simultaneously. The following list of words, compiled by Kerry L. Johnson and reproduced here with his kind permission, have been shown to be the most influential. If you look at advertising in magazines and newspapers and on advertising hoardings and billboards, and listen to television and radio adverts, you will see and hear these words being used repeatedly.

Word	Effect
1 Discover	This generates interest, evokes a feeling of opportunity and suggests a better life.
2 Good	This is not a high-powered word, which is the secret of its success; it evokes stability and security. If something is good for your clients, they will want to buy it. If it's good, it's not bad. Everyone wants to be associated with what's good.
3 Money	Few people feel they have enough and everyone wants more.
4 Easy	What everyone wants is more simplicity and the ability to do things more easily. If your product can make something easier for potential purchasers, they will be more likely to buy it.
5 Guaranteed	Most people fear taking a risk. They want to know that, if your product doesn't work out, they can get their money back.
6 Health	'If I've got my health, I've got everything.' If a product promises financial, emotional or physical health, it offers a big plus. To many people, this is more important than money.

(Continued)

Word	Effect
7 Love	Said to 'make the world go round', love is important in everyone's life and is a prime selling enticement.
8 New	If it's new, it must be better, improved and at the 'cutting edge'. Unless a product is specifically targeted to evoke nostalgia, anyone trying to sell something old-fashioned meets with limited success.
9 Proven	Although we like new things, we want reliability as well. We want something that has been tested and proven not to be harmful in any way. We need to know that it will neither break down nor require a lot of servicing. We don't want to doubt that something will work.
10 Results	We want to know exactly what we're getting for spending our money.
11 Safe	This closely parallels health. We all value our lives and if a product is safe, or our assets are safe, we are much more trusting.
12 Save	Saving money is almost as important as making money. If a company can't promise that you will make money with a product, it usually promises to help you save money. Saving is better than spending.
13 Own	We all like to own things. Owning is better than buying because it implies possession rather than more spending. When you present a product, talk about owning it rather than buying it.
14 Free	We love to say that you can't get something for nothing, but we don't believe it! 'Free' is an instant eye-catcher, something that compels you to look or listen further. If you can use the word 'free', pointing out that your customer will get something for nothing, you will get that customer's attention immediately.
15 Best	If you know that a product has been shown to be the best in any way, shape or form, be sure to make your customer aware of it. Something that has been shown to be the best in any context exerts a powerful pull on us to possess it for ourselves.

Because all these words work so well, both in writing and verbally, keep a list of them by your telephone so that you can drop them into a conversation and thus become instantly more influential!

More convincers

In Chapter 11 you discovered that people have preferred channels of communication – visual, hearing or feeling. Not only will they speak in these channels, but they also like to be communicated with, and influenced, in their preferred channel. If you are in a one-to-one situation and you become aware from listening to the other person's language and watching their eye movements which channel they fit into, then you will need to think about the following:

- **Visual people**
  What evidence do they need to see in order to be convinced? Can you show them examples, pictures, charts, diagrams, or even a short video clip? Don't use long verbal explanations with visual people, because they will lose interest quickly. They will also notice your appearance in far more detail than hearing or feeling people, so be meticulous about how you present yourself.
- **Hearing people**
  What do they need to hear from you to be convinced? Hearing people like to be 'talked through' things in steps, procedures and sequences, so structure your presentation in that way. Also, vary your voice tonality, speed and volume, as this will appeal more to them.
- **Feeling people**
  What do they need to feel in order to be convinced? These people will go with their gut feeling and they like to be tactile when evaluating something. If you can give them a sample of your product to touch, they will appreciate that. They are

'hands-on' learners, so if you can demonstrate something to them and then give them the chance to have a go for themselves, this will work well. Feeling people will notice the quality of a handshake, so make sure that yours is firm without being a bone-crusher.

The law of reciprocity

It is human nature that when someone has done us a good turn, we feel a need to reciprocate and do something for them. This is known as the law of reciprocity. In terms of communication, if you show a genuine interest in somebody by asking them questions and listening attentively to their replies, there will more than likely come a point at which they will say something like, 'So what about you? What do you do?' People like to be listened to (this is the 'good turn' you are doing for them), so on no account lapse into level 1 listening.

In his book *7 Habits of Highly Effective People* (1989), Stephen Covey defines habit number 5 as 'Seek first to understand, then to be understood'. He states that most people listen with the intent to reply rather than to understand, and this affects the quality of their listening. He also says that we tend to be keen to put our point across and be understood rather than first wanting to understand the other person. If you find yourself at a networking event, you will see this happening constantly. If you make sure that you are the person who asks questions and really listens to the answers, you will make a very positive impression on the other attendees.

The law of scarcity

If we think something is in short supply, we want it. Even if it is only rumoured that there could be a shortage of a particular commodity, we may feel a need to 'stock up' in case it runs out altogether. You will have seen this happening with, for example, petrol. If it is reported in the media that service stations may run short of fuel for some reason, immediately queues will form. People will sit in their cars in a queue for an hour or two (burning fuel), sometimes just to top up an almost-full tank. As a result, the service station runs out of fuel and the rumoured shortage becomes a reality.

How could you use this 'law'? If you are launching a promotion of some kind, think about imposing some limitations to create scarcity and thereby increase desire. For example:

● 'Only seven places remaining!'
● 'Offer must close at midnight on Friday!'
● 'Discontinued model – only two left at this price!'

Emotional triggers

Just as we tend to buy what we *want* rather than just what we *need*, so emotions play a key part in influencing our behaviour. For instance, Bob Geldof activated our emotions and feelings of guilt with his Live Aid appeal, raising £40 million to help alleviate suffering and starvation in Ethiopia.

Another curious and amusing example of an emotional trigger is the interesting phenomenon of cute cat pictures becoming widespread on the Internet. Several different, corroborative sources now suggest that, if you have a business page on Facebook and you would like to attract more visitors, posting a photo of a cat on there will do the trick! Yes, honestly. I suspect a photo of a cute kitten sitting on your keyboard may be even better, but apparently this works. Do with this as you will!

Summary

In this chapter you have learned some proven practical and effective persuasion techniques.

To be influential, we have to know how to communicate successfully. One of the most important communication skills is the ability to listen well. If you identified yourself as a level 1 listener, you now know that this is a skill you need to practise!

The FAB and AIDA techniques also work well, so familiarize yourself with them so that they will come naturally to you in an influencing conversation. It's also worth learning how and when to use the 15 most influential words.

By presenting information to people via their preferred channel of communication, you can increase your powers of persuasion. The laws of reciprocity and scarcity and emotional triggers also present opportunities to be influential.

Fact-check (answers at the back)

1. What is level 3 listening?
   a) Speaking more than listening ❏
   b) The best one to use in a one-to-one conversation ❏
   c) The best one to use when presenting to a group of people ❏
   d) Being focused on your own internal dialogue ❏

2. What does FAB stand for?
   a) Feature, Advantage, Benefit ❏
   b) Feature, Adaptability, Brightness ❏
   c) Fitness, Advancement, Benevolence ❏
   d) Flexibility, Assistance, Benison ❏

3. What does AIDA stand for?
   a) Administration, Influence, Design, Action ❏
   b) Audience, Interest, Designer, Animation ❏
   c) Attendance, Individuality, Desire, Activity ❏
   d) Attention, Interest, Desire, Action ❏

4. How many words have been identified as the most influential when used in marketing?
   a) 15 ❏
   b) 18 ❏
   c) 25 ❏
   d) 35 ❏

5. How should you influence a visual person?
   a) With visual evidence ❏
   b) By asking them to sing along with you in a duet ❏
   c) By using long verbal instructions ❏
   d) By being tactile with them ❏

6. What is the law of reciprocity?
   a) Seeking first to be understood, before understanding ❏
   b) If you do someone a good turn, they will naturally want to reciprocate ❏
   c) People like to be listened to, so use level 1 listening ❏
   d) Stocking up in case something runs out ❏

7. What is the law of scarcity?
   a) It means that there is plenty for everyone ❏
   b) If we think something is in short supply, we'll decide we don't want it ❏
   c) Scarcity makes a commodity less desirable ❏
   d) If we think something is in short supply, we want it ❏

8. What are emotional triggers?
   a) Small brain pulses that release a stimulus ❏
   b) External signals to stop buying ❏
   c) Appeals to feelings of guilt ❏
   d) Photos of snakes and other reptiles on your Facebook business page ❏

9. Who make the best influencers?
a) Those who talk the most ❏
b) Those who listen well ❏
c) Level 1 listeners ❏
d) Those who avoid words like good, love and new ❏

10. Why should you listen attentively?
a) To find out whether the other person is using influential words ❏
b) To pick up another person's 'cues' and then match to them in order to influence ❏
c) To indicate that you have a strong character and you will not allow the other person to leave until they have agreed to your proposal ❏
d) To avoid having to say anything ❏

7 × 7

1 Seven quotes by influential people

- 'Be the change you wish to see in the world.' Mahatma Gandhi
- 'Keep away from small people who try to belittle your ambitions. Small people always do that, but the really great make you feel that you, too, can become great.' Mark Twain
- 'Logic will get you from A to B. Imagination will take you everywhere.' Albert Einstein
- 'If you look at what you have in life, you'll always have more. If you look at what you don't have in life, you'll never have enough.' Oprah Winfrey
- 'Our greatest weakness lies in giving up. The most certain way to succeed is always to try just one more time.' Thomas Edison
- 'I like things to happen; and if they don't happen, I like to make them happen.' Winston Churchill
- 'You don't learn to walk by following rules. You learn by doing, and by falling over.' Richard Branson

2 Seven key ideas to become more influential

- Become a blogger and share your expertise; position yourself as a trusted resource. Blogs create the perfect environment for an influential, interactive relationship. Think of it as your own public relations forum. An additional benefit is it may generate actual PR. Business bloggers often receive requests for interviews or quotes from journalists who consider them industry experts.
- Develop an influential charisma. How do respected world-class leaders generate a positive impact when making

speeches? Watch their body language, gestures, style of speaking, pauses for effect, etc and experiment with replicating them for yourself.

- Think of your last significant purchase. What exactly influenced your buying decision? Was it how the product/service was marketed? The written word? Maybe the spoken word? Was it a word-of-mouth recommendation from someone you trust? What can you learn and adopt from these sources of influence?
- Carry out a regular 'shoe review'. The smartest outfit can be let down by scuffed, dirty shoes. Invest 20 minutes at the weekend to clean the shoes you will be wearing in the coming week. If they still don't look smart after cleaning, it's time to turn them out.
- Make a list of famous, influential people that you admire and then check your local library for their biographies and autobiographies. For each one you read, jot down five key elements that contributed to their success, e.g. beliefs, values, strategies, decisions, etc. Then create a written plan to adopt as many of these proven traits as possible for yourself.
- Continually review and expand your networks, both informal (friends of friends) and formal (networking groups). The opportunities for being influential are unlimited when you network regularly.
- Social media provides a huge opportunity to be influential. On Facebook, join groups with which you have a shared interest. Start by following discussions and contributing short comments. Then build up to initiating discussions and eventually, starting up groups of your own.

3 Seven tips for making influential presentations

- Remember that feeling nervous is normal – in fact you need adrenaline to make a 'sharp' presentation. Everyone gets butterflies when presenting but it's the professionals who can get them to fly in formation!

- The symptoms associated with nervousness are identical to those associated with excitement, e.g. racing heart, sweaty palms, dry mouth. Instead of telling yourself that you are nervous, substitute the word 'excited' and you will feel quite different.
- If you need to read from a sheet of paper during your presentation, hold it in both hands with your hands pulling away from each other so that the paper is held taut. This prevents it from shaking and gives an impression to your audience (and to you) that you are confident and in control.
- Be a lighthouse. Make eye contact with your audience by looking around in sweeping arc-shape movements. This maintains a connection with them and there are bound to be some friendly faces looking back at you.
- Always have a glass of water to hand. Then if you experience a dry mouth or you need to pause momentarily to recover your composure, taking a sip of water fills the pause and looks completely natural.
- To avoid 'death by PowerPoint', follow the 5 × 5 rule. Use bullet points of no more than five words each, with a maximum of five bullet points per slide. Keep the overall number of slides used to just enough to support the content that you are delivering verbally.
- Practice makes permanent. The surefire way to become a confident, competent, persuasive presenter is to seek out opportunities to present and make the most of them. Toastmasters is a non-profit organization developing public speaking and leadership skills through practice and feedback in local clubs. For further details, check out their website at www.toastmasters.org

4 Seven ways to be a more influential networker

- When you introduce yourself at a networking event, say your first name twice to make it more memorable, e.g. 'My name is Alex, Alex Smith.'

- It is very easy to forget someone's name shortly after being introduced because your mind is busy processing your initial perception of them. When you know you are about to hear a name for the first time, 'prime' your memory by saying to yourself, 'I am about to hear this person's name and I *will* remember it.'
- Always have an 'elevator pitch' prepared. This is a very short statement, one minute long at most, that describes what you do in terms of how you help your clients successfully overcome their business challenges. This generates far more interest than just saying your name, job role and where you work.
- At networking events, it is essential to mingle and then keep moving around and introducing yourself to as many people as possible. Ensure that you maintain a genuine interest in the people you are meeting and always be seeking mutually beneficial collaboration opportunities.
- Collect business cards from everyone you speak to and then follow up with a personalized e-mail within 24 hours. If you jot down a few words on the cards relating to each person, then you can incorporate that into your e-mail and thus generate the personal touch.
- When someone tells you about their business, ask how you could identify their ideal client with a view to brokering a beneficial introduction. This will almost certainly invoke the Law of Reciprocation and they will be thinking about what they can do for you.
- If you identify a collaboration opportunity, ask the other person whether you can schedule a time for a 'coffee on the phone' chat. This assumes that at some time, probably around 11 am, they will pause for a coffee and in those few minutes, there is an opportunity for the two of you to explore mutually beneficial opportunities over the telephone. This is less 'in your face' than asking a busy person for a face to face meeting and they will respect you for that. If the conversation goes well, then they are far more likely to be amenable to a follow-up meeting.

5 Seven things at which the best social media influencers excel

- They persevere and put in the time that is needed. They understand that nobody gets famous overnight and they are prepared to spend countless hours on social media building their brands and their influence.
- They become the 'go-to' source of valuable content. They get to know their followers and share content that will benefit them. Influencers always keep their audience in mind when they post.
- They use social media to help others rather than to promote themselves. And yet in doing this, they have provided value and a service, and have thus indirectly promoted themselves.
- They contribute to the social media community whenever possible. They engage with the people who connect with them, and give back, thereby positioning themselves as a direct source of valuable knowledge and support.
- They only post positive comments. They never use social media to criticize, condemn or complain. This generates a very positive perception and increases followers.
- They consistently post high-quality content and in doing so, build a high quality reputation for themselves. They are seen as experts in their field.
- They recognize that whilst none of these things is difficult, consistency and constant focus are required and they are committed to provide these in bucketfuls.

6 Seven things to avoid

- Being 'needy'. Avoid being so focused on the outcome of a situation that it takes on the drama of a being a life or death scenario – it repels people.
- Being over confident. Even if everything has been going well during a persuasive conversation, never assume that the outcome is a foregone conclusion. People can be very unpredictable.

- Being a quitter. You must be prepared to be patient in order to achieve your outcomes. Many people need to take time to consider their decisions and just because they haven't said 'yes' yet doesn't mean that they won't. Countless goals are abandoned so close to their successful achievement because of impatience with the process.
- Being a 'limpet' – holding on to a situation that you believe you are influencing positively but in reality, is never going to come good. It is far better to recognize that you have done your best but that other influences outside of your control are determining the outcome and it is time to leave.
- Losing control and your temper when things aren't going how you want them to, and in particular, when there is a personality conflict. Even if you are in the right, you will not look good if you have allowed yourself to get drawn into a volatile situation.
- Talking more than listening. You have two ears and one mouth and it is essential you use them in that proportion. When you really listen to others, you gain insights into what is important to them and clues as to how they are most likely to be influenced.
- Making assumptions – there will always be at least a 50 per cent chance that your assumption is incorrect. Never attempt to persuade or influence someone based on an assumption. Check it out first for accuracy.

7 Seven best resources

- Holly Weeks' *Failure to Communicate: How Conversations Go Wrong and What You Can Do To Right Them* (Harvard Business Press, 2010). Difficult conversations cause stress and jangle nerves. This book serves as a reference for leaders from every profession.
- Dr Robert Cialdini's *Influence: The Psychology of Persuasion* explores the six universal principles of persuasion and how to use them to become a skilled persuader.
- Roger Fisher and William Ury's *Getting to Yes: Negotiating an Agreement without Giving In* has been in print for over 30 years and has helped countless people achieve win/win agreements both at work and in their private lives.

- Website http://www.businessballs.com is an invaluable resource for up-to-date thinking on business training and personal development in a business environment.
- http://www.theinvisiblegorilla.com/gorilla_experiment. html is a video clip that demonstrates how easily we can be influenced by our intuition into not seeing something obvious that is right in front of us.
- Daniel Pink's *Drive: The Surprising Truth About What Motivates Us* is an exploration of the secrets of high performance and personal satisfaction at work and at home.
- Sally Hogshead in *Fascinate: Your 7 Triggers to Persuasion and Captivation* promotes the concept that fascination is one of the most powerful ways to attract attention and influence behaviour, and explains how companies can use these concepts to make their products and ideas irresistible to consumers. .

PART 3
Your Public Speaking Masterclass

Introduction

*'There are certain things in which mediocrity
is not to be endured, such as poetry, music,
painting, public speaking.'*

Jean de La Bruyère, seventeenth-century French moralist

**Public speaking is the ritual humiliation of one person by a
group of onlookers before whom he or she must orate, laying
themselves open to embarrassment, belittlement and ridicule.**

Does this sound about right?

If it does, then it's time to do something about it because
public speaking really doesn't need to be an ordeal. It can,
and should, be stimulating, self-affirming, empowering and
even enjoyable. It can also provide a great boost to your self-
confidence and to your self-esteem, the benefit of which can
be enjoyed in all aspects of your work life, and beyond. Not
only that, but accomplished public speakers are much valued
and sought-after by the majority of businesses, who recognize
that excellent communication skills are a key tool in today's
workplace.

Mastering the art of public speaking, then, will strengthen your
contribution to your company, and your perceived value within
it, as well as boosting your confidence and providing you with
a new and exciting outlet for your skills. So what type of public
speaking are you hoping to excel at?

Whether you need to present to just a few people at an in-
house meeting, or to thousands at a global conference, the
principles are the same, and once you have mastered them
you will be able to use them in a variety of situations. You will
find that your self-belief receives a healthy boost when you can
stand in front of an audience and confidently deliver a speech
with clarity, dynamism and panache. You will also find that
over time your voice becomes stronger and clearer, allowing

you to make yourself noticed and heard in *any* situation. In turn, your contribution to your company will be better heard and acknowledged, fully realized and even rewarded.

As you develop a reputation within your company as someone with excellent public speaking and presentation skills, you may even find yourself being asked to present on the company's behalf at conferences and seminars. This can be a great way to get yourself noticed, both in your company and beyond, and can provide a very useful entrée to networking. It's also a consummately transferable skill which can help to make you an attractive acquisition should you at any time decide to move on from your current employment.

So there are a great many reasons to want to become excellent at speaking in public – but is it possible to learn how to do it? Happily the answer is 'yes' because public speaking is an art, not a science. It doesn't matter what your current level of experience or ability might be – with diligent practice you will be able to master the art of engaging, dynamic public speaking – and then reap the rewards for years to come.

CHAPTER 14

Writing
your speech

Good public speaking does not require stimulating material – it requires that the material you have is delivered in a stimulating way. And this means that it needs to written and structured in a stimulating way. Depending on your subject matter, it may not be possible to fill your speech with exciting material – but it's always possible to ensure that you compose your speech in such a way as to make it interesting to listen to. To do this, you will need to adhere to some fundamental principles, and it's worth investing the necessary time early on to ensure that the material you are going to deliver – the speech you hope people will want to listen to – is as good as it can be.

Preparing a good speech, and in good time, will also help you to combat any nerves you may experience (and it's highly likely you will, since these, left unmanaged, are one of the most common roadblocks to good public speaking).

Finally, it's important to remember that material that is written to be spoken is very different from material that is written to be read, both in style and content, and mastering the techniques for writing a great speech will in turn help you to master the techniques for great delivery.

The basics

What makes a great speech?

There is a difference between making a great speech and making a speech great. Making a great speech requires fantastic delivery, whereas making a speech great requires fantastic writing. Of course, it naturally follows that the better your speech is written the more likely it is that you will be able to deliver it to maximum impact. So let's look at how to write a great speech.

There are three stages to writing a successful speech:

1 Tell them what you are going to tell them.
2 Tell them.
3 Tell them what you have told them.

If this sounds like a recipe for a repetitive and boring speech, remember that your audience won't be familiar with the material, as you are, and in some cases may not even be familiar with the subject area, so it's important to give them every opportunity not only to listen to what you are saying but to take it in. Following this simple three-stage approach will also ensure that you adhere to two basic principles of speech-writing:

1 All the information you want to convey should be **confined to the body of your speech.**
2 Audiences need to hear your key message **at least three times** for it to really sink in.

Of course, you will need to tailor your format to your audience (e.g. if you will be addressing a mixed group, some of whom are very familiar with your subject and some not at all, you will need to find suitable middle ground so as not to bore the former or leave the latter stranded) but you should always aim to structure your speech in three distinct sections:

1 introduction
2 speech
3 conclusion.

Introduction

This should comprise no more than:

- introducing yourself to your audience
- introducing your audience to the key tenets of your speech.

It's important that you keep the introduction to just that, an introduction, and that you don't begin to explore any of the topics your speech will cover. By introducing all the key areas of your speech you are ensuring that nothing in your speech will come as a surprise (unless this is intended – and this is a technique that should be used rarely and sparingly), which in turn means that your audience will be prepared and should therefore be receptive to what you have to say.

Speech

This is the main body of your material and should contain all the key parts of your speech – everything you want people to take away from your speech should be here. You will introduce the themes, and go over them again in your conclusion, but this is where they should be described in detail.

Conclusion

This is your opportunity to sum up the key points and reiterate them so that they stay firmly in your audience's mind. Don't try to go over everything you've said – keep it tight and focused on only the main points – and don't ever try to introduce new points here.

Getting started early

Proper planning and preparation prevents poor performance.

The earlier you start working on your speech, presentation, or whatever form of public address you will be giving, the better your delivery will be. It's a common mistake to believe that preparing your material in good time is important only to ensure that what you are saying is as good as it can be.

In reality, preparing your material in good time also allows you to ensure that how you say it is as good as it can be. Leaving it to the last minute, or, worse still, just 'winging it' on the day, is a recipe for disaster.

 TIP *When it comes to public speaking, there is no such thing as being over-prepared.*

Preparing your speech in good time allows you to become familiar with your material. This is crucial for good, confident public speaking as it:

- allows you to lift your head from your notes and speak directly to your audience, making all-important eye contact
- gives you confidence in your delivery, knowing that what you are saying is interesting
- allows you to read from brief, headline notes and memory joggers, so that you don't have to write out the entire speech and read it verbatim
- ensures that you can stay calm, relaxed and in control without the fear of losing your place and stalling your delivery
- helps to settle your nerves since you can go into it well-practised and sure of your ability to do a good job
- ensures that you don't omit anything important, which you then have at the back of your mind for the rest of your speech
- ensures that you don't ad lib, which serves only to give an impression of unprofessionalism – unless you are very, very good at it
- gives you the time and opportunity to rehearse your speech so that you're familiar with every aspect of it.

 TIP *Prepare well, and prepare early.*

Initial preparations

Since it's never too early to start, there are a number of things that you should get under way right now. These will help you to focus on the task ahead and prepare some necessary groundwork:

1 Begin sketching out a **draft plan** of your speech – however rough. This should be regularly updated.
2 Ask any colleagues, bosses, stakeholders and so on. whether they want to be **consulted** on your speech. If there are specific items they want you to include, then the sooner you know about it the better.
3 **Know your audience.** This is important so that you can pitch your speech appropriately – so if you're not sure who will be attending then find out.
4 **Begin practising speaking out loud** – and loudly – whenever you're on your own. At first, it will sound odd to you but the more you do it the more normal it will become.
5 Line up some **willing volunteers** in front of whom you can practise making your speech, preferably people who are used to public speaking and from whom you can receive constructive criticism.

While a friend or partner may seem an obvious candidate, a colleague with a knowledge of your subject area is likely to be a better choice since they are better placed to spot any errors, superfluous material or repetitions – and they are likely to be less forgiving and more vocal in their criticism!

Starting and finishing strongly

You don't need to be a professional speech-writer to write a great speech. By thinking about what you want to say well in advance, structuring your thoughts carefully, and continually improving your speech over time, you will soon discover that everyone can write a great speech.

Get into the habit of always carrying with you a pocket-sized notebook devoted exclusively to your speech and jotting down thoughts as and when they occur to you. You can structure them later – the important thing is to capture them before you forget them.

The beginning and end of your speech are the parts that are likely to be most clearly remembered so you will need to make sure these are particularly strong.

It's crucial to have a **strong start** to your speech in order to:

- grab your audience's attention
- help them to relax (which will help *you* to relax)
- break the ice
- make your audience want to listen to your speech.

It's crucial to **finish strongly** in order to:

- bring your speech to a definite conclusion
- ensure a smooth handover to the next speaker (where applicable)
- end on a high note
- leave the audience wanting more.

Structuring your speech

You will need to divide your speech into sections so that it takes your audience on a journey. What this looks like will, of course, depend on the material you are delivering but try to ensure that your speech flows neatly from one section to the next. By breaking it down in this manner you will make it easier for:

- your audience to follow
- your audience to digest
- you to focus on the key content in each section.

You will also need to give some thought to the length of your speech. Making the speech unnecessarily long is a trap into which inexperienced speech-givers commonly fall, in the mistaken belief that:

- they will appear in command of their subject by demonstrating the scope of their knowledge
- they will have time to 'get into it' and calm their nerves
- they will give their audience value for money
- there won't be time for any awkward questions and answers!

The truth, of course, is that the value of the speech lies in the quality, not the quantity, of the material and, crucially, in the quality of the delivery.

TIP *A short, punchy speech delivered with dynamism, with a few key messages that shine out, will be remembered long after an endlessly wordy, albeit worthy, speech has been forgotten.*

Keep your speech short, relevant and 'fat-free' and your audience will thank you for it. It will also help to ensure that your message is clearly defined, and that it does not get lost in a jungle of superfluous material padding out your speech.

> **'If you can't write your message in a sentence, you can't say it in an hour.'**
> Dianna Booher, US communication expert

Remember that:

- a short speech...
  - will be more memorable
  - will leave the audience wanting more
  - might be a pleasant surprise!
- a long speech...
  - may make the audience restless
  - can appear self-indulgent
  - is likely to obscure the important points.

TIP *Don't forget that your speech may not exist in isolation – and that any audience has a maximum tolerance for listening! Your audience may already have heard one or more speeches and may have more to listen to after yours, so make your speech stand out by keeping it tight, focused and punchy.*

Setting the tone

'They may forget what you said, but they will never forget how you made them feel.'

Carl W. Buechner, US theologian

When writing your speech it's important to bear in mind how you want to come across to your audience – not simply how it sounds to you. Think about whether you want your speech to be regarded as:

- authoritative
- sincere
- professional
- humorous
- no-nonsense
- friendly
- insightful
- witty

... and so on. In reality, you will probably want it to be a mixture of several things, and it easily can be, but you must be careful to avoid a mixture of tones cancelling each other out so that your speech just appears bland. In order to avoid this, you will need to ensure that you:

- decide what the predominant tone of each section should be
- keep each section defined and unique
- begin and end on an upbeat note to hook your audience.

It's certainly important to inject some colour into your speech since orations without variety, interest and impact are difficult to listen to and easy to forget. Striking the right balance between writing a speech which is dry and dispassionate and one which is gushing and effusive is a fine art, but one which will make all the difference between an end product which is run-of-the-mill or truly memorable.

Writing your speech – advanced techniques

To give your speech that extra dimension that will elevate it above and beyond the majority of speeches, and make it truly memorable, you will need to employ some more advanced speech-writing techniques. Remember that many members of your audience may well listen to speakers on a regular basis, so to stand out from the crowd you will need to use some 'tricks of the trade' which will help you to change a good speech into a great speech through a process of enhancements and fine-tuning.

Fine-tuning

Great speeches aren't written, they're rewritten. You simply can't expect, or even hope, that you will be able to compose a great speech at the first attempt. Even if you plan the outline with great care and precision and then work diligently over time to fill in the blanks, you can be sure that the speech you end up with will be markedly different from your first draft (it may even bear no resemblance to it at all!). This is because you will need to employ a continual and ongoing process of revision and reworking, fine-tuning your speech by crafting it until you have smoothed off all the rough edges.

> **'Great speeches aren't written, they're rewritten.'**

The most effective way to do this is to revise your speech regularly, and often, keeping it always somewhere at the back of your mind and practising delivering it at every opportunity, even when this is just inside your head (e.g. when out for a walk or at the gym). This will help you in a number of ways. For example, you will:

● become **increasingly familiar** with your material, ultimately allowing you to give your speech with minimal need for notes and enabling you to maintain eye contact as much as possible

- become increasingly used to delivering your speech, helping to **settle your nerves**
- be constantly on the lookout for ways in which your speech **can be improved,** particularly by adding important material you had overlooked and deleting any extraneous material.

It's impossible to overstate the importance of removing any, and all, material which doesn't need to be there. Material which is simply acting as padding, which is unnecessary filler, which serves no particular purpose, may be repeating a point already made or which you will make better elsewhere, which creates 'run-on' sentences by not knowing when to stop so that the sentence would clearly have been punchier and easier to listen to and better remembered if it hadn't been allowed to go on so long, material which repeats itself, material which goes on too long, material which repeats itself, which starts to appear in love with the sound of its own voice, which repeats itself and goes on far too long...

You get the picture? This is one of the most common pitfalls in speech-writing, often because people worry that they won't have enough to say, or because they are (often subconsciously) creating a quantity of material which they hope will compensate for a lack of quality, either in the speech or, more usually, in their ability to deliver it. Sometimes people simply want to include every relevant fact and overlook the crucial point that they don't need to say everything they know on any given topic in every speech.

Indeed, falling into any of these traps of including too much material is hugely detrimental since your audience will simply start to tune you out! You have probably experienced this yourself when listening to an uninteresting speaker drone on and on and on, or someone who simply tries to convey far too much information in their speech. No matter how hard you try to concentrate on what they are saying you find your mind wandering, and their material, no matter how good, is wasted. Worse still, if some of the speech is good but surrounded by an obscuring mask of detritus they run the risk of all of it being lost.

The best way to counter any of these potential pitfalls is simply to keep going over your speech and honing it: reworking, editing, paring, rewriting and recrafting until it's lean, interesting and the right length – not for you, but for your audience. By doing this, any pointless material or repetition will stand out a mile and you will find yourself wanting to cut it before it begins to grate, or to bore you. In this way you will be keeping only the very best all the time, and by adding to it as and when thoughts occur you can also be sure to cover all bases, while being ever mindful of keeping it to an appropriate length.

> ### 'Always be shorter than anybody dared to hope.'
> Rufus Daniel Isaacs, 1st Marquess of Reading,
> barrister and British Foreign Secretary

When new material occurs to you, capture it immediately. You can work out later on where best in your speech to put it – the important thing is to make sure that you get it committed to paper before you forget it.

Sometimes you will want to leave your speech for a few days to gain perspective, and this can be very valuable (provided it doesn't become an excuse for not working on it!), but it's important not to leave it too long, or too frequently. Try to get into the habit of updating your speech on a regular basis; otherwise, you might go for weeks without looking at it if you don't think of anything new to add to it. In particular, try to ensure that you revisit your speech after:

- presenting it to anyone who is helping you to practise
- adding new material (check for repetition)
- leaving it for a few days (to gain perspective).

At the very least, you should aim to revise your speech once per week. If your command of the subject is excellent (which should be taken as read if you are going to speak publicly on it), and if you are continually thinking about how to improve it, then you shouldn't find the process of writing your speech too difficult or daunting.

> **'Grasp the subject, the words will follow.'**
> Cato the Elder, ancient Roman statesman

Injecting variety

Any audience has a maximum tolerance for listening, so it's a good idea to add some variety to your speech to help break it up, particularly if it's lengthy or one of several speeches to which your audience will be listening that day.

Good ways to achieve this include:

- using props
- showing slides
- playing music
- showing video clips.

TIP *Be careful not to overdo it! If your entire speech is filled with props, slides, music and so on, then this becomes the norm and ceases to add variety.*

Adding variety helps to keep your speech fresh and differentiate it from any other speeches. It also:

- creates interest for the audience
- breaks up your speech
- divides your speech into sections.

TIP *Remember to use only things which are directly relevant to your speech, and support or embellish it.*

By thinking this through at an early stage you can ensure that everything you use is really justified and not just there for show, and that it's properly worked into your speech.

Where possible, it is also a good idea to add some **humour** to your speech. This can be a great way to:

● break the ice
● add variety
● help your audience to relax
● help you to relax
● keep your audience entertained – and thus engaged.

Tailoring your speech to your audience and venue

If possible, you should try to get some idea of the people who will comprise your audience so that you can tailor your speech to suit them. Pitching a speech at the right level is crucial for ensuring that your audience:

● don't get bored by hearing things they already know or that they don't understand
● hear something genuinely new and interesting
● remember what you have said.

In the same way, if you have the opportunity to scope out the venue beforehand, it will help you to tailor your speech to the specifics of the venue:

● **For a very large venue with a sizeable audience:**
  You will need to remember that not everyone will be able to see your face so don't rely on this to communicate feelings or ideas – make sure they are obvious from your words.
● **For a very small venue with a small audience:**
  This can easily become overly familiar, or preachy and worthy – you will need to ensure that you write your speech with a suitable degree of formality and so on.

Summary

However good you are at public speaking, your overall performance can only ever be as good as the speech you have written allows you to be. Of course, a bad speech can be delivered with panache and dynamism, but it will still be a bad speech. Imagine how much better it would have been if the speech itself had been good to begin with. So the quality of the speech you prepare will be a limiting factor in determining how good your performance will be, and how memorable your speech will be.

In addition, knowing that you have a great speech to deliver will help to build your confidence for the moment when you step up to deliver it. Having a really interesting speech removes a good deal of the pressure on you as a speaker since you will not need to 'sell' your speech to the audience, but rather to ensure that they have every opportunity of hearing it clearly and delivered with confidence.

The speech you write will therefore form the bedrock of everything else to do with giving your speech, so it really is worth investing the necessary time and effort to get it as good as possible.

In the next chapter, we will begin to master the art of delivery...

Fact-check [answers at the back]

1. Your speech should...
a) Dot your themes about in a random fashion ❏
b) Employ a clear, linear structure ❏
c) Simultaneously cover as many topics as possible ❏
d) Make it difficult for your audience to follow so they will have to concentrate ❏

2. The key themes of your speech should...
a) Be confined to the introduction ❏
b) Be confined to the main body of the speech ❏
c) Be confined to the conclusion ❏
d) Be in the introduction, the main body of the speech and the conclusion ❏

3. With public speaking it is...
a) Poor practice to prepare too much in advance ❏
b) Good to practise a little ❏
c) Good to practise a lot ❏
d) Impossible to be over-prepared ❏

4. To begin with, speaking aloud when you are on your own will seem...
a) Entirely natural ❏
b) Odd and ridiculous ❏
c) Better than remaining silent ❏
d) Comforting ❏

5. It's crucial to have a strong start to your speech in order to...
a) Grab your audience's attention ❏
b) Remind yourself what your speech is about ❏
c) Make sure that the microphone is working ❏
d) Wake everyone up ❏

6. Your speech should take your audience on a journey because...
a) Everyone likes a story ❏
b) It makes it easier for your audience to follow ❏
c) They may be unfamiliar with the local area ❏
d) They probably don't get out much ❏

7. It's preferable to keep your speech short because...
a) There is less chance of making mistakes ❏
b) If your delivery is boring, at least there will be less of it ❏
c) It will be more memorable ❏
d) You get paid the same anyway ❏

8. You will need to go back over your speech because...
a) You may have omitted something vital ❏
b) You may have included something untoward ❏
c) Great speeches aren't written, they're rewritten ❏
d) You never get things right first time ❏

9. It's good to inject variety into your speech because...
a) Otherwise your speech will be boring ❑
b) Your audience may have poor concentration ❑
c) Everyone loves juggling ❑
d) It creates interest for the audience ❑

10. It's good to tailor your speech to your audience so that...
a) They are not being told things they already know ❑
b) It can't be used again ❑
c) It can't be plagiarized ❑
d) They can keep up if they are slow ❑

CHAPTER 15

The basics of public speaking

For many people, simply standing in a large room and speaking out loud seems very odd and even rather disconcerting. Hearing your own voice – loud and the only sound in the space – can be very off-putting at first, and it's something you will need to get used to, and comfortable with, before speaking in public.

It's essential that you are at ease with this element of public speaking as it forms the bedrock for the more advanced techniques we will look at later on – without it, it will be extremely difficult to employ successfully the methods which will captivate and inspire your audience. Happily, it's something you can get used to fairly quickly and easily, as are learning to command the space and eliminating bad habits.

Other techniques such as using the actor's method of projection and supporting your voice take a little longer to master, but they are perfectly achievable – and if you are willing to put in the hours you will be amazed just how much progress you can make in one week.

As you master the techniques set out in this chapter, you will begin to develop your own style and, importantly, grow in confidence until the thought of feeling embarrassed at hearing your voice bouncing off the walls is just a distant memory.

Getting used to speaking aloud

There is only one way to get used to speaking out loud and to hearing the sound of your own voice (which will at first sound and feel unfamiliar to you) and that's to do it. Try it the next time you are alone – **if you are alone now then read the rest of this chapter out loud.** At first you are likely to feel:

- self-conscious
- that you're showing off
- acutely aware of the sound of your voice.

This is natural and to be expected and will wear off only with repeated practice, so every time you find yourself alone try speaking out loud.

 Most people are rarely conscious of hearing their own voice in everyday situations, but when it's the only sound in the room and everyone is listening to you you will hear it in a whole new light – and it's something you need to get used to.

It doesn't matter what you say – the object of the exercise isn't to practise your speech but just to get used to the actions of speaking aloud. So don't be put off by not being able to think of anything to say; say whatever comes into your head or, alternatively, just grab a book or newspaper and start reading it aloud.

Don't worry if you feel ridiculous (and you almost certainly will at first), just keep going – it's only with repeated exposure that you will begin to feel comfortable with hearing yourself speaking out loud, and if you can't get comfortable with it in this environment just imagine how you are going to feel when you have an audience looking back at you – and listening to your voice.

Try speaking out loud whenever you are on your own. This will:

- force you to concentrate on your voice
- give you an opportunity to get used to hearing yourself
- make it seem normal!

Rehearsing in front of other people

'All the real work is done in the
rehearsal period.'

Donald Pleasence, English actor

Practising giving your speech in front of a small, invited audience is vital preparation for giving your speech in front of a real audience. You can start with just one person and build up to a few colleagues, family members or close friends. Initially, you are likely to feel:

- nervous
- awkward
- embarrassed
- self-conscious.

This is entirely natural (indeed, it would be unnatural if you didn't!) but it will subside with practice and experience, leaving you free to concentrate on delivering your speech with dynamism and élan; and this will give you the best possible chance of ensuring that your message is heard and remembered. You might even be pleasantly surprised and find that you *enjoy* giving your speech. And remember that it's far better to get past this hurdle now than to face it for the first time when you are standing in front of an expectant audience.

 TIP *The more you practise, the easier it gets.*

Using cue cards

One of the most important techniques to master for good, confident public speaking is the use of cue cards. By having the outline of your speech written out in front of you, you will have the reassurance of not having to remember your entire speech – something which is a recipe for disaster no matter how good your memory is, since the pressure of the occasion can make the minds of even the most confident speakers go blank. Equally disruptive to fluent public speaking is to have your entire speech written out in full for you to read to your audience. Doing so provides a number of unnecessary potential pitfalls:

- It will be difficult to establish and maintain good eye contact with your audience since your eyes will necessarily be cast down most of the time, reading.
- Spontaneity will be lost if you are reading verbatim and your audience might just as well sit in their seats reading a copy of your speech instead of listening to you delivering it.
- Your speech-giving can all too easily morph into a homily, making it seem condescending or overly worthy to your audience.
- It's easy to lose your place in a speech which you are reading word for word, and this can cause an embarrassing hiatus, making both you and your audience nervous.

While you should, broadly speaking, stick to the script and avoid improvisation, it's always a good idea to tailor your speech to each audience, perhaps including something topical or particularly relevant to the place in which you are speaking. This is much easier to do if you are speaking freely from headline overviews than if you are reading aloud an essay.

So what makes a good cue card?

Depending on the length of your speech, it's likely that you will need a number of cue cards, and this can be used to your advantage to help you break your speech down into manageable sections. Always keep in mind that a good speech is one which is easy to listen to and remember, as well as one which is easy to give. By breaking your speech down into logical component parts you will be making it not only easier to deliver but, crucially, easier for your audience to receive.

So your speech is likely to consist of a stack of cue cards, each focused on a different area of your speech, and each containing sufficient information for you to know instantly what you will be saying next without providing so much that it causes you to pause while you read what you have written.

The secret to creating a great cue card can be broken down into seven points:

1 Size

It should be sufficiently large to fit enough information that you avoid the need to move on to a new card every two minutes, and to enable you to use a size of writing that you are able to read easily at a glance. It should also be small enough that it fits comfortably in your hand and doesn't obscure your audience's view of you (that is particularly important if you are speaking from a raised dais).

2 Clarity

The clearer the words on the page, the clearer your speech will be. It's a simple fact that, if you can glance at your cue cards and glean all the relevant information in a moment without breaking stride, then your speech will remain fluent and easy to listen to. To achieve maximum clarity you will need to:

- use a clear, easy-to-read typeface
- keep the text large enough to read at a glance
- underline all headings and subheadings
- highlight key words and phrases in the text
- use plenty of spaces and line separation to prevent the text from becoming too dense
- clearly number each card in sequence
- mark each card with a coloured dot in one corner using a different colour for each section (important if you are giving a long speech covering a number of different subject areas).

3 Detail

How much information should each bullet point contain? Include too much and you will find it hard to see the wood for the trees – and there is a very real possibility that you will simply end up reading aloud what you have written, verbatim. Include too little and you may well find yourself struggling to remember what exactly the point was that you wished to make! Therefore, including just the right amount of detail is extremely important – how much this is will depend on your preference, your style of delivery, and your ability to recall information (particularly facts, statistics, etc.). To find out what is going to work best for you, simply do a trial run.

4 Focus

By having the topic or subtopic highlighted at the top of each of your cue cards, you will give yourself a handy reminder of the focus for each section of your speech, ensuring that they are always easy to see and always front of mind.

5 Direction

Just as actors have a director to help them to get the most out of their performance, and annotate their scripts in order to remind themselves where they need to go, when they need to pause, and so on, you, too, should mark up your cue cards with similar reminders. Which points require more emphasis? When should you pause? When is it crucial to look up and make eye contact?

6 Quality

This refers to the quality of the card you use and not the quality of your speech, though one should reflect the other. By using really good-quality card you will be able to:

● hold them steady without fear of them bending away from you
● rest them on a lectern without fear of them blowing away
● see clearly what you have written without a strong backlight at subsequent pages showing through
● avoid distracting your audience by them trying to read your notes.

It also helps to convey an image of professionalism which will put your audience at ease. Remember to use smart blank cards with plain backs.

7 Back-up

Plenty of great speeches have been ruined by the speaker mislaying their cue cards. Always ensure that you carry a spare set and always keep the two sets separate. It's a good idea to also carry a memory stick with your speech backed up on it, and, if possible, to have it on a computer back at the office which you can access remotely.

> # Warning!
>
> Prepare your cue cards carefully, and double-check that everything on them is as it should be. Even one slight error in preparing your cue cards can make all the difference when it comes to *pubic speaking* (sic) and under the pressure of the occasion this can be all that is needed to throw you off balance causing you to stumble over your words, laugh or dry up altogether.

Making eye contact

Establishing and maintaining eye contact with your audience members is one of the most important aspects of good public speaking – of any kind. Any speech-giver who fails to make eye contact with their audience risks distancing them, and leaving them unengaged. Imagine watching someone giving a speech in which they fail to make eye contact and imagine how that makes you feel – and what impression it gives you of them. They will seem disinterested and aloof and you will be far less likely to care about what they are saying.

Making eye contact allows you to:

- engage with your audience
- establish a rapport with your audience
- make each audience member feel included
- deliver your speech with dynamism.

It will also help you to:

- look confident
- look interested
- feel less nervous
- keep your head up!

Failing to establish eye contact creates a damaging separation between the speech-giver and their audience, while making and maintaining good eye contact does the opposite, drawing them in and engaging them. Remember that you don't need to do this all the time, but that the more you can manage it the better your speech will come across.

Addressing a large audience

If you are addressing a large gathering then you might not be able to look directly at each and every member of your audience but that doesn't matter – what matters is that every member of your audience will feel involved just by knowing that you're making eye contact with someone in the audience. Try to move your gaze around so that you take in different people and different sections of your audience as your speech progresses.

Facial expression

Appropriate use of facial expression can be used to help you to convey any number of meanings which will help to support what you are saying. Of course, you will want to avoid your speech turning into a comedy routine of strained expressions and gurning, so the trick is to keep them to a minimum and keep them appropriate. On the other hand, a speaker who is resolutely unanimated runs the risk of appearing disinterested, or even bored, with their own speech!

It's important to do what feels natural to you, so don't force it – just be mindful that, if your face reflects the tone of what you are saying, it will help to support your message, and the audience will be more likely to receive it well.

Correct posture and relaxation

By standing tall, and looking relaxed and confident, you are more than halfway to getting a good reception from your audience. Whether or not this translates into a good response to your speech will depend on its contents and your skill as a speaker, but by establishing the basics early on you will be giving yourself the best possible chance.

TIP *If a speaker looks cowed and worried, their audience is likely to be sceptical about their ability to deliver an engaging speech, and also about the quality of their material. If a speaker stands tall and appears relaxed and in control, then the opposite is true.*

Avoiding fidgeting

Fidgeting needs to be avoided at all times as it's distracting to the audience and a clear sign of a nervous speaker, as well as taking attention away from what you are saying. The best way to avoid fidgeting is to practise speaking aloud while looking at yourself in a mirror, or better still employ the services of someone to watch you as you practise, in order to identify the ways in which you fidget.

Every speaker is different and will fidget in different ways, so it's important to learn what yours are and then to establish ways of eradicating them. Some of the more common ones are listed in the table below, together with ways to avoid them.

It's important to remember that fidgeting is not restricted to physical movements – it can also manifest itself in other ways, such as nervous laughter, frequent swallowing, unnecessary coughing, lengthy unintended pauses or gabbling, and so on. Try to give yourself plenty of time to identify the problem areas for you and don't be tempted to ignore them, in the hope that they will just go away over time. However tiresome it may be to work on them, it's much easier to do so when you are practising than when you're standing in front of a room full of people, and it really will make a huge difference to the quality of your presentation. Remember the Russian army motto:

'Train hard, fight easy.'
Aleksandr Suvorov, Russian general

Ways of fidgeting	How to avoid them
Shuffling feet, or regularly shifting weight from one foot to the other	Plant your feet firmly, shoulder-width apart, and imagine that they are nailed to the floor. Concentrate on standing tall, imagining a thread joined to the top of your head pulling you up. This will keep your feet firmly planted and improve your posture.
Playing with hair, fiddling with jewellery, etc.	Keep your hands firmly on the lectern or on your cue cards. Playing with your hair or other types of fiddling are often subconscious, so don't allow your hands to wander.
Scratching, or wringing hands	Usually a reaction to nervousness. Ensure that you have employed the relaxation techniques in this book (see Chapter 19) and remember to take deep, calming breaths, before your speech and during it. Keep your hands firmly on your cue cards or lectern.
Flailing arms	Usually the result of trying to emphasize a point, particularly when you feel nervous about your ability to convey your message. Occasional use of gestures can be beneficial but lots of imprecise movements will only distract your audience so keep your arms still unless you wish to make a deliberate movement – and then make it clear, clean and quick.
Rapid blinking	Employ the relaxation techniques, focus on your key messages, and concentrate on making eye contact with members of the audience. Focus on one person and try to imagine that they are the only person in the audience, and deliver a part of your speech to them. Then choose someone else and do the same... and so on.

Clarity

You will want to make sure that every word you say is heard and understood, and it's important to remember that clarity of speech and careful annunciation are just as important as volume. Trying to listen to someone who mumbles, and trying to understand them and concentrate on what they say, is very difficult and quickly becomes wearing. If your audience have to work hard to understand you, they will:

- be devoting their attention to trying to catch what you are saying rather than to understanding its meaning
- quickly tire and their attention will start to wander
- think less of you as a speaker.

So practise speaking aloud to see if you are naturally clear in your speech.

If you are not, this is something you will need to work on by practising tongue twisters, speaking aloud sections of text ensuring that you clearly annunciate every vowel sound and every consonant, and by strengthening the muscles in your tongue and jaw. You will also need to practise speaking loudly, and make sure that your voice doesn't lose any clarity as the volume increases.

Putting your audience at ease

If your audience is relaxed and comfortable, they will be more receptive to your speech, and the more confident you appear to be, the better this will be achieved. Remember that it doesn't matter how you *feel* – it's how you *look* that counts. A swan might be paddling furiously under the water but on the surface it appears to be gliding effortlessly. By learning to walk confidently to the podium or lectern and smiling at your audience with certainty and confidence, radiating an unshakeable belief in your ability to give a good speech, your audience will relax and you will have achieved a significant victory before you even begin.

Avoid the classic trap for the unwary and inexperienced of telling your audience that you are not used to making speeches, or that you are nervous. Novices do so in the hope that it will:

- lower the audience's expectations
- make you feel better
- break the ice
- get the audience on your side (through sympathy).

It's a mistake which actually has the opposite effect, but it's amazing how often it's made (even by people who are not new to speech-giving!). What saying so actually does is:

- make your audience feel uncomfortable
- make your audience nervous *for* you and *about* you
- undermine your speech
- undermine you as a speaker.

Furthermore, pre-empting your audience's view that your speech won't be good is a great way to ensure that's how they remember it – even if it was actually excellent.

> '*Why doesn't the fellow who says "I'm no speechmaker" let it go at that instead of giving a demonstration?*'
>
> Kin Hubbard, US cartoonist and humorist

Setting the tone

The tone of your speech is crucial to helping you to convey its message in the quickest and clearest way possible. If you include too many 'ice-breaker' jokes or stories, particularly early on in your speech, you run the risk of undermining the content; and if you are hoping to inspire your audience to do something you hope they will see as enjoyable, then an overly serious tone might seem depressing and undermine your message. So it's important to determine:

- the overall tone you wish your speech to convey
- the tone of any individual sections, or subsections
- how you hope your audience will feel on hearing your speech
- what actions, if any, you hope your speech will produce.

Later in the book we will look at some of the ways in which the tone of your speech can be established, but it's important to remember to identify early on what you want it to be.

Keeping to the script

Many an otherwise excellent speech has been undermined, sometimes disastrously, by the speech-giver straying from their script and inadvertently saying something detrimental or damaging. A quick aside, an ad lib, a moment of lost concentration and discipline, and the whole speech can all too quickly go horribly wrong. Often, such asides are the result of nervousness, leading to the speaker trying to add something extra to make the speech more interesting if they feel their audience isn't responding in the way they had hoped.

It's therefore very important to stick to the script. If you are satisfied that the speech you are giving has been as well written and rehearsed as it could be, then you will have every reason to feel confident about it – and no reason to stray from what you have planned to say.

Keeping to your script will ensure that:

✓ you say everything you wanted to

✓ you keep your speech tight and focused

✓ you look and sound confident and in control

✗ you don't say anything you may later regret

✗ you don't dilute your speech with poor material

✗ you don't go on too long.

> **'No one ever complains about a speech being too short!'**
>
> Ira Hayes

Resisting the temptation to hurry

There are four primary reasons why speech-givers feel an (often overwhelming) urge to hurry:

1 nervousness at having to give their speech
2 lack of confidence in their abilities

3 lack of confidence in their material through:
   - fear that it's not sufficiently interesting
   - concern that their audience may disagree or identify factual errors
4 fear about overrunning their allotted time.

It's important to remember, however, that hurrying your speech is detrimental for a number of reasons:

- It can make you appear nervous.
- It makes it more difficult for the audience to hear what you are saying.
- It makes it more difficult for the audience to follow what you are saying.
- It may come across as breathless and disjointed.
- It denies you the important ability to:
   - clearly separate sections of your speech
   - use pauses to add emphasis to important moments.

Therefore, in order to eliminate the temptation to hurry you will need to eradicate the reasons behind it, allowing yourself the freedom to give your speech to the best of your ability, and giving your audience the freedom to listen to it to the best of theirs.

It is good practice to get into the habit of letting out several deep, slow, controlled sighs to completely fill your lungs with air before you start speaking. This will help you to:

- *start with a good strong voice*
- *maintain a consistent flow of air*
- *slow down your heart rate*
- *distract you from being nervous.*

The following table will help you address the usual reasons that lie behind hurrying:

Reasons for hurrying	How to avoid them
Nervousness	Practise the techniques in Chapter 19, and remember that you are likely to want to hurry – so force yourself to go slower than you want to (50 per cent is usually about right).
Lack of confidence in your abilities	By practising the techniques given here you will soon be able to write, and deliver, a great speech – so focus on that and be confident in your abilities.
Lack of confidence in your material	If you have researched your subject thoroughly and taken the necessary time to carefully write and structure it, you have every reason to be confident that it's both interesting to your audience and factually correct.
Fear of overrunning	Provided you have practised your speech out loud and timed it to ensure that it's a suitable length, you can be confident that you will not overrun. Find out well in advance how long you are expected to speak for, and whether you will be required (or want) to take questions from the floor, and then aim to make your speech 10 per cent shorter.

Practice makes perfect

'It takes one hour of preparation for each minute of presentation time.'

Wayne Burgraff, US philosopher

Delivering a speech well is a skill which needs to be learned and practised. You can master the principles of public speaking in a week but the more you practise – and keep practising – the better you will become. How much practice you will need to put in will depend on a number of factors, including your:

● previous experience
● natural aptitude
● starting level of confidence.

The best thing to do is to get into the habit of practising speaking out loud. Try to practise saying your speech out loud, and implementing the techniques you will learn in this book, as often as possible. It doesn't matter where you are or how long you have got – every extra bit of practice will be valuable to you and for several reasons:

- The more often you hear yourself speaking out loud – and loudly – the more natural it will seem.
- The more frequently you practise your speech the more familiar – and more comfortable – with it you will become.
- Practising saying your speech regularly will better enable you to see if and where there are any gaps.

Remember, whatever your starting position, the more practice you put in the better your speech will be. So, practise early and practise often.

Summary

The basics of public speaking can be quickly learned, and as you practise putting them into action you will begin to develop your own style of delivery. Before long you will be thoroughly familiar with hearing your own voice loud and clear in a room, and confident of speaking with authority to a small audience. Using your cue cards to prompt you, you will be able to deliver your material without rushing, and with a flair which hooks the audience and keeps them engaged.

Remember that many of the techniques in this chapter can be practised wherever you are, and with however much time you have to spare. Imagine that you are on a business trip and find yourself in a hotel room with ten spare minutes – grab the opportunity and start speaking aloud.

Remember that it's not important what you say – you can just read the room service menu – but that you are using the opportunity to practise, practise, practise. Before long you will find that the techniques become second nature, and your speech-giving will flourish as a result.

In the next chapter, we will build on what we have begun in this chapter!

Fact-check [answers at the back]

1. When you first start rehearsing in front of other people you are likely to feel...
   a) Elated and uplifted ❏
   b) Confident and self-assured ❏
   c) Nervous and self-conscious ❏
   d) Short and fat ❏

2. It's important not to read your speech, but to use cue cards to prompt you, because...
   a) They allow you to maintain good eye contact with your audience ❏
   b) Speaking while reading causes headaches ❏
   c) Cue cards are lighter to hold ❏
   d) You may not be able to read your writing ❏

3. All headings and subheadings should be underlined because...
   a) They act as quick reminders of the key themes in each section of your speech ❏
   b) It makes them seem more important ❏
   c) Your audience may ask to examine your notes afterwards ❏
   d) You need to remember to shout them ❏

4. Establishing and maintaining eye contact with your audience is important because...
   a) If you can see them, they can see you ❏
   b) It allows you to engage with them and make each person feel included ❏
   c) You can gauge their reaction and speed up or slow down ❏
   d) They won't leave if they know they are being watched ❏

5. It's important to look relaxed and confident because...
   a) It will divert attention from your speech ❏
   b) If you rush through your speech, no one will notice ❏
   c) It will inspire confidence about you in your audience ❏
   d) It makes you look sexy ❏

6. Fidgeting is to be avoided because...
   a) It's distracting, and a clear sign of a nervous speaker ❏
   b) It saps your energy ❏
   c) You may lose your place in your speech ❏
   d) It can make your audience dizzy ❏

7. Clarity of speech is important because...
   a) It shows you have had a good education ❏
   b) Your audience can concentrate on *what* you're saying, not just on trying to hear you ❏
   c) It allows you to whisper ❏
   d) You won't need to use a microphone ❏

8. Avoid telling your audience that you are unused to public speaking because...
a) They are likely to leave, to go and hear someone who isn't ❏
b) It will be obvious anyway from your delivery ❏
c) It will make your audience nervous *for* you and *about* you ❏
d) They will still boo if you are rubbish ❏

9. It's important to keep to the 'script' because...
a) It avoids any copyright issues ❏
b) It was written by a professional scriptwriter ❏
c) Your audience has a copy and will be following it ❏
d) It will keep your speech tight and focused ❏

10. Hurrying your speech is detrimental because...
a) You are being paid by the minute ❏
b) It can make you appear nervous, and your message may be lost ❏
c) Speaking slowly allows you to speak more quietly and save your voice ❏
d) You are not supposed to finish before lunch is ready ❏

CHAPTER 16

Advanced public speaking techniques

Having learned the basic techniques of public speaking, you can now move on to the more advanced practices. These are the techniques which will elevate your speech from solid and professional, to dynamic and engaging. Having your speech heard and understood is one thing, but delivering it in a way which will captivate and inspire your audience is another – and it's this which will mark you out as a great public speaker.

By learning to use expression and inflection to convey meaning and tone effectively, and through mastering the arts of pausing and phrasing to give your speech real clarity and precision, you can deliver a speech which will be easy to listen to and difficult to forget. Add to this the techniques of varying your pace, pitch and volume, learning how to use audio-visual and multi-media materials and props, etc. to best advantage, and how to spotlight and eradicate any bad habits you might fall into, and you will be fully equipped to develop your own style of presenting with flair.

And when you feel confident that you can deliver any speech, in any venue, to any audience, you should begin to really enjoy public speaking, too.

Dynamic expression and presentation

> *'Acting should be bigger than life. Scripts should be bigger than life. It should all be bigger than life.'*
>
> Bette Davis, US actress

Even the best speech can be marred by an uninspiring speech-giver; indeed, it can actually be difficult to listen for any length of time to someone whose presentation is flat and monotone. Furthermore, if the speaker appears to lack interest in their own material, why should their audience be any different? By injecting some energy and passion into your speech, and by mastering the techniques for dynamic expression and presentation, you can ensure that your speech receives the attention it deserves from your audience.

The techniques outlined in this chapter will enable you to deliver your speech in a manner which is:

- engaging
- sincere
- passionate
- inspirational
- memorable.

Remember that no one technique alone will suffice – it is the combination of methods and approaches which will elevate your speech-giving.

Make sure that you practise your speech early – and often – to discover the combination of techniques which:

- best suits your style
- allows you to achieve the desired tone
- best communicates your message
- makes you feel most comfortable and confident
- will most appeal to, and suit, your audience.

TIP *Experiment with different combinations of techniques until you find your preferred style. Remember that you can also use these techniques to tailor your delivery for every speech you make, and for every audience.*

Effective use of pauses and phrasing

> *'It's not so much knowing when to speak as when to pause.'*
>
> Jack Benny, US comedian

A much overlooked aspect of public speaking is knowing when *not* to speak. Just as someone talking too quickly is difficult, and tiring, to listen to, and their message is often lost as a result, so someone talking without pausing runs the very real risk of having their audience tune them out and switch off.

Effective use of pauses, on the other hand, helps to break up the pattern of your speech so that it's pleasingly phrased, doesn't run into one never-ending sentence, and is easily absorbed. Pauses will also:

- allow your audience to take in what you have said
- give your audience time to digest your message
- build anticipation and expectation of what you will say
- break up any long sections into manageable chunks
- prevent you from gabbling, and your speech from running away from you
- allow you to prepare for the next part of your speech.

TIP *If you wish to inject some humour into your speech, try using a 'pregnant pause' – pausing at the end of a phrase to build suspense before a punch line.*

261

Varying your pace, pitch and volume

Pace

Varying the pace of your delivery helps to maintain your audience's interest. It can also help to underline what you're saying.

Speaking **slowly** is ideal when:

- you are saying something serious
- you need to be solemn
- you want to add extra gravity to your message
- what you are saying is complex.

Speaking **quickly** is ideal when:

- you want to keep your message light
- what you are saying will be familiar to your audience
- you are using humour
- you are saying something upbeat.

TIP

Whatever pace you are aiming for, the temptation is to rush – particularly if you are nervous. So remember to go more slowly than you think you should. A good rule of thumb is to halve the speed you think feels right, and halve it again if you are nervous.

Remember that it's important to keep to the appropriate pace for what you are saying, but that any pace will become boring if it's maintained for too long. Varying your pace is key.

Pitch

Another way to help to convey your message effectively is to vary the pitch of your voice according to the content of your speech and the effect you are hoping to have.

Use a **low** pitch to help convey:

- seriousness
- solemnity
- genuineness.

Use a **high** pitch to help convey:

- lightness
- humour
- excitement.

As with pace, varying the pitch of your voice will help to keep your audience interested and engaged, and will also help you to best convey your message. Combining different speeds of delivery with different vocal pitches can really help to generate different feels to your speech, so practise to find out which are most useful to you, and most appropriate for your speech.

 The exact pitch of your voice will depend on whether your voice is naturally deep (low pitch) or naturally light (high pitch). Being aware of this will help to prevent you from delivering your speech with an unwanted vocal message.

Volume

Often people are under the misconception that volume is something they won't need to concern themselves with, particularly if they will be presenting to a small group in an enclosed space, or if they will be using a microphone. In fact, effective use of volume is just as important as effective use of pace and pitch, and once again the key is to use it to add variety – speaking at just one level for your entire speech can quickly have a soporific effect!

Keeping your voice varied and interesting

The need to vary your volume is especially acute if your voice is naturally very low, or devoid of cadence. Injecting variety into the volume of your delivery can be a great way to prevent any monotone creeping into your speech patterns, and to ensure that your voice is interesting to listen to over a sustained period.

Dropping your voice can have the effect of making your audience listen harder to what you're saying and can help to give emphasis as a result; equally, raising your voice can have the effect of driving home your message. These techniques can be employed (and can be just as effective) whether or not your voice will be amplified, but be careful not to overuse them.

Effective use of vocal tone and inflection

Vocal tone

The tone of your voice is the underlying message implicit in what you are saying – regardless of the content. It's therefore vitally important to be aware of the tone since it can convey an unwanted or unintended sentiment. By learning to use it to your advantage, however, you can colour your voice with meaning, emotion and feelings, such as:

● sincerity
● gravitas
● pride
● fear
● excitement
● warmth
● humour.

This will enable you to convey the appropriate sentiment quickly and openly, and it will actively support your message.

 Identify the primary sentiment for each section of your speech and determine how you will achieve it – then highlight it in your notes.

Inflection

The inflection in your voice means the rising and falling patterns you create in your speech. This is important to:

● help paint a picture of what you're saying
● introduce vocal variety
● keep your audience interested
● underline the most important parts.

By modulating your voice you can help to ensure your manner of speaking is interesting to listen to, and that the content of your speech is delivered with maximum impact.

Appropriate use of audio-visual and multi-media materials and props

The key word here is 'appropriate'. Many a speech is marred by inappropriate use of these tools, most commonly through overuse. This is usually because the speaker:

- wants to use them as a distraction to take the focus off themselves
- is unconfident in their material or their ability to deliver it
- feels that using these tools makes their speech seem more 'professional'
- feels that using these tools validates their material
- feels that it's required of them, a necessary part of every good speech
- thinks it will give them a nice break!

Think about it from the audience's point of view, though – if they are presented with a series of slides, a PowerPoint presentation or a video clip and cannot immediately see its relevance and why you are using it, it will set off alarm bells for them over the quality of your speech.

Put simply, these tools are often used as an excuse for not having great material or for the inability to deliver it well, and this is easily spotted by an astute audience. They should therefore be avoided unless you have a very good reason to use them, and if you do you must know exactly why it's better to communicate your material in this way rather than delivering it though your speech.

So what constitutes appropriate and inappropriate use?

Appropriate use

- showing video clips of people giving their opinions on a subject, first-hand
- showing photographs which would be difficult to describe
- succinctly communicating a lot of data – but only if the data really needs to be shown
- displaying objects which are best seen 'in the flesh'
- giving your audience a breather.

Inappropriate use

- demonstrating anything which could be better presented through your speech
- use of data-rich presentations which are:
  - unnecessary
  - difficult for your audience to take in
  - better presented as handouts for later consumption
- any form of overuse
- time-fillers
- giving yourself a breather.

TIP A good rule of thumb is to ensure that anything which you elect to communicate in this way cannot be better communicated in a different way, and particularly through your speech, and that you're using these tools for the benefit of the audience and not yourself.

Overcoming mistakes

> *'Do not fear mistakes. You will know*
> *failure. Continue to reach out.'*
>
> Benjamin Franklin, US Founding Father

If standing in front of a large group of people and speaking is something you don't do on a regular basis, it's highly probable that you will make a mistake (or several!). That doesn't matter – what matters is how you deal with them. Remember that everyone makes 'mistakes', even when speaking casually to friends in a relaxed environment.

How often have you found yourself with a frog in your throat, or mispronouncing something, or that a word or phrase came out differently from the way you had intended? It happens to everyone and it's no big deal – but when you're standing in front of a group of people, and the whole point of what you are doing is speaking, it can suddenly take on huge significance.

Try thinking of it from the audience's point of view though – or from your point of view if you were a member of the audience. If you heard a speaker make a mistake, would you mind? Would you think less of them for stumbling over a word or momentarily losing their place in their speech? Of course, you wouldn't. What you would care about is how they dealt with it. If they seem to go to pieces, or are terribly embarrassed or apologetic, or as a consequence rush through the rest of their speech, you may quickly begin to lose confidence in them as a speaker – even though you might empathize with them and be glad that it's them and not you in that situation!

If, on the other hand, they quickly and calmly get themselves back on track you will admire them for it, and here's the really interesting thing – you will admire them more because of it. So making a mistake is not always a bad thing, provided you deal with it well.

The key to dealing with mistakes is to have thought through as many of them as possible in advance, and know how you will deal with them if and when they occur. Study the table below.

Common mistakes	How to overcome them
Stumbling over words	Just repeat them, more slowly. Remember to take your time – the audience will be happy to wait and you need to ensure that you don't stumble over your words repeatedly.
Losing your place in the 'script'	Take your time to find it again. Your notes should be clearly labelled and numbered, so finding your place shouldn't be difficult or take long – but the more you try to rush, the harder it will be. Remember: 'More haste, less speed.'
Never lifting your head	Make regular eye contact. If you realize after a while that you haven't been making regular eye contact with your audience, just begin to do so from that point. It can feel strange to suddenly begin to do this partway through your speech, but it's much better than not doing it at all.
Speaking too quietly	Deliver every word to the back of the room. This is easier if you are using a microphone but even then the levels may not have been set up for you, so you may find you still need to be aware of delivering your words loudly, clearly and with confidence.
Panicking	Take a deep breath and carry on. It's not uncommon for a speaker to panic, and usually the horrible feeling of panic rising through your body, constricting your throat and flooding you with fear, quickly passes. Taking a deep, slow breath can help, as can taking a sip of water. Then just carry on, remembering not to rush.
Fidgeting	Stand still and tall, and keep your hands occupied. Remember that fidgeting is a sure giveaway that you are nervous, and it's distracting to your audience and makes them concerned about your ability to deliver. Concentrate on standing still and keeping your hands on your notes or on the lectern.

By knowing how you will act if the situation arises, you can prepare yourself for how you will react; and by preparing yourself thoroughly for what you will do in each situation, you will give yourself every chance of dealing with it in a professional manner. Even if something completely unexpected happens, by preparing yourself to deal with the unexpected you will have put yourself in a position to deal with it calmly and confidently.

Eliminating bad habits

Every speaker, whether seasoned or new to speech-giving, will need to be mindful of the likelihood that they will develop bad habits with regards to their public-speaking technique. The best way to keep on top of this, and to remedy it as and when it occurs, is to ask a colleague to watch you every so often and to give you honest feedback. Some points for them to consider include:

● Have you started to rush your words?
● Have you developed any distracting fidgeting?
● Are you shuffling your feet?
● Are you audible?
● Are you gabbling?
● Are you making eye contact with your audience?
● Do you look nervous?
● Are your speech and your message coming across clearly?

It is possible to keep an eye on these things yourself, but it really is much better having someone do it for you since they will be devoting all their efforts to it, and not trying to give a good speech at the same time! Many a speaker has come unstuck during the course of giving their speech because they were trying to evaluate themselves as they gave it. Also, an 'outside eye' is better placed to notice bad habits.

Impress!

As a starting point, ask the person assessing you whether you 'IMPRESS' them as you speak:

Inflection – is your speech being delivered with interesting vocal variety?

Movement – are you guilty of shuffling your feet or fidgeting?

Pause – is your speech broken up with appropriate pauses, or are you rushing through it?

Reach the back of the room – is your speech audible, both in terms of volume and clarity?

Eye contact – are you lifting your head from your notes and taking in your audience?

Stand tall – do you look interested and alert? Does your body language convey the right impression?

Speak slowly – are you taking your time and getting your message across or are you gabbling?

By combining and employing these advanced techniques, you will soon develop a style which really works for you. As you gain in confidence, try pushing the techniques further and further – then rein them back in to their most productive point for you. With regular practice you will soon be able to master the art of successful, dynamic public speaking.

Summary

Once you have mastered the basics of public speaking, it's time to practise the more advanced techniques, the successful employment of which will elevate your speech from simply 'good' to 'outstanding'. By learning the principles of using your voice and face to put your speech across to your audience in a way which is engaging and memorable, you will be able to create and deliver speeches which people will look forward to hearing, and talk positively about long after.

And by learning how to identify and get rid of your bad habits, and how to pre-empt and overcome any mistakes which might occur, you will put yourself in the enviable position of being able to do full justice to every speech you give.

In the next chapter, we will consider how you can maximize the impact of your speech...

Fact-check [answers at the back]

1. It's best to use a combination of presentation techniques because...
   a) You spread your chances of using a good one ❑
   b) Each one is rubbish on its own ❑
   c) The audience might not understand some of them ❑
   d) This will allow you to achieve the desired tone and style ❑

2. Effective use of pauses will...
   a) Build anticipation and expectation of what you will say ❑
   b) Spin out your speech so you don't need to write much ❑
   c) Create convenient snack breaks for you ❑
   d) Fool the audience into thinking you have forgotten what comes next ❑

3. Varying the pace of your delivery helps to...
   a) Confuse the audience ❑
   b) Unsettle the audience ❑
   c) Maintain your audience's interest ❑
   d) Stop the audience from going to sleep ❑

4. Using the appropriate vocal pitch and volume will...
   a) Pre-empt what is coming ❑
   b) Keep the audience engaged and help to underline your message ❑
   c) Confuse the audience ❑
   d) Quickly become boring to listen to ❑

5. The tone of your voice is...
   a) Crucial to the speed at which you convey information ❑
   b) Best when it's patronizing or condescending ❑
   c) The underlying message implicit in what you are saying – regardless of the content ❑
   d) Impossible to regulate in cold conditions ❑

6. A mastery of vocal inflection will help you to...
   a) Become more supple over time ❑
   b) Swallow large food items without risk of choking ❑
   c) Bend reverentially on one knee ❑
   d) Paint a picture of what you are saying ❑

7. A common reason for the overuse of audio-visual and multi-media materials and props is...
   a) You have got lots so you might as well use them ❑
   b) Wanting to use them as a distraction to take the focus off yourself ❑
   c) You might disappoint technology fans if you don't ❑
   d) Everyone loves a puppet show ❑

8. You are likely to make some mistakes when speaking in public because...
   a) You are rubbish ❑
   b) You refuse to practise and love to 'wing it' on the day ❑
   c) Everyone does – no matter how good they are ❑
   d) People will be heckling ❑

9. If you do make a mistake...
a) There is nothing you can do ❏
b) You should give an immediate, heartfelt apology ❏
c) It's best to stop there and then ❏
d) It doesn't matter – just carry on ❏

10. You are likely to develop some bad habits over time because...
a) You are careless ❏
b) It's a natural effect of repeating any action ❏
c) You are naturally slipshod in your work ❏
d) It's peculiar to public speaking but happens to everyone ❏

CHAPTER 17

Delivering your speech with maximum impact

Now that you have learned how to write a great speech, and learned the techniques of public speaking, it's time to learn how to deliver your speech with maximum impact, in order to create the maximum effect.

You have the necessary tools at your disposal but putting them into practice requires a new set of skills. Imagine someone being trained to be a soldier – getting fit and learning how to use a weapon are necessary skills, but putting them into practice on a battlefield is something else altogether. The tools and techniques outlined in the previous chapters will have provided you with a valuable new skill set – now it's time to learn how to employ those skills to transform your speech-giving from competent to truly memorable.

In this chapter you will learn how to command the space from start to finish, to engage with your audience, to look confident (despite how you might be feeling!), and to deliver your speech with dynamism and élan. But we will also look at some of the practical issues such as getting to know the venue (whether or not you are able to visit it in person) and preparing for unexpected eventualities.

Checking out the venue

If possible, it's a great idea to scope out the venue in advance. Getting the 'lie of the land' will help you in a number of ways:

● Seeing the venue, and where you will stand to give your speech, will help to settle your nerves.
● You will be able to determine the size of the space, and whether or not you will need (and be able to have) amplification.
● You will be able to determine how far you may have to walk to get to the podium from your seat – and how long that will take.
● You will be able to see whether there are any 'hidden' surprises.

It's particularly valuable to check out the venue if you are nervous about giving your speech. There will be enough pressure on you on the day without adding any surprises or unwelcome complications, and most venues are happy to let people visit to orient themselves within the space where they will be giving their speech.

It's amazing what a difference it makes to how you will feel on the day if you can enter a space you already know. If you know where everything is, where you will be speaking from, how far away the audience will be, the acoustics, and so on, you will feel exponentially more relaxed about giving your speech. You will also have the advantage of it feeling like 'home' to you, while it's unfamiliar to everyone else. See whether you can practise your speech while you are there – a dry run *in situ* is a wonderful confidence boost.

Other ways of learning about the venue

If you're unable to visit the venue in person before the day, you may be able to see photos or even a video clip of it online. Some venues provide this on their website, while you may be able to find footage of people giving a speech in the venue on popular sharing sites such as YouTube.

Failing this, you may know someone who has been there, or else call the venue with a set of questions which will

> help to give you the 'lie of the land' in advance. In the
> worst-case scenario, where none of this is possible, en-
> sure that you arrive at the venue extra early to give your-
> self time to orient yourself and to begin to feel familiar
> with the space.

Making sure that you're heard

When it comes to listening to speeches, there is little more aggravating than not being able to hear the speaker – and from the speaker's point of view, there is nothing more aggravating than working hard to give a great speech only for it not be heard. Most venues will have checked the sound levels and provided amplification if necessary but this is not always the case, so make sure that you arrive early and take the time to ensure that your speech gets heard.

If you're going to use a **microphone** you will need to learn how to use it properly, and even if you feel you don't need one because you have a loud voice, unless the venue is really intimate it's usually best to use a microphone. This will:

- take the pressure off you having to project
- make you sound more relaxed, confident and in control
- allow more vocal expression and subtlety
- allow you to continue over any interruptions!

TIP *If you have a particularly soft or quiet voice, you may find that you need to use a microphone when other people don't. This may not be provided automatically by the venue. Contact them in advance and request a microphone be made available. That way, if you find you don't need it, it doesn't matter – but, if you do, it will be there waiting for you.*

Fortunately, there is no great mystery to using a microphone effectively, and even if you have never used one before and do not have time to practise with it before giving your speech it shouldn't present too many problems, provided that you remember the basic principles given in the table below:

How to hold it	Hold it in a comfortable, open fist, ensuring that you don't obscure the mesh. Try to keep it vertical so that you are speaking across the top of it.
Where to hold it	The top of the microphone should be just in front of your chin.
How to speak into it	Speak normally, keeping your voice at a constant volume, and be careful not to breathe loudly as this can be picked up by the microphone.

The seven giveaways of a nervous speaker

Controlling your nerves is important, and we will look at this as a separate topic in Chapter 19, but it's also important that you don't *look* nervous. Appearances count for a lot when you are speaking in public – if you can get the audience to relax and believe in you as a good speaker, then you are already halfway there. Creating a good impression is vital – you will want to look calm, confident and in control.

Several things, however, can undermine this. These are some of the most common giveaways you will want to avoid:

● fidgeting
● rapid swallowing
● frequent coughing
● nervous laughter
● not lifting your head up
● avoiding eye contact
● speaking too quickly.

 If you appear nervous, your audience will be nervous – which in turn will make you even more nervous! If you appear calm and confident, your audience will relax – and so will you.

Keeping the audience on your side

By applying the techniques we have looked at, you can get the audience on your side and feeling relaxed from the outset, so their expectation will be of an interesting, engaging and enjoyable speech.

In many ways, that's the hard part done – what you have to do now is to keep it going. To do so there are some key points to remember:

- Keep smiling – even if you feel it's going badly!
- Make eye contact with as many people as possible.
- Remember not to fidget, or shuffle your feet.
- Don't be tempted to rush – take your time and let your audience soak up and appreciate your speech.
- Keep to the script – this will ensure that your material is first-rate.
- Try to ensure that you sound like you are confident and enjoying yourself.

There is no reason to suppose that your audience will be hoping you fail – so give them 'permission' to relax by appearing confident and in control at all times.

Engaging with the audience from start to finish

A bored speaker is a boring speaker. It's hard work and off-putting listening to someone who seems uninterested in their material, or who gives the impression that they don't really want to be giving their speech at all. On the other hand, listening to someone who seems genuinely interested in their material, and who gives the impression that they genuinely want to communicate it, can be energizing and inspiring; there is also a much greater chance that you will remember what you have heard.

So, engaging with your audience right from the word go, and continuing to do so throughout your speech, is crucial to ensuring that your message is heard and that your audience is stimulated. We have looked at ways of achieving this but it's worth looking at some of the pitfalls and pratfalls which can get in the way and undermine your hard work.

Reason for lack of engagement	Solution
Lack of ownership	If you haven't written the speech yourself, or have written only a part of it, you may not feel that you have much invested interest. If you feel disconnected from your speech, then so will your audience, so you will need to find a way to include only material for which you can feel real ownership.
Heard it so many times before	If you are to give a speech you are used to giving, there is a real danger of it coming across as flat and uninspiring. Worse still, you may give the impression that even you are bored with it! You will need to be mindful of the fact that your audience will be hearing it for the first time – so you need to deliver it as though you are doing so for the first time, too!
Don't believe in what you are saying	In a worst-case scenario, you may be giving a speech which includes material you disagree with. Sometimes this is unavoidable, such as when you are giving a speech on behalf of a company and need to reflect the views of a number of stakeholders. You will need to remember that for those people the material is accurate and important, and that is how it must be delivered. Never be tempted to use the speech-giving as an opportunity to make known your opinion of their views. You will need to ensure that you have ownership of this material, so try to ensure that you fully understand their point of view.
Hate giving speeches	Giving speeches may be a highlight of your working year. For many people, however, it's a worry or a chore rather than a delight. If this is the case for you, you will need to be mindful of the reason why you are giving it, of its importance to you and to your company, and of the audience members who are giving up their time to hear it. Then dig deep, remember the techniques for dealing with nerves and appearing confident, and try to enjoy your speech-giving as much as possible.
Need to be doing something else	The time pressure of modern working life often means that we feel that we really don't have the time to attend conferences, or give speeches. If this is the case for you, you will need to be clear about your priorities and commit to giving speeches only when you have the time and desire to do so fully. If you have no choice but to give a speech, even when you don't have the time, you will need to understand why this is being prioritized by your bosses, and then concentrate fully on giving the speech well and resolving any conflicts later on.

Varying your delivery

Imagine driving across a vast desert, with nothing to break the journey, no stops, and no interesting scenery along the way. You would soon be bored, and shortly after that you would mentally switch off, driving on autopilot and subconsciously waiting for the journey to end. This is what it's like listening to a dull speaker, someone who talks in a flat monotone, who doesn't break up their speech, and who doesn't use any of the tools and techniques for injecting variety into their delivery.

By using your voice to paint a picture of what you're saying for your audience, and by using your facial expression and body language to communicate your interest in, and passion for, your subject, you will be able to hook the audience and keep them interested. And by adding vocal variety to your delivery you will be able to take them on a journey which is enjoyable and stimulating.

Using the actor's method of projection and voice control

One of the fundamentals of acting, which every student of the theatre is required to learn before they can progress, is voice control. If an actor can't be heard, and heard clearly, then it really doesn't matter how good their acting is, it will just be wasted. The same is true of speech-givers, and so the same consideration must be given to mastering voice control.

It's likely that you will be using a microphone if the venue in which you are giving your speech is large, so it's not so important to conquer the more advanced techniques of what is known as 'bellows breathing', diaphragm control and supporting your voice for clear projection – but control of your voice is crucial. This is because it will allow you the flexibility to deliver your speech in exactly the way you want to, the way which you know will best put it across. You won't be restricted by limitations on what you can do with your voice, which might otherwise hamper your delivery.

The best way to achieve complete control of your voice, and at the same time increase its vocal range to enhance the scope of techniques in your armoury, is to practise vocal exercises. There are a great many of these, and details of a wide range can be found on the Internet, but to get you started here are a few of the most fundamental:

Exercise	What to do	How it helps
Yawning	Yawn, stretching your mouth as wide as possible, and vocalize as you exhale.	This is one of the best exercises for expanding and relaxing your throat, vital for the creation of a clear, pure, unconstricted sound.
Tongue stretches	Open your mouth wide, and stick out your tongue as far as it will go. Then try to touch your nose, your chin and each ear with it, in turn. Then use your tongue to describe a large circle.	These will help you to improve the mobility and the strength of your tongue – the primary organ of articulation.
Deep breathing	Stand with your feet shoulder-width apart and relax. Breathe in through your nose and inhale a really big lungful, concentrating on feeling your chest expand. Hold it for a few seconds and exhale slowly through your mouth.	This will help you to relax, and will encourage your lungs to take in more air, allowing you to better support your voice.
Vocalizing your breathing	As above but begin the exhalation as a gentle hum, and try to feel it tickling your lips. Gradually increase the volume of the hum and then open your mouth and allow the sound out as an extended 'aaahh'. Hold the note for as long as you can.	This is a great way to practise generating a clear, true sound, and to train your vocal muscles and responses to work properly to allow the sound to travel undisturbed from your body to your audience's ears. It also helps in the development of the intercostal muscles, important for breath control.
Shoulder rolls	Stand with your feet shoulder-width apart and relax. Lift your shoulders up towards your ears, then back to neutral, then push them down as far as they will go. Back to neutral before pushing	Tightness in the shoulders is a sure-fire way to create tension in your body, and this will lead to a tightness in your voice. This exercise, practised regularly, will help to increase

	them forwards and backwards, and finally describing large circles with them.	the range of motion in your shoulders, and your ability to keep them relaxed.
Jaw extensions	Stand with your feet shoulder width apart and relax. Allow your jaw to relax so that it drops slightly, then swing it gently from side to side.	Any tension in your jaw will adversely affect your ability to deliver your speech since it tightens your mouth, making proper articulation difficult to achieve.

Try timing yourself on the 'Vocalizing your breathing' exercise. Start from the moment you exhale (as humming) and continue through the open mouth exhalation until you run out of breath. Over time you should be able to reach 30 seconds or more. Try to make sure that you keep your mouth really wide open and your throat relaxed, so that the sound produced is clear and unimpeded.

Commanding the space

This is predominantly a matter of confidence – not of *feeling* confident, but of *looking* confident. As long as your audience thinks you are confident they will relax and be more receptive to your speech. Commanding the space, then, is an important factor in establishing the framework for a successful speech. The following techniques will help you to accomplish it:

● Walk confidently and with purpose to the podium.
● Lift your head and take in the audience.
● Smile, and look relaxed.
● Breathe deeply, and slowly, and support your voice for a strong, clear delivery.
● Stand still and avoid fidgeting.
● Speak slowly and clearly.
● Make eye contact with your audience throughout your speech.

Remember the three Cs: by following these simple steps you can appear calm, confident and in control, allowing you to command the space.

Essential preparation

By getting yourself prepared well in advance, both practically and psychologically, you will feel more confident about your speech-giving. In addition to visiting the venue and practising your speech *in situ*, you will need to prepare your cue cards, together with any additional physical material such as slides or props – as well as thinking through as many potentially speech-ruining eventualities as possible and ways to deal with them. This will help you to relax and to deliver your speech to the very best of your ability.

If you will be using **props**, it's best to prepare these as soon as possible. Doing so will give you time to:

● practise with them
● make sure you know how they work
● work them seamlessly into your delivery
● make sure you can get all the items you need.

If you are using **technical** items (sound, lighting, slides, etc.), be sure to check:

● that there will be a power outlet to hand
● whether they require time to warm-up
● that you have a backup plan if they fail to work!

 Using additional and unexpected elements to complement your speech can provide an extra dimension and add variety.

Remember that using these extra elements can help to break up your speech and add interest but they should never be the mainstay – a ratio of 80–90 per cent speech to 10–20 per cent additional elements is a good rule of thumb.

Stepping stones

For your speech to be really well received, and long remembered, it's crucial that your delivery is first-rate. As a useful checklist for delivering your speech with dynamism, use the 'STEPPING STONES' acronym:

Smile – nothing says you are confident of giving a great speech as quickly as the appearance that you are calm, in control and looking forward to giving it – and a relaxed smile does just that.

Tone – establishing the desired tone early on is a great way of managing the audience's expectations, and conveying the subtext of your speech.

Energy – no one likes to be faced with a lifeless speaker. Do a good warm-up before you start, and attack your speech with verve, enthusiasm and lots of energy.

Pace – remember not to rush. Your audience will need time to take in, and soak up, what you are saying.

Pause – this will help to emphasize the most important parts of your speech, and give your audience the opportunity to properly digest it.

Inflection – injecting vocal variety into your speech is crucial to ensure that it's pleasant to listen to, and easy to remember.

Nerves – getting your nerves under control, and even using them to your advantage, can really help to give you the edge in making a great speech.

Give out the right attitude – the audience will respond well if you appear calm, confident and collected, and enthusiastic about your subject and the opportunity to talk about it.

Style – try to make sure that nothing you say or do, or the way in which it's said or done, is ever bland. Think through each part of your speech to see how you can add style and interest.

Try not to fidget – there are few things more off-putting to the audience than distracting fidgeting, so make sure that you have identified your weaknesses in this area and work to eliminate them.

Observe the audience – monitoring the audience is a great way of making sure that you are on track and that they are keeping up; adjust your delivery accordingly.

No distractions – stay focused on your delivery and ensure that you have eliminated any obvious potential distractions (e.g. turning off your mobile phone or pager, and reminding the audience to do likewise).

Energy and enthusiasm – give out lots of energy and your audience will feed off it and respond accordingly. Similarly, if you are enthusiastic about your subject, so will your audience be.

Say it with confidence – with everything in place you have every reason to feel confident that you will deliver a truly memorable speech.

Summary

No matter how good you become at writing a great speech, and no matter how accomplished you are at each of the public-speaking techniques we have looked at, if you can't deliver your speech with maximum impact then all the rest will have served little or no purpose. Delivering your speech with dynamism and flair is crucial to first-rate public speaking. By mastering the techniques of getting – and keeping – the audience on your side, and of commanding the space while delivering your speech with vocal variety and ensuring that you are heard, you will be well on your way to becoming on orator of some distinction.

By visiting the venue in advance, where possible, or at least researching it as thoroughly as you can, you will be prepared for what lies ahead and can begin to plan accordingly. Better still, try out your speech *in situ*.

In the next chapter, we will be looking at how best to practise your speech.

Fact-check [answers at the back]

1. Checking out the venue in advance is useful because...
   a) It will help to settle your nerves ❏
   b) You will know where it is ❏
   c) You will know where the toilets are ❏
   d) You can find the nearest exit for a quick escape ❏

2. Practising your speech in the venue is a good idea because...
   a) You can leave prompts around the room ❏
   b) It will help to settle your nerves ❏
   c) You will know if you can see over the lectern ❏
   d) People will be fed up of you practising it elsewhere ❏

3. You should always arrive early and check the sound levels because...
   a) The venue's last use may have been as a disco ❏
   b) You do not know how loud your voice is ❏
   c) You can take the appropriate steps to ensure that your speech can be heard ❏
   d) You will know if you should have brought a microphone ❏

4. Unless the venue is really small, it's a good idea to use a microphone because...
   a) It will save you having to project, allowing more vocal expression and subtlety ❏
   b) It makes you look more professional ❏
   c) It prevents you from fidgeting with your hands ❏
   d) It allows you to sing as well as to speak ❏

5. Appearances count for a lot when you are speaking in public because...
   a) They take attention away from what you are saying ❏
   b) Looking professional and confident helps the audience to relax and to believe in you ❏
   c) If you look good, no one will care how good your speech is ❏
   d) You might go on somewhere nice afterwards ❏

6. It's important to start confidently and to set an appropriate tone because...
   a) Even if it all goes horribly wrong, at least you started well ❏
   b) Otherwise the audience may not know what you are talking about ❏
   c) You can fool some of the people all of the time ❏
   d) It settles the audience and improves their perception of you ❏

7. It's important that you are interested in your material because...
a) It will help to prevent you from dozing off ❑
b) A bored speaker is a boring speaker ❑
c) Otherwise you may be tempted to talk about something else altogether ❑
d) No one else will be ❑

8. It can be useful to employ the actors' method of projection and voice control when...
a) There is no amplification available ❑
b) You start to become sleepy ❑
c) You start to become bored ❑
d) You decide you would rather be an actor ❑

9. It's important to talk slowly and clearly because...
a) Some of your audience may be hard of hearing ❑
b) People may want to take notes ❑
c) It allows you to confidently command the space ❑
d) Some of your audience may be foreign ❑

10. You can feel more confident about your speech-giving by...
a) Getting yourself prepared well in advance, practically and psychologically ❑
b) Having triplicates of all your notes ❑
c) Having it all recorded and mouthing to the soundtrack ❑
d) Getting someone else to do it for you ❑

CHAPTER 18

Practising your speech

How often have you heard it said that 'Practice makes perfect'? And yet it's amazing how many people think that simply writing their speech is sufficient preparation for giving it! If you're unused to public speaking, it's especially important to familiarize yourself with your speech, and the way in which you intend to deliver it, in order to give yourself the best possible chance of success.

Speech-giving is a skill which needs to learned, and then practised, just like any other skill – and you shouldn't expect it to come quickly or feel natural straight away. You wouldn't expect to be able to drive a car the first time you sat behind the wheel, no matter how much you had read about the process. You would know that practical experience is the only way to master the skill – and that it takes time, repetition and hard work. It's exactly the same with learning to give a great speech.

By practising your speech, you will grow in confidence while honing your technique to ensure that you deliver it to the very best of your ability. Don't feel that you need to wait until your speech is finished to start practising either – the sooner you start the better; and the more practice you put in, particularly in front of a few people, the more confident you will become.

Practice makes perfect

Delivering a speech well is a skill which needs to be learned and practised. How much practice you will need to put in will depend on a number of factors, including:

- previous experience
- natural aptitude
- level of confidence.

However, no matter what your starting position, the more practice you put in the better your speech will be. So, practise early and practise often.

Saying it out loud

Remember that one of the things which often throws people when they are unused to giving speeches is hearing the sound of their own voice out loud – if you're not used to public speaking, you will be amazed how odd this sounds at first! Most people are rarely conscious of hearing their own voice in everyday situations, but when it's the only sound in the room and everyone is listening to you, you will hear it in a whole new light – and it's something you need to get used to.

Fortunately, it's something which can be practised any time you're on your own, for example when driving your car or while doing the housework. It doesn't matter what you say: just get used to speaking out loud, and loudly. If you find it difficult to think of things to say, try listening to an all-talk radio station and simply repeating whatever is being said.

By giving yourself the opportunity to get used to hearing your own voice (and one which forces you to concentrate on it), you will quickly become comfortable with it, and even make it seem normal.

There will be enough things to contend with when you are standing in front of an audience to give your speech, without adding to them by being startled at the sound of your own voice. Worse still, if you are, it will almost certainly make you self-conscious, so get used to it early. Bear in mind that, if your speech is recorded, your voice on playback will sound very different from the way it sounds in your head – another reason people become overly self-aware. Remember, though, that this is the way it sounds to everyone else all the time – for them the shock would be if they heard your voice the way you hear it.

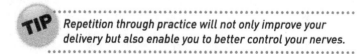

TIP *Repetition through practice will not only improve your delivery but also enable you to better control your nerves.*

Gaining in confidence

'How often in life we complete a task that was beyond the capability of the person we were when we started it.'

Robert Brault, US writer

As you practise, your confidence level increases to a directly proportionate degree. So the more you put in the more you get out. And the tougher you make your 'training', the bigger the rewards will be, and the easier it will be to give your speech on the day.

As you gain in confidence you will:

- start to feel more relaxed
- start to look more relaxed
- slow down your delivery
- make more eye contact with your audience
- make better use of pauses
- add more variety to your delivery
- control your fidgeting
- begin to actually enjoy giving your speech!

Using a mirror to highlight bad habits

'The world more often rewards the appearance of merit than merit itself.'

François de La Rochefoucauld, French writer of maxims

Looking as though you know what you are doing is half the battle. Appearances can be deceptive, and you can use this to your advantage if you don't feel confident. Remember that projecting a positive image will help your audience to relax – which will help you to relax.

One of the best ways to monitor your appearance is to use a mirror, preferably one which is full-length. This really is an invaluable tool in helping you to get used to standing tall, and still, and looking confident. It will also highlight any bad habits you may have, or which creep in over time, so try to get into the habit of practising in front of a mirror on a regular basis.

TIP *Smaller mirrors can be angled to focus on different areas in turn, for example face, hands and feet.*

Practise delivering part of your speech, paying particular attention to whether you:

- stand up tall
- shuffle your feet
- fidget
- shift your weight from one leg to the other
- play with your hands
- breathe more rapidly, or less deeply
- feel self-conscious.

By observing and monitoring your appearance you can help to eradicate any distracting habits you may have while building your confidence and losing your inhibitions.

Rehearsing in front of other people

The next step on from practising in front of a mirror (or perhaps filming yourself) is to practise in front of other people – rehearsing your speech in front of an audience is vital preparation for any speech-giver. You can start with just one person and build up to a few people, such as colleagues, family members or close friends. Initially, you are likely to feel:

- nervous
- awkward
- embarrassed
- self-conscious.

This is entirely natural but will subside with practice and experience, leaving you free to concentrate on presenting your material with passion and dynamism, and – I hope – to enjoy doing so. You will find it all but impossible to give of your best if you cannot relax, and all but impossible to relax if the first time you give your speech in front of an audience is when you give your speech on the day. Remember that, however bad going through this process makes you feel, it's far better to get past this hurdle now than to face it for the first time when you actually stand up to present your speech for real.

There is no substitute for practice and the more often you can practise in front of other people the better you will get. Practising in front of other people has the additional bonus that you are able to receive constructive criticism from them. Make sure that you ask them for this in advance so that they know you want to hear what they think, and ask them to be completely honest – no matter how much you may not like hearing what they have to say, it's better to hear it from them than from members of the audience on the day when it's too late to do anything about it.

Try using different people as your 'practice audience', when possible, so that:

● you don't become too familiar with them
● they don't become too familiar with your speech
● you receive the widest possible range of feedback.

Projecting a positive image, and the need to exude confidence

When you stand up to make your speech the audience becomes *your* audience. First impressions are critical, and the secret is that, no matter how you feel inside, the audience will perceive only what you project to them. Think of yourself as an actor, and the person who will be giving your speech as a character. Think of the characteristics you would want them to have as well as those characteristics you wouldn't want them to have:

✓ confident	✗ nervous
✓ in control	✗ dreading having to give the speech
✓ pleased to be there	✗ worried they are going to make a fool of themselves
✓ looking forward to giving the speech	✗ impatient to get it over with

'I'm no good at public speaking, but if I can assume a role and speak as that person, then I'm fine.'

Jason Wiles, US actor

By thinking of yourself as an actor playing a character you can help to distance yourself from the real you, the person who may be unconfident, unused to speech-giving, or nervous. You can then decide what impression you want your audience to have of you, and create exactly that. Appearances can be deceptive – so use that to your advantage.

Remember that many professional actors are extremely nervous before they perform, but because they appear confident and relaxed, people assume that they are.

Learning to exude confidence

Even if you do feel confident, you will need to *exude* that confidence so that your audience will:

- feel that they are in safe hands
- relax
- be free to concentrate on what you are saying.

This becomes a kind of virtuous circle, with the audience's positive response to your confidence further reinforcing that confidence:

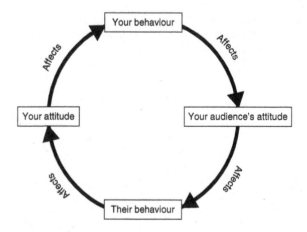

This is sometimes known as the 'Betari Box'.

Memorizing the key points

Memorizing the entire speech is pointless and unnecessary. Besides, if you give speeches frequently, it will be all but impossible to learn them all, and a tiring waste of time. Your speech will come across better if you know it extremely well but work from cue cards to jog your memory, allowing a degree of freshness and spontaneity into your delivery.

There are, however, two potential pitfalls with this approach:

1 You may lose your place on the cue card, or find the cards to be out of sequence.
2 You may read the headline reminder on the cue card and not be able to remember what it refers to.

If you can get into the habit of memorizing your speech's key points, however, even if you do lose your place, or realize that the cue cards have been reordered, you should be able to carry on regardless while buying yourself valuable time to regroup.

If you cannot remember what the card is prompting you to say, it can be trickier, but the situation can be avoided by memorizing not only the headline but some key sub-points, too.

Make sure that you memorize all your speech's headline prompts, as well as at least a couple of sub-points for each one.

Summary

We all know the old adage that 'practice makes perfect' and it's certainly true when it comes to public speaking. The more you can practise, and the more realistic you can make the opportunities, the more you will find yourself gaining in confidence and even beginning to enjoy delivering your speeches.

The act of practising what you will have to do on the day has a wonderfully calming effect, aiding you in being able to project a positive image and to exude confidence – which in turn will help the audience to relax, which will help you to relax.

In order to create this positive circle, you will need to ensure that you are as familiar with your speech as you possibly can be, and that you're confident with the way in which you stand, your deportment, and the way you look overall. By using a mirror to highlight any bad habits you can practise ways to counter them.

Remember, when it comes to public speaking there's no such thing as too much practice.

In the next chapter, we will look at two issues that can derail the speech-maker, nervousness and tension.

Fact-check [answers at the back]

1. How much you will need to practise depends on...
   a) How long your speech is ☐
   b) Previous experience, natural aptitude and confidence level ☐
   c) Your level of stamina ☐
   d) How well you can be seen from the back of the room ☐

2. A recording of your voice sounds different from the way it sounds in your head so you will need to...
   a) Cancel excess background noise ☐
   b) Get used to the sound of your recorded voice when you practise your speech ☐
   c) Add loud background music or sound effects to your recorded voice ☐
   d) Get someone else to record these bits for you ☐

3. Repetition through practice will not only improve your delivery but also...
   a) Make you less afraid of the sound of your own voice ☐
   b) Allow you to learn your speech by heart ☐
   c) Enable you to better control your nerves ☐
   d) Improve hand/tongue co-ordination ☐

4. The more you put in, the more you...
   a) Wish you hadn't ☐
   b) Need to carry ☐
   c) Become tired and irritable ☐
   d) Get out ☐

5. As you gain in confidence you will:
   a) Be able to finish your speech in half the time ☐
   b) Start to look, and feel, more relaxed ☐
   c) Completely lose your nerves ☐
   d) Become a full-time after-dinner speaker ☐

6. Using a mirror to practise will enable you to...
   a) See the different ways in which you fidget ☐
   b) Do your hair at the same time ☐
   c) Keep an eye on your figure ☐
   d) See whether anyone is standing behind you, laughing ☐

7. Practising in front of other people is likely to make you feel...
   a) Like giving up ☐
   b) Awkward and self-conscious ☐
   c) Ill ☐
   d) Like a professional ☐

8. No matter how you feel inside, the audience will perceive only...
   a) What you project to them ☐
   b) What they had imagined you to be like ☐
   c) Themselves ☐
   d) One other ☐

9. By exuding confidence your audience will...
a) Like you better as a person ❏
b) Think you are smug and patronizing ❏
c) Feel that they are in safe hands, and relax ❏
d) Need sunglasses ❏

10. Memorizing your entire speech is...
a) Great fun ❏
b) Achievable in 30 minutes ❏
c) Pointless and unnecessary ❏
d) Useful for reciting at parties ❏

CHAPTER 19

Dealing with nerves

It's OK to be nervous. In fact, it's a definite advantage for any speech-giver. The reason is a simple biological reaction to your anxiety – your brain triggers the 'fight or flight' mechanism and your body floods your system with adrenalin, giving you an all-important edge – provided you can learn to control it.

Remember that even professional actors get nervous before going on stage, but it's this nervousness which enables them to perform to the very best of their ability. So it is with your speech-giving – the nervous energy the situation creates for you allows you to deliver your speech with power, passion and clarity.

A dull, lifeless speaker is usually one who has given their speech so many times they know it backwards and no longer get nervous, or someone who is overcome with nerves. Any speaker who delivers a dynamic and impassioned speech is almost certain to be nervous, but able to use this to their advantage.

So feeling nervous about giving your speech is a good thing – the trick is to not allow the adrenalin to overpower you, nor the situation to overcome you, but to learn to harness the feeling of fear and use it to your advantage.

Understanding nerves
Why it's good to be nervous

Pretty much everyone gets nervous before a public appearance. Whether it's your first time standing in front of an audience ready to give a speech, or whether it's something you do on a regular basis, you can expect to get nervous. Indeed, as odd as it sounds, you should actually hope to get nervous! This is because the mechanism which creates nervousness is triggered by 'fight or flight' impulses, which provide the energy and 'buzz' which will enable you to give a great performance.

> *'I get nervous when I don't get nervous. If I'm nervous I know I'm going to have a good show.'*
>
> Beyoncé Knowles, US singer

So it's not only perfectly natural to get nervous before giving your speech; it's actually necessary in order to be able to deliver it to the best of your ability.

Some of the tell-tale symptoms you might experience include:

- racing heart
- wobbly legs
- 'butterflies' in your stomach
- 'knotted' feeling in your stomach
- sweating
- weak legs
- feeling of loose bowels
- shaking
- shortness of breath
- tight shoulders
- tight neck
- clenched jaw
- headache
- dry mouth
- feeling sick
- feeling faint or light-headed
- feeling of detachment from your limbs.

After reading this list two reactions are common:

- experiencing some (or all!) of the symptoms
- wishing you hadn't read the list!

It's important to remember that you're unlikely to experience all of these symptoms and, as to be forewarned is to be forearmed, it's better to know what to expect so that you will realize what is happening if you do experience them. Some people are more prone to nervousness than others and will experience it more easily, and some people experience the symptoms more acutely than others (which can include vomiting, diarrhoea and fainting). For most people, though, it's just an uncomfortable feeling of being jittery and on edge, coupled with some mild physical symptoms.

Everyone is different...

Everyone is different and will react differently to each situation, and past performance isn't necessarily a good indicator – some people who can jump out of an aeroplane for a parachute jump, or swim with sharks, without so much as batting an eyelid, go to pieces when they have to speak in public. However it affects you, and to whatever degree, it's important to remember that the reactions caused by the stress of the situation are there for a reason and can be used to your advantage if correctly managed.

What happens when I get nervous?

When the 'fight or flight' response is triggered, several things happen at once, and almost immediately. Some of these are in addition to those we have looked at, while others are their cause:

- Adrenalin and glucose flood into your bloodstream.
- Your heart rate and blood pressure increase.
- Your pupils dilate to allow in as much light as possible.
- The veins in your skin constrict to send more blood to major muscle groups (responsible for the 'chill' sometimes associated with fear).
- Your muscles tense.
- Extra oxygen is taken into your lungs.
- Less essential systems (such as the digestion and immune systems) shut down to allow more energy for emergency functions.

How can I use this response to my advantage?

The sudden introduction of large amounts of adrenalin and glucose into your bloodstream can help to provide you with a 'cutting edge' for your delivery:

- They will provide you with huge amounts of energy (short-term).
- They will provide you with an enhanced level of focus and concentration.
- Your awareness and perception are raised to a new level.
- Your body is being supercharged, ready to give a great performance.

If you find yourself starting to experience the symptoms of nervousness, try to remember that this is a good thing – then take a few deep breaths to keep the symptoms under control.

Channelling your adrenalin

In order to make your nervousness work for you, you will need to ensure that you can channel the vast amounts of energy with which your body is being flooded. Learning to control your nerves in this way can be the difference between delivering a fantastic speech with dynamism and élan, and becoming rooted to the spot with fear, unable to speak.

- The first thing is to get used to delivering your speech in front of other people. This will get you used to the feeling of being nervous (albeit to a lesser degree than you are likely to feel when in front of a large audience), and will allow you to see some of the ways in which you respond under pressure.
- Learn to recognize the feelings you experience when you are nervous:
  - What are they?
  - When do they come?

- How do they manifest themselves?
- How long do they last?
- Are they a help or a hindrance?
● Practise seeing your body's physical reaction to the anxiety you are feeling in positive ways where appropriate, and to devise coping strategies where it is not. The table below will help you:

Physical reaction	Positive or negative	How to use it to your advantage	How to cope with it
Heart racing	Positive	Your heart is pumping blood to your muscles ready to give a great, energized speech	
Butterflies in stomach	Positive	Your body is flooding your system with adrenalin ready to tackle the task ahead with energy and élan	
Dry mouth/ scratchy throat	Negative		Have a glass of water to hand
Feeling sick	Positive	Your body is shutting down non-essential processes so that all your energy can be devoted to giving a memorable speech	

Remember that the unpleasant physical symptoms which accompany the anxiety are there for a reason – it's your body giving you an edge, heightening your senses and your speed of thought, ready to deliver your speech to maximum effect.

Understanding tension

Why it's crucial to release tension

'If nerves are a public speaker's best friend, tension is his worst enemy.'

David Windham, public speaking expert

While nervousness is a positive aspect of public speaking which can help to energize you and to give you that all-important edge, allowing tension to creep into your body can be damaging. But is it possible, under such stressful circumstances, to relax?

> *'True relaxation, which would do me the world of good, does not exist for me.'*
> Gustav Klimt, Austrian painter

Relaxation can be hard to come by under such circumstances, and indeed it should be avoided anyway since it will merely counter all the positive aspects of your nervousness. What is possible, however, and certainly desirable, is the ability to rid your body of potentially harmful tension. Tension in your body and in your voice, while attempting to speak in public, will manifest itself in a number of different ways:

Tension in your **body** may:

- make you look nervous
- make you want to fidget
- impair your breathing
- make you feel unwell
- make you too rigid
- make your audience nervous.

Tension in your **voice** may:

- make you sound nervous
- make it difficult to control
- make it sound strained
- make you feel unwell
- make it too quiet or too harsh/shrill
- make your audience nervous.

So it's important to try to relax to rid your body – and your voice – of tension. Being relaxed puts you in control of the mechanics of speech-giving, enabling them to work for you and enabling you to give a fantastic, controlled speech.

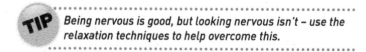

TIP *Being nervous is good, but looking nervous isn't – use the relaxation techniques to help overcome this.*

Simple relaxation techniques

The following exercises can be done individually to focus on one specific area, or as a group.

Symptom	Exercise	Result
Tightness in shoulders	Shrug tightly, then relax. Repeat. Move shoulders in large circles.	Promotes relaxation through whole body; aids the appearance of being relaxed; helps to relieve tension from chest, allowing lungs to fill properly.
Tight voice	Yawn – as widely as possible and vocalize with an 'ahhh' sound.	Throat is relaxed; voice does not sound strained; vocal flexibility is improved.
Heart palpitations; shortness of breath	Breathe deeply – hold for ten seconds – and relax. Repeat.	Slows down heart rate; helps to get breathing under control; allows you to sound relaxed and in command.
Tightness in neck	Tip your head forward so that your chin is on your chest – circle head slowly in a large arc. Repeat in opposite direction.	Relieves tension in neck; relaxes throat; improves vocal quality.
Butterflies in stomach; general nervousness	Clench and relax different muscle groups in turn – important ones include forearms, buttocks, quadriceps, stomach, shoulders.	Tempers nervousness; rids tension to promote general relaxation and feeling of well-being; keeps you in control.
Clenched jaw	Swing jaw from side to side, first with mouth open, then closed.	Relaxes jaw; allows the mouth to fully open so sound can freely exit.

The importance of a good warm-up

The importance of a thorough warm-up cannot be underestimated. Not only will it relieve tension but it will prepare you, physically and mentally, for the task ahead. It will also help to channel your adrenalin so that it doesn't overwhelm you, but instead allows you to use it to your advantage. It's imperative that you devote sufficient time to doing a good warm-up so that your body and your voice are ready for the task ahead, and so that you rid both of any damaging tension.

Warming up your **voice** will:

● make it clearer
● allow you to be heard by everyone
● make you sound relaxed
● prevent strain
● put you in control.

Warming up your **body** will:

● help you to relax
● release pent-up adrenalin
● help to prevent you shaking
● get rid of any 'wobbly' feeling
● put you in control.

Remember: professional actors always warm-up before a performance – so should you.

The table below gives some useful warm-up exercises. Over time you will learn which ones are most important for you, and you will be able to tailor them to your needs. Always work within your own limitations and never strain yourself – these should be used as a *gentle* warm-up, not as an exercise routine!

Area of focus	Warm-up exercise
Whole body – general	Stretch up with your whole body, lifting your hands as high as you can, pointing your fingers towards the ceiling – be sure to go up on to the tips of your toes. Feel your whole body stretch – then drop gently down, bending at the waist and keeping your knees slightly bent, so that your head is hanging down in front of your knees and your arms are hanging down in front of your legs. Very slowly unfurl your spine, one vertebra at a time, until you are standing upright, ensuring that your head is the last thing to come up. NB: *Be sure to do this slowly so that you avoid getting dizzy or experiencing 'head rush'.*
Lateral stretch	Stand with your feet shoulder-width apart and let your arms hang down by your sides. Slowly lean to one side allowing your arm to hang freely so that it slides down your leg, then very slowly come upright again. Pause to regain your balance, then repeat on the other side.
Shoulders	Stand with your feet shoulder-width apart and relax your shoulders. Now shrug tightly, lifting your shoulders up to your ears. Hold this for a few seconds, then relax. Repeat. Let your shoulders relax, then try to push them down another few inches, hold for a few seconds, then relax. Repeat. From a neutral position, push your shoulders forward as far as they will comfortably go, hold for a few seconds, then relax. Repeat. From a neutral position, push your shoulders back as far as they will comfortably go, hold for a few seconds, then relax. Repeat. Roll your shoulders in large circles, front to back, then back to front. Repeat.
Neck	Tip your head forward so that your chin is on your chest – circle your head slowly in a large arc until it's back resting comfortably facing forward. Repeat in the opposite direction. NB: *Be sure not to push your head further than is comfortable in any direction, and be particularly careful not to strain your neck muscles by pushing your head back too far.*

(Continued)

Area of focus	Warm-up exercise
Mouth and face	Screw your face up as tightly as possible, trying to make it as small as you can. Relax. Now try to make your face as big as possible, raising your eyebrows and opening your mouth as widely as you can. Relax, and repeat. NB: *This is one to do when you are on your own, as it is impossible not to look comical while doing it!*
Lips	Open your mouth as wide as you can, giving it a firm but comfortable stretch, then pinch your mouth, pushing your lips forward. Repeat. Keeping your teeth together, blow air through your mouth so that your lips ripple (as if you are doing an impression of a horse blowing out!).
Tongue	Stick your tongue out as far as it will go. Move it up, as if you are trying to touch your nose with it. Then move it down, as if you are trying to touch your chin with it. Next move it to the left, as if you are trying to touch your left cheek with it. Finally move it to the right, as if you are trying to touch your right cheek with it. Stick your tongue out as far as it will go and move it in large circles, first one way and then the other.
Jaw	Relax your jaw and swing it gently from side to side, first with your mouth open, then with your mouth closed.
Voice	Stand with your feet shoulder-width apart and relax. Inhale through your nose, slowly and deeply – hold for ten seconds – then exhale slowly, through your mouth. Relax and repeat. Yawn, as widely as possible, and vocalize as you exhale with a long, steady 'ahhh' sound. Take a deep breath and hum, gradually making the sound louder, then open your mouth and turn the sound into a long, steady 'ahhh' sound. Keep this going for as long as you feel comfortable, concentrating on keeping your mouth open and your jaw relaxed so that the sound you create is pure and uninterrupted.

Confidence tricks

There are a number of 'tricks of the trade' employed by professional public speakers to give them an air of confidence. Remember that if you appear confident your audience will feel that they are in safe hands and will relax – allowing you to do the same. These are some of the most popular techniques used by professional speakers:

- Know your speech thoroughly – and stick to it.
- Have a glass of water to hand.
- Don't drink alcohol to calm your nerves – it can make you more relaxed but it also dulls your senses. Use the relaxation techniques instead.
- Fight the temptation to rush your speech:
  - speak slowly
  - don't forget to pause.
- If wearing a tie, undo your top button (hidden behind the tie).
- Pick out one person at a time from your audience and deliver that part of the speech directly to them.
- If you feel nervous, picture the audience members naked!
- Keep your feet still.
- Keep your hands firmly planted to, or resting on, the lectern, or firmly gripping your cue cards.
- Don't speak over laughter.

TIP *Remember these rules to appear calm, confident and relaxed – even if you're not.*

The confidence ladder

As you gain in experience of speaking in public, you will find that you also gain in confidence about doing so:

Gain in confidence → Voice becomes stronger → Voice becomes clearer → Diction improves → Get a positive reputation → Gain charisma → Desire to do more public speaking → Gain in confidence...

Two-minute warm-ups that can be done anywhere

There is no substitute for a good, thorough warm-up. It will help to rid your body and your voice of potentially damaging tension while preparing them for the task ahead, and employing a familiar routine will help to calm your nerves. So why would you ever want to do a warm-up lasting only two minutes?

- **You may not be able to do your warm-up immediately prior to giving your speech.** Is it best to do it as close as possible to the moment of delivery, but if there has been a delay then a quick two-minute warm-up is perfect for getting things back up to speed, and provided the delay hasn't been too long this sort of 'turbo-charge' warm-up should suffice.
- **Sometimes, despite your best efforts, it's impossible to complete a proper warm-up** (e.g. if you weren't expecting to speak and someone suddenly asks you to do so at zero notice). In this situation a two-minute warm-up, basic as it is, is certainly better than nothing, and it will provide you with the opportunity to gather your thoughts and focus on your speech while preparing your body and your voice for the undertaking.

 These super-quick warm-ups can be performed anywhere – if there is nowhere more suitable to hand, then the venue's toilets will do perfectly well.

Physical warm-up

Deep breathing

- Stand up tall, relax your body and breathe in deeply.
- Hold for ten seconds and slowly release.
- Repeat five times.

Stretching

● Stretch as high as you can reach, on tiptoes. Relax.
● Stretch your arms as wide as you can. Relax.
● Repeat five times.

Scrunching and stretching your face

● Scrunch and stretch your face really tight, pinching it in.
  Relax.
● Scrunch and stretch your face as wide as possible, lifting
  your eyebrows and opening your mouth. Relax.
● Repeat five times.

Vocal warm-up

Yawning

● Open your mouth really wide and yawn loudly, vocalizing the
  sound as you exhale.
● Repeat five times.

Humming

● Hum one steady note, starting softly and growing louder.
● Repeat, but this time open your mouth widely allowing the
  sound out fully.
● Repeat five times.

Lip and tongue mobility

● Stick your tongue out and move it in large circles.
● Repeat your favourite tongue-twister.

 TIP *Use this time to think through your speech ready to deliver
it to maximum effect.*

Summary

One of the main stumbling blocks for anyone unused to speaking in public is the act of controlling their nerves when standing up in front of an audience. While it's good to be nervous, it's not good to look nervous or to be overwhelmed by nerves, so learning to control them is crucial; and by doing so you can harness their considerable power and energy and use them to your advantage.

By employing the techniques described in this chapter to harness the energy and edge gifted to you by nervousness you will be able to minimize the likelihood of having the occasion marred by a debilitating 'attack' of nerves, while at the same time elevating your speech-giving to a whole new level. In order to make sure that you give yourself, and your speech, the best possible chance of success you should aim to master the techniques as fully as possible, and as soon as possible, so that when you need them they will be second nature to you, ready and waiting – an essential part of your speech-giving arsenal.

In the last instalment in your journey towards being a great speech-giver, we will be looking at the common pitfalls and how to avoid them.

Fact-check [answers at the back]

1. It's good to get nervous before delivering your speech because...
a) Looking nervous will elicit sympathy from the audience ❑
b) Shaking helps to control your voice ❑
c) It charges your body with energy ❑
d) It helps you to lose weight ❑

2. Tell-tale symptoms of nervousness commonly experienced include...
a) Blackouts ❑
b) Stomach feeling 'knotted' or having butterflies in it ❑
c) Double-vision ❑
d) A feeling of tranquillity and calm ❑

3. Learning to channel your adrenalin is important because...
a) You can save it for later ❑
b) It can get messy if not reined in ❑
c) It can be used to your advantage ❑
d) Otherwise you might become hysterical ❑

4. Tension in your body may...
a) Make you feel relaxed ❑
b) Be good for your voice ❑
c) Make you appear taller ❑
d) Make you look, and feel, nervous ❑

5. Tension in your voice may...
a) Make it louder ❑
b) Make your voice sound strained, or shrill ❑
c) Make it clearer ❑
d) Give it a pleasing tone and resonance ❑

6. Being relaxed puts you in control of...
a) The audience ❑
b) The mechanics of speech-giving ❑
c) Your company ❑
d) Your finances ❑

7. Being nervous is good but...
a) It's not that good ❑
b) It's not for everyone ❑
c) Looking nervous isn't ❑
d) Only at weekends ❑

8. A good warm-up will...
a) Relieve tension and prepare you for the task ahead ❑
b) Help to counter the air conditioning ❑
c) Be invaluable preparation for running a marathon ❑
d) Inspire the audience to get fit ❑

9. It's inadvisable to drink alcohol before giving your speech because...

a) It's usually very expensive at large venues ❏

b) You may be so nervous you won't want to stop ❏

c) If the lights fail, you may have to recite your entire speech by heart ❏

d) It dulls your senses, and diminishes your capacity to give a great speech ❏

10. Two-minute warm-ups can be useful because...

a) Warming-up for any longer will tire you ❏

b) After two minutes your body can't get any warmer ❏

c) They can be done quickly, anywhere ❏

d) Warming-up for any longer is just a waste of time ❏

CHAPTER 20

Common mistakes and how to avoid them

Despite all your best efforts, dedicated practice, and careful preparation for giving your speech, it's a fact of life that something can still go wrong with some part of your speech-giving at some point. This is almost inevitable if you give speeches regularly due to the number of possible chances for it to happen; and even if you give speeches only rarely the odds are still high, since you won't have had the necessary practice to build up a store of experience which can help to prevent the possible pitfalls and pratfalls of speech-giving.

So either way, it's highly likely that you will be faced with challenging moments and experiences with which you will have to deal. Part of the key to doing this successfully lies in being as prepared as possible, thinking through all the eventualities which might occur to trip you up. Even though you won't be able to picture them all, thinking through as many as possible will help to get you into the habit of being ready to deal with the unexpected.

The other part is adopting the best mindset to spot mistakes early and deal with them swiftly, so that they will have the minimum possible impact on your speech, or even go unnoticed.

Trying to ad lib

Ad libbing – making unscripted remarks off the cuff – is a skill best left to the professionals. They make it look easy but don't be fooled – it's an incredibly difficult art to master and, unless you can do it brilliantly, it can all too easily go wrong and make you look amateurish.

You are almost always better off sticking to the script. Besides, if you have worked hard to write a great speech, and practised hard to be able to deliver it with dynamism and professionalism, why wouldn't you want to stick to the plan and give a speech which you know is great?

 TIP *It's extremely difficult to ad lib really well, and if it's not brilliant it can all too easily fall flat.*

The biggest danger with ad libbing is that in the heat of the moment, under the pressure to perform and filled with adrenalin, you may say something you wish you hadn't. Many speeches have been ruined in this way – and even careers.

Some of the most common reasons for ad libbing are that you:

● feel the speech is going badly and needs a 'lift'
● feel under pressure to be funny or to keep the audience entertained
● feel insecure about your material
● are answering a question from the floor.

This last point is worthy of further consideration. Obviously, you can't prepare your answers to questions you haven't heard, so how can you ensure that you don't say something you might later regret?

The answer lies in the preparation of your material. If you know your subject inside out, then there is no reason why you shouldn't be able to answer any question you may be asked without straying into dangerous territory; and if you don't know the answer it's better to say so than to guess (and risk being shown to be wrong, perhaps in front of the entire audience).

Crucially, you should always keep your answers short and to the point – it's when you begin to ramble and waffle that errors are likely to creep in, and that includes saying something which is factually correct but which you really don't want your audience to hear.

 TIP *It only takes an unguarded second to say the wrong thing – but you might regret it for ever.*

Allowing interruptions

Heckling during business speeches is uncommon but not unheard of, and usually occurs during a question and answer session. Someone may call out their question unbidden, or ask a further question once you have moved on to someone else's question, and all too easily you can succumb to the 'snowball effect'. This is where you allow one person to interrupt your speech, in whichever way, and then others quickly jump on the bandwagon – and before you know it you have been made redundant, left to just stand at the front looking awkward and trying to regain control of the situation.

It's crucial, therefore, that you retain control of the situation at all times, for your sake and for the sake of the audience. If you allow a situation of heckling or multiple calling out to occur, several unwanted things happen:

- The focus and direction of your speech are lost.
- The flow and momentum of your speech are lost.
- Your audience is left isolated and bewildered.
- You have lost control and will almost certainly become more nervous.
- You will end up firefighting, with all the structure of your argument eroded.

The most alarming aspect of this situation is the speed with which it can happen; and if you don't nip it in the bud right away it can very quickly spiral out of control. The key, then, is to ensure that you are always:

- alert to the possibility of it happening
- ready to deal with it quickly and firmly
- determined not to let it happen, even if that means risking appearing rude by talking over your audience to restore order.

Regaining control

Don't be afraid to take command of the situation and speak over people to regain control – your audience will be grateful that you did, and you will appear confident and in command. This will, in turn, help to settle your nerves, and you will have turned a potentially damaging situation into one which has allowed you to shine.

Straying from the subject

'His speeches left the impression of an army of pompous phrases moving over the landscape in search of an idea.'

Anon.

If yiu ahve carefully written your speech and diligently worked on perfecting your delivery, you are far better off sticking to the 'script' – wandering off at a tangent is a great way to add an unnecessary element of uncertainty to an occasion which was otherwise meticulously planned and practised. Depending on how far from your core themes you stray, you might find you are covering tangential topics on which you had not intended to encroach, or you may even wander away from your subject altogether! Veering away from your intended speech will:

At best:	At worst:
● dilute the contents of your speech	● have little or nothing to do with your subject
● lose the focus of your message	● appear self-indulgent
● make you seem less competent	● make your speech unreasonably long
● confuse the audience.	● leave the audience bewildered or bored.

Maintaining good speech-giving discipline will ensure that your speech always remains focused and targeted, and that you appear confident and in control – so stick to the subject and keep to the script.

 Give the best speech you're able to give by delivering the speech you had intended to deliver.

Relying on, or misusing, technology

You may well wish to employ some form of technology in your speech, and indeed this can be an excellent way of communicating information quickly and easily, or more directly and accurately than would otherwise be possible. This can also be a good way to add variety, create intrigue and, importantly, to give you a break! However – and it's a big 'however' – all technology is susceptible to Murphy's Law: 'If it can go wrong it will go wrong!' So always make sure you have a back-up to hand in an appropriate format, to prevent your speech grinding to an unscheduled stop, e.g. if you intend to show a PowerPoint presentation, ensure that you have a print-out of it to hand – but also have all the data available in a format which allows you to give out the salient points, without floundering and trying to describe each slide.

It's also important to remember that while the inclusion of technological aids can help to elevate your speech, it should never be its mainstay. It's best used sparingly, and only when it's unquestionably the best way to communicate the information you wish to deliver to your audience, or when you wish to inject some variety into your speech. It can help to give you a pause during your speech (particularly useful if your speech is lengthy), but it must never be apparent that this is why you have included it! Any technology you employ:

Must be:

✔ relevant
✔ audible/visible to everyone
✔ the best way to communicate specific information
✔ ready to start and finish instantly
✔ clearly relevant.

Must not be:

✗ the mainstay of your speech
✗ generic
✗ gimmicky
✗ used as 'filler'
✗ relied upon!

Another common pitfall with using technology to bolster a speech is over-use. This can:

● make your speech cluttered
● slow you down
● draw emphasis away from what you're saying.

It should therefore be kept to a minimum and used sparingly, only being included if it's:

● completely relevant
● entirely appropriate
● going to complement your speech – not undermine it.

Contact the venue in advance to let them know of your technological requirements, and to determine whether or not they can be accommodated, and if you will need to bring everything or if it's all supplied. Be careful to ensure there is an adequate power supply, not only in terms of wattage but also location, and that there are a sufficient number of power sockets where you need them.

What to do if you begin to feel overwhelmed

'The best way to gain self-confidence is to do what you are afraid to do.'

Anon.

Despite diligent practice and preparation, you won't be able to replicate exactly what it will be like on the day due to a number of factors which are either beyond your control or else all but impossible to create in advance, such as assembling a suitably large audience to hear your speech. And by not having experienced the conditions exactly, prior to giving your speech, there is always the possibility that the occasion might overwhelm you.

By thinking through the reasons for this in advance, and by being as prepared as possible to combat them, you can minimize their impact and give yourself the best possible chance of staying on top of the situation.

In addition to an unexpectedly large audience, other factors to be aware of include:

- **N**ervousness – you may have experienced a degree of this when practising but you are almost bound to experience it to a greater degree when you are giving your speech 'for real'.
- **A**tmosphere – each venue, and each audience, creates its own unique atmosphere. These can help to lift your performance but can also threaten to undermine it if it all becomes too much.
- **S**ense of occasion – the speech you are giving may be important for your company, for the occasion you are presenting at, and for you. The more important the occasion, the more likely it is that you may feel overwhelmed by it.

- **A**udience – will there be someone in the audience you are particularly nervous about presenting to? Might there be a surprise VIP guest on the day?

Remembering '**NASA**' will help you to be ready for extra pressures you may experience on the day – fortunately, combatting them is not rocket science!

Similarly, remembering '**SPACE**' may help you to maintain a cool, calm temperament, and to keep your composure, whatever the situation:

- **S**tand tall, with your feet firmly planted, shoulder-width apart, and maintain a good posture.
- **P**lace a glass of water to hand to keep your mouth from drying.
- **A**void drinking alcohol to calm your nerves – it doesn't work and leaves you less in control.
- **C**ontrol your breathing – take several deep breaths before you begin, and one whenever you pause.
- **E**nsure that you take your time – don't rush, and pause when you need to, to compose yourself.

Becoming distracted

You may have practised until you are almost perfect with your speech-giving every time you run through it, but rest assured that on the day, given the additional external factors that will impact your delivery, it's very easy to become distracted. If you are used to attending speeches then you will probably have seen it for yourself – a speaker who allows their attention to wander, even for just a second, and gets caught out by not realizing that a film presentation was about to end, or by not being able to find their place in their notes, or even by not being able to remember what they were talking about! It happens, but it needn't happen to you.

One of the most common reasons for a sudden loss of concentration is the occurrence of negative thoughts. One minute your speech is going really well and you are getting your nerves under control, the next doubts are starting to creep in and you are beginning to wonder whether the audience is enjoying what you are saying. Are they finding it interesting? Useful? Are they wishing they hadn't come?

And the next thing you know there is an awkward silence as everyone waits for you to continue with the speech. In order to prevent this, it is crucial that you approach your speech with the most positive attitude possible. You have worked hard on writing a great speech; you have worked hard on delivering a great speech; now all you have to do is to believe in yourself and maintain your concentration and your focus.

Another typical reason for losing your concentration is the other side of the same coin – complacency. Your speech is going really well, you have every reason to believe that the audience is thoroughly engaged with what you are saying, and you are so relieved that you allow your guard to drop. It takes only a second and suddenly you are floundering, and kicking yourself for allowing these self-congratulatory thoughts into your head.

The trick to not letting your mind wander like this is to keep focused on what you are saying, and to have decided before you begin that you are not going to try to read the audience's reaction to your speech while you are still giving it, but to leave that until after it is finished.

The third pitfall people fall into when distracted is allowing themselves to ramble. You shouldn't be reading your speech verbatim, but taking the headline notes on your cue cards and expanding on them. This means that you have the licence to either keep your message short and to the point, or else to ramble – and risk losing your audience's interest in the process.

So make sure that you have an idea of how much time it should take to cover each of your points and try to ensure that you don't allow yourself to go beyond it.

Summary

Although it's impossible to ensure that you will never, ever, make a mistake – indeed, it's highly probable that at some point you *will* make a mistake – it's possible to ensure that these are kept to a minimum, and that you know how to deal with them when they do occur so that their negative impact on your speech is minimized. You can also minimize the likelihood of needing to add unrehearsed elements to your material by ensuring that you don't rush your speech; and by taking just one question at a time, and by dictating the quantity of the input from the audience, you can maintain control of the situation.

Make sure that any technology on which you rely is working properly and can be catered for at the venue (and never, ever rely on anything which relies on batteries!) and keep to your subject and to the way in which you have rehearsed your speech to ensure that the material won't let you down.

Keep your focus, take some deep breaths if you begin to feel overwhelmed, and concentrate on delivering your speech the way you have practised, and you will have every reason to believe that your speech will go really well – mistakes or no mistakes.

Fact-check [answers at the back]

1. Ad libbing is a skill...
a) Which can be mastered in minutes ❏
b) Best left to the professionals ❏
c) You should aim to employ in every speech ❏
d) Essential to public speaking ❏

2. The biggest danger with ad libbing is that...
a) In the heat of the moment you may say something you wish you hadn't ❏
b) It can become addictive ❏
c) You may be tempted to recite stories not connected to your speech ❏
d) The audience might want to join in ❏

3. Allowing interruptions to your speech can ruin...
a) Your day ❏
b) You chances of promotion ❏
c) The flow and momentum of your speech ❏
d) Your ability to get it over with quickly ❏

4. Wandering off at a tangent to your speech is a great way to...
a) Underline the key points ❏
b) Explore new territory ❏
c) Keep the interest of anyone who has heard it before ❏
d) Add an unnecessary element of uncertainty to your delivery ❏

5. Veering away from your intended speech will...
a) Add a welcome element of intrigue and mystery ❏
b) Lose its focus and confuse the audience ❏
c) Allow you to cover multiple topics ❏
d) Allow you to save some material for another time ❏

6. It can be useful to incorporate technology into your speech in order to...
a) Use up time so you don't have to prepare such a long speech ❏
b) Communicate specific information concisely and clearly ❏
c) Show off your mastery of information technology ❏
d) Keep your audience awake ❏

7. Technology should only be employed in your speech when...
a) You run out of ideas ❏
b) You become bored of your own material ❏
c) It's completely relevant and entirely appropriate ❏
d) It's free ❏

8. You should never, ever rely on...
a) Anything which relies on batteries ❏
b) The venue to provide lunch ❏
c) Your own ability to give a great speech ❏
d) Your boss ❏

9. If you begin to feel overwhelmed by the occasion you should...
a) Reconsider undertaking public speaking engagements ❑
b) Stop, and seek medical help ❑
c) Control your breathing, and take your time ❑
d) Faint ❑

10. A little humour in your speech is great, but too much may...
a) Create so much laughter your speech can't be heard ❑
b) Be inappropriate and come back to haunt you ❑
c) Underline your key themes ❑
d) Be a blessing in disguise ❑

7 × 7

1 Seven top tips

- There are three parts to every speech: tell your audience what you are going to tell them; tell them; and then tell them what you have told them.
- Get into the habit of always noting down your ideas as and when they occur to you, no matter where you are or what you are doing. You may not remember them later.
- Divide your speech into manageable sections, and pare each one down to the bare bones. Then keep it simmering until only the richest material remains.
- Your speech should be the right length – not for you, but for your audience.
- Breathe deeply. This will help to slow you down, and calm your nerves, as well as supporting your voice for effective delivery.
- Rehearse in front of other people, and begin at the earliest opportunity.
- Memorize the key points of your speech – but don't learn it by heart.

2 Seven ways to control nerves

- Remember that being nervous is a good thing – the energy it creates allows you to deliver your speech with power, passion and dynamism. Don't be afraid of nerves.
- Learn to recognize the feelings you experience when you are nervous, and practise seeing your body's physical reaction to the anxiety you are feeling in a positive light.
- Use simple relaxation techniques immediately before giving your speech to rid your body of tension, and to ensure that you don't look nervous.
- Thoroughly warm up your body, and especially your voice, before giving your speech.

- Check out the venue as soon as possible, and make sure that you have somewhere to rest your notes, and a place for a glass of water.
- Try out the 'confidence tricks' to learn which ones work best for you – then memorize them, and practise them often.
- Remember to keep things in proportion – everyone gets nervous when speaking in public, but nobody ever died of it!

3 Seven pitfalls to avoid

- When it comes to speeches, longer doesn't mean better. Keep it short, sharp and focused.
- Silly gimmicks, unnecessary props and questionable humour have no place in a good speech.
- Ad libbing. Even the very best comedians sometimes come unstuck doing this; the rest of us shouldn't even try.
- Don't gabble.
- Frequent coughing, nervous laughter and fidgeting are sure signs of a nervous speaker. Keep your body and your voice under control.
- Never permit interruptions or succumb to distractions.
- Do not stray from the script – this will often lead to a speaker straying from the subject.

4 Seven things to do today

- Great speeches aren't written – they're rewritten. Allow yourself plenty of time by getting your speechwriting under way at the earliest opportunity, and then improve it continually with subsequent amendments.
- Ask colleagues, bosses, stakeholders and so on whether they want to be consulted on your speech, and whether there is anything specific that they want you to include.
- Find out who your audience will be – if you know whom you will be giving your speech to, you can pitch it appropriately.
- Begin practising speaking out loud – and loudly – whenever you are on your own. The more often you do it, the more normal it will become to you.

- Find some colleagues to whom you can practise giving your speech, and from whom you can receive constructive criticism.
- Start practising giving your speech in front of a full-length mirror.
- Buy some cue cards, and start practising reading from them while maintaining eye contact with your audience.

5 Seven ways to look like a pro

- Start and finish strongly.
- Make eye contact with your audience, often, and throughout your speech.
- Stick to the script.
- Colour your voice through inflection, and vary your pace, tone, pitch and volume.
- Never be afraid to pause. It can help to undermine a point, or to build expectation and focus on what you are about to say.
- Don't rush your delivery.
- Command the space. Look confident by walking purposefully to the podium, looking your audience in the eye, and remembering to smile.

6 Seven inspiring speakers

- Nelson Mandela (1918–2013), South African President 1994–9, anti-apartheid activist and revolutionary
- Steve Jobs (1955–2011), entrepreneur, and cofounder, Chairman and CEO of Apple Inc.
- Winston Churchill (1874–1965), British Prime Minister 1940–45 and 1951–5
- Mother Theresa (1910–97), founder of the Missionaries of Charity Roman Catholic religious order
- Martin Luther King, Jr. (1929–68), civil rights campaigner, activist and humanitarian
- John F. Kennedy (1917–63), President of the United States of America 1961–3

- Billy Crystal (1948–present), actor, comedian and nine-times Master of Ceremonies at the Academy Awards (Oscars)

7 Seven great quotes

- 'A speech is like a woman's skirt: it needs to be long enough to cover the subject matter, but short enough to hold the audience's attention.' Anon.
- 'How often in life we complete a task that was beyond the capability of the person we were when we started it.' Robert Brault
- 'It takes one hour of preparation for each minute of presentation time.' Wayne Burgraff
- 'His speeches left the impression of an army of pompous phrases moving over the landscape in search of an idea.' Anon.
- 'Be sincere, be brief, be seated.' Franklin Delano Roosevelt
- 'There are certain things in which mediocrity is not to be endured, such as poetry, music, painting, public speaking.' Jean de La Bruyère
- 'Always be shorter than anybody dared to hope.' Lord Reading

PART 4

Your Successful Meetings Masterclass

Introduction

Business is all about conversations. Whether you are in manufacturing, a service industry, farming, a local or national government department, working as a sole trader or are the chief executive officer of a global organization, we all ultimately do business by talking to each other. We can hold our conversations one to one or in groups, in small, formal or informal gatherings, in major conferences or through social media. We cannot avoid meetings!

The online dictionary service, dictionary.com, defines a meeting as:

1 the act of coming together
2 an assembly or conference of persons for a specific purpose
3 the body of persons present at an assembly or conference
3 and, rather interestingly:
4 a hostile encounter; duel.

Whatever our reason for meeting others, a vast number of people feel that they are wasting time in meetings when they could more usefully be getting on with their work. Yet a well-managed, purposeful meeting can be highly motivating. This book will show you how to achieve that and will help you enormously in your professional career.

Whether you are participating or chairing, this Part will help you to develop the skills you need to make meetings effective and get the most out of them.

CHAPTER 21

Why meetings?

If all else fails, we can always have a meeting. Meetings have become the standard default means of exchanging information and sharing ideas at work, and often we do not consider the alternatives that could save us time and allow us to achieve more.

In this chapter we're going to set the scene for the rest of this section. We'll look at why we hold meetings, whether formal or informal, and explore some of the best reasons for meeting with others. In each case we'll spend a little time looking at how those meetings can successfully achieve their aims. We'll look, too, at less useful reasons for holding a meeting.

We'll look at how much time we spend in meetings, and how much of this people feel is wasted time. We'll see how we can determine whether a meeting is the most appropriate channel for achieving a business objective or whether alternatives may be preferable.

What's a meeting?

In the ideal world, a meeting is a chance for people with shared or developing interests in a common theme to come together to further develop those interests. By the end of the meeting, something should have changed – participants may have agreed on something new, discovered something new or changed their thinking about something. Whatever the purpose of the meeting, it should result in some change, whether immediate or as a result of the meeting.

A meeting should:

- have a purpose
- bring together people with shared interest in achieving that purpose
- result in change.

A good meeting is action focused. It's not simply a talking shop, but a productive mechanism for making things happen. Just as the best production line streams out high-quality goods as efficiently and effectively as possible, so the best meeting generates focused actions as efficiently and effectively as possible.

> **Effectively – doing the right things**
> **Efficiently – doing things right**

A waste of time

It has been estimated that 11 million meetings take place in the USA every day1 and that most professionals attend nearly 62 meetings per month.[1] Research suggests that more than 50 per cent of this meeting time is wasted time.[2]

If each meeting is just one hour long, this means that people are spending 31 hours (around four working days) every month in unproductive meetings.

344

Most people meeting regularly say they daydream (91 per cent), miss meetings (96 per cent) or miss parts of meetings (95 per cent). Many (73 per cent) say they bring other work to meetings and 39 per cent say they have fallen asleep during meetings.[3]

Whether or not it is reasonable to extrapolate these figures for other nations based on their relative population size, you can see that meetings have received a bad press over the years, and quite deservedly so.

Bad meetings lack purpose and focus and are badly chaired; the agenda is unclear or absent, dominant people use the meeting as a platform for their own political interests and others feel that they have no voice.

Meanwhile, everyone's *real* work piles up as the meeting grinds on inexorably to a stuttering finish. Does this sound familiar?

Reasons not to hold a meeting

Let's think about some good reasons not to hold a meeting (although we often do) and get these out of the way, so that we look positively at good reasons to meet and how those reasons can be translated into productive effort.

Actually, it doesn't matter on which day of the week the meeting is held. The regular monthly, weekly or (alarmingly) daily meeting suffers from the very reason it was initiated – its regularity. The first time a team decides to meet regularly, there is relative enthusiasm. People see the point. It's a chance to get together as a team, talk about things of mutual interest and share information which may be useful to others. It doesn't take long for meetings to turn stale and for people to start attending out of a sense of duty or fear of reprisals. People go over the same old ground, jokes are repeated and the same people use it as a platform for their own intentions whether or not these are relevant to the subject of the meeting.

I once had a client that was a sales-driven organization obsessed by its weekly figures and reactive to any slight short-term change in its profitability. One of its sales teams held a regular Monday morning meeting. The team's manager told me that this was a motivational event, designed to kick-start the week on a high. He encouraged me to attend to see how it worked in practice.

He began by announcing that Terry (name changed to protect the innocent) had exceeded his sales target by 4 per cent.

'What do we say to Terry?', he exclaimed.

'Hurrah!', they all shouted.

'Now Joan missed her target by 2.5 per cent. What do we say to Joan?'

'Boo!', they all cried.

I later asked him what he thought he was doing. 'Motivating Joan', he said.

Regular meetings tend to reflect short-term thinking. For example, a sales team will meet once a week to discuss the sales figures of the previous week. The danger in focusing on the short term is that you miss longer term trends and read too much into glitches or exceptional situations. It's important, of course, to rectify immediate problems, but it's more important to assess how an organization is performing over a longer period.

The sole purpose of the 'blame fest' seems to be to point fingers at any hint of underperformance. If you think in the short term, you're more likely to find fault with individuals based on a single error or on a single week in which they appeared to underperform. The blame fest is a power play for the person who runs the meeting and is desperately embarrassing for participants, who may wonder 'Will it be my turn this time?' While teams often perform well for limited periods under pressure, they do not perform well out of fear, and blame fests simply make people frightened.

Perhaps controversially, meetings are not a great forum for information sharing. We have excellent electronic tools for just this. (E-mail is not one of them! When a person leaves, the vital information buried in their account disappears from sight.) Often, organizations hold meetings to share information because they think their employees do not read important e-mailed information. If a piece of information is relevant to someone's job and they either do not read it or do not act it on it, then that becomes a management issue rather than a reason to hold meetings.

It may be that e-mail is simply not the right medium for disseminating information. Equally, it may be that too much information is sent too often, written in language people do not understand, the e-mails are too long, the distribution list is too broad, the content isn't relevant or it's just plain boring...

One example of useful information-sharing software is Lotus Notes, which is designed to allow teams to share information using 'databases' which are really information-sharing or knowledge management repositories. In organizations where Notes is well used, teams are kept completely up to date on everything their members are doing. They do not need to meet to share this knowledge – they already have it, whether they are working in the same location or are geographically spread.

Reasons to hold a meeting

Let's explore some of the better reasons for holding a meeting. They are in no particular order, and it may be that within your organization you are aware of other good reasons. Make sure that they meet the three criteria that we set out a little earlier.

Here are two different scenarios:

1 A board of directors must decide whether to spend a large amount of money on something which may be risky for their business. If it works, it could result in a massive increase in profitability. Failure could mean financial disaster. The directors have always worked well together, buying into the company's strategic vision and understanding how actions

taken in one area of the business will affect work in the other areas.

2 The manager of a team working in a single location has been approached by a stationery company offering printer paper at lower cost and at a slightly lower quality.

Which of these decisions merits a formal meeting? One, both or neither? What criteria would you apply to determine whether it's appropriate to hold a meeting to make these decisions?

Here are some ideas:

1 Could the decision be taken by one person alone?
2 Do they have authority to make the decision?
3 What are the potential outcomes of the decision?
4 How many people do the outcomes affect?
5 If the wrong decision is made, what would happen to the decision-maker?
6 Is it morally acceptable for one person to make the decision?
7 Is it commercially wise for one person to make the decision?
8 Does any single person have the expertise to make the decision alone?

On that basis, it should be clear that in the first scenario, a meeting of all the directors is necessary. In the second scenario, the manager should be able to make the decision alone. We can take democracy at work too far!

Collaborative decision-making is a useful purpose for a meeting, where it is right and proper that the decision should fall to more than one person. Enlisting a wider group of people to make decisions brings its own problems, which we'll see when we look at chairing skills. It also brings different perspectives, which can be useful for seeing an argument from more than one side.

Your long-established team is about to undertake a new project. Members know each other very well and have worked on many projects in the past. The team leader has e-mailed details of the project to you all and has assigned project roles and responsibilities. You are happy to start on the new project but something doesn't feel right. What's missing?

At the start of any new project, whether involving a new or established team, it's useful to meet and talk through how you will work together. Team members may spot issues which have not been addressed by the team leader, may want to ask questions about project specifics and may even feel that the first meeting is the formal start to the project.

At the end of a project, it's great practice to hold a debrief meeting.

A bad debrief ends up as a blame fest, in which people have to account for mistakes they have made along the way.

A good debrief is all about what is called *double-loop learning*. Imagine you go to the doctor because you have a rash on your hand. A bad doctor gives you some cream and tells you to apply it three times a day and the rash will disappear. A good doctor examines you more thoroughly to understand the underlying causes of the rash. *Single-loop learning* addresses symptoms, sticking a plaster over the problem in the hope that it won't recur. Double-loop learning finds the underlying cause of a problem and changes systems or processes so that the problem cannot recur.

A good project debrief will:

1 Blamelessly discover the underlying causes of problems which occurred during the project and change working practices so that the problems cannot recur in future projects.
2 Discover the things which worked well and determine whether they can be built into new 'best practices'.

Ten people are brought together to form a new team. Some have met before, some are complete strangers to each other and some know others only by name or by reputation. It's useful for any new team to meet and get to know something about each other. Give them time to chat, mix socially, talk one to one and discover something about each other, both professionally and personally.

New teams are said4 to go through a number of stages – 'forming', 'norming' and 'storming' – before they reach the intended goal of 'performing'.

At the forming stage, they are polite and a little formal, evaluating and trying to understand each other. At the storming stage, politeness is replaced by some jostling for position, and team members become more assertive in carving out the most appropriate role for themselves. At the norming stage, people have begun to find their feet, roles and responsibilities are clearer and ways of working have been established.

Because the team has been set up to perform at its best, it's important to get through these early stages as quickly as possible. One way to speed up the process is to get the team members together as early as possible so that they can assess each other face to face.

> As a consultant to many organizations, I am often asked to give opinions. This is a reasonable request – I can often bring a fresh perspective based on experience of working with many other organizations in the same or different sectors.
>
> Sometimes, however, I am asked to ratify silly decisions made by senior people who have played the dangerous business game of 'ready, fire, aim!' They have made a decision and probably realized it was inappropriate but, having announced it to their staff, lack the courage or humility to admit that there may be a better option and bring me in to agree to it so they can tell their staff that an outside consultant told them it was the right decision...
>
> If you meet others to seek their expertise, use their views and experience to help shape your own decisions rather than as a validation of a misguided decision which you've already put into operation. (And beware of the consultants who *will* ratify your thinking because they want the fee.)

Traditionally, teams worked in the same place. Globalization and expansion of organizations, a need to serve people locally and a desire to cut costs have led to increasing numbers of people working from home, only occasionally visiting an office, and geographically scattered teams with few opportunities to meet up. This increase in 'virtual teams' can result in people feeling isolated and dissociated from both each other and the organization. It is important for a new virtual team to meet each other face to face. Just as for the new team working in the same physical space, members will go through the forming, storming and norming stages, but physical separation of the virtual team makes this extremely difficult.

Bring them together at the outset and, whenever possible, arrange other opportunities for them to meet. As we'll see in Chapter 24 there are ways to bring them together virtually, too.

We negotiate constantly at work. Each of us wants something a little different (or completely different) and we negotiate to get the possible deal. It is far easier to negotiate face to face because it allows us to see, in the moment, others' reactions to our ideas. Globalized markets mean that often we have to negotiate by telephone, video conference or other virtual means. Whatever the chosen medium, the meeting is the basis for our negotiations.

It's unlikely that you know the answer to every problem which faces you at work. Luckily, if your network is good, you'll know someone with more expertise than you. Meet them and draw on their experience. Try not to influence their decision as you state your problem – present it objectively, as factually and as clearly as possible. The most useful experts ask good, often penetrating, questions before offering advice. Often they will not tell you the course of action to take, but help you to understand the consequences of the options available to you so you can make an informed judgement.

A team leader or manager has agonized over a solution to a problem and has determined a possible action. They now ask others to come and help them to work through their solution to identify its strengths and weaknesses.

Summary

When you invite others to a meeting you are taking some of their most valuable resource – time. Time is short and time is money. You cannot afford the luxury of time in a meeting if your time would be better spent elsewhere.

Equally, you cannot afford to work in isolation from others because the organization isn't all about *you*.

If you are in a position to decide on the best way to tackle a business issue, consider the three criteria for a meeting: purpose, bringing people together who have shared interests in achieving that purpose and bringing about change. If others decide on your behalf that a meeting is the best channel to resolve an issue and you can't see how a meeting would achieve that objective, then have the courage to question its validity.

At every level in an organization, it's worth considering two things: stewardship and legacy. Nobody stays in an organization forever, and most organizations are unlikely to last forever! You are the temporary steward of an organization. If you continue to adopt practices which you know are inappropriate or inadequate, then you are perpetuating and institutionalizing mediocrity and thus your legacy to others will be poor.

Picture this: you have a new member in your team, a fresh-faced youth who asks in all innocence 'What's the purpose of the Monday morning meeting?' If your truthful answer is 'We've always had a Monday morning meeting' and you can think of no more positive reasons for it, then shame on you! It's terrible stewardship and a woeful legacy...

Fact-check (answers at the back)

1. One of the primary purposes of meetings is:
    a) To help people to feel important in their work ❑
    b) To result in change ❑
    c) To motivate people whose morale is low ❑
    d) To help people to network more widely in the organization ❑

2. A meeting is the best way to:
    a) Share information ❑
    b) Provide a platform for senior people to air their views ❑
    c) Kick-start a virtual team ❑
    d) Manage an organization ❑

3. Research suggests that the percentage of meeting time which people feel is wasted is:
    a) 50 per cent ❑
    b) 20 per cent ❑
    c) 30 per cent ❑
    d) 70 per cent ❑

4. Which of the following is typically not a good basis for a meeting?
    a) Collaborative decision-making ❑
    b) The regular weekly meeting ❑
    c) Project initiation ❑
    d) Seeking opinions and expertise ❑

5. Which of the following is a potential benefit of a project debrief meeting?
    a) Zero-loop learning ❑
    b) Single-loop learning ❑
    c) Double-loop learning ❑
    d) Triple-loop learning ❑

6. At the 'storming' stage in a team's evolution, team members:
    a) Ignore each other in favour of their own political ends ❑
    b) Display anger and become aggressive ❑
    c) Complain about colleagues behind their backs ❑
    d) Try to establish their own position within the team ❑

7. One of the key reasons for a virtual team meeting is:
    a) To stave off the boredom which members feel when working alone ❑
    b) To help team members avoid a feeling of dissociation from the rest of the team ❑
    c) To ensure that the team members are actually doing some work ❑
    d) To give them a chance to gossip ❑

8. What's the biggest danger in attending a meeting at which your expertise is sought?
    a) That you have simply been invited to ratify a silly decision ❑
    b) That your expertise will be ignored ❑
    c) That you will disagree with others who share different opinions ❑
    d) That you don't know your subject sufficiently well ❑

9. A meeting whose purpose is for a group to make a decision collaboratively is most appropriate when:

a) Individuals are scared of taking individual responsibility for a decision and so need group support ❏

b) The team members are not clever enough to make decisions on their own ❏

c) It would be commercially unwise for one person to make the decision alone ❏

d) It is important for team members to believe that the organization is democratic ❏

10. Which two ideas should you constantly review as a professional person?

a) Stewardship and legality ❏

b) Stewardship and legacy ❏

c) Stewardship and legitimacy ❏

d) Stewardship and leadership ❏

CHAPTER 22

Preparing for a meeting

You may have experienced being asked to attend a meeting whose purpose is unclear and wondering why you were invited at all. The key to a successful meeting is careful planning and thoughtful preparation.

Preparation may be the responsibility of either the Chair of the meeting or a participant. Some Chairs actively prepare for meetings and some delegate the responsibilities to others. With an increasing trend in rotating the chairing of meetings, it's quite likely that you will be called upon to prepare a meeting at any stage in your career.

In this chapter we'll look at everything you need to do to make a meeting work. Meticulous planning at this stage reaps rewards in terms of meeting success. Participants who are able to find their way easily to a venue, are made to feel welcome (or, at the least, expected) when they arrive and feel that some thought has gone into the organization of the meeting (or, at the least, do not notice any problems) tend to contribute more.

We'll call those attending a meeting 'participants' and not 'attendees', which suggests someone attended to rather than taking an active part, or 'delegates', which implies that someone has delegated their attendance. Ideally, meeting participants should attend through choice!

Starting with purpose

Start your preparation by determining the purpose of the meeting:

- Why and by whom is it believed to be necessary?
- What are the intended outcomes?
- Is it time critical?
- What will happen if it fails to meet its objectives?
- What might contribute to its success?

The agenda

The agenda sets out the purpose of the meeting (if the participants don't already know), the topics to be discussed, who leads on each topic and usually some logistical arrangements which may be reiterated in a separate invitation. It is worthwhile including them as an additional page in the agenda because busy people often neglect to print invitations and may miss important details such as venue and timing.

   The agenda should list all participants and any special roles they will have in the meeting.

Here's a sample template for an agenda:

- Meeting subject
- Meeting objectives
- Meeting organizer (with contact details)
- Meeting recorder
- Names of invited participants
- Venue, date and time
- Pre-meeting reading
- Apologies for absence
- Action points and matters arising from last meeting
- Specific topics to be discussed, with brief detail, topic owners and allotted timings
- Details of next meeting

Let's look at each item in turn. The first items are all scene setters, designed to give background information to those attending:

- Meeting subject
  - For example: Meeting of the finance subcommittee to determine the level of funding for the new wing of Cell Block H.
- Meeting objectives
  - For example: 'We are charged with allocating funds towards completion of the new building. All budgets must be completed by 3 March and so it is vital that we reach our final decision at this meeting to get budget approval.' This, combined with the meeting subject, is our statement of purpose.
- Meeting organizer (with contact details)
  - The name of the meeting owner. It may be the Chair, the Chair's personal assistant, one of the participants or another interested party. Include telephone and e-mail details and a title or role – something to make clear the involvement of this person to participants who may not recognize the name.
- Meeting recorder
  - The name of the person who will record the significant points arising from the meeting.
- Names of invited participants
  - Participants like to know who else will attend a meeting so they can prepare properly for it. Would you prepare more or less rigorously if you had to present an argument designed to influence your friends or your organization's Board of Directors?
- Venue, date and time
  - Where the meeting will be and when. We'll look at venue and timing in more detail shortly.
- Pre-meeting reading
  - Any essential background reading. Ensure that you send the background material when you send out the agenda.

The second set of items outline what will happen, in sequence, during the meeting:

- Apologies for absence
  - It's usual to record who has notified the Chair of their absence before the meeting. This way they can be eliminated from the list of unexplained absentees who should be contacted after the meeting to explain their absence.
- Action points and matters arising from last meeting
  - The best Chair, as we'll see in Chapter 24, follows up on action points to ensure that they have been completed. In this part of the meeting, participants briefly describe how they have tackled the actions to which they agreed at the last meeting. It's also a place to raise any serious issues which demanded thought from the participants after the last meeting.
- Specific topics to be discussed, with brief detail, topic owners and allotted timings
  - How many topics to include in an agenda is a matter of judgement. The list must be manageable within the allotted time. You will have to make your best guess at how long a topic will take based on, for example, the complexity and critical nature of a topic, the level of interest and knowledge of the participants and other local factors. If in doubt, reduce the number of topics on the agenda to be safe.
- Arrange/announce details of next meeting

Any other business?

No! Notice that the traditional item, any other business (AOB), is not included here. Meetings must be purposeful and AOB dilutes that purpose.

AOB has long been an excuse by the vocal minority to hijack a meeting, using it as a platform to address their own political agendas or introduce topics they were too lazy to bring to the attention of the meeting organizer before the meeting. Often the person who raises other business is the least prepared for the meeting. In reality, many meetings spend longer discussing other business than dealing with scheduled topics.

The absence of AOB has several benefits:

1 The meeting remains purposeful and on topic.
2 The meeting can run to time. AOB can create long extensions to a meeting.
3 Everyone is open with each other about the meeting.
4 There can be no surprises. Meeting participants should have time to prepare for a topic before the meeting, and AOB prevents that preparation. The only person likely to be prepared to discuss the other business is the person who raises the topic, and there is a considerable danger of them railroading participants into agreement with something which they have not considered in sufficient detail to make an informed decision.

The only reason for other business to be discussed comes when an emergency arises between the distribution of the agenda and the meeting date. If this is the case, the person involved should raise the issue with the Chair and, if sufficient people see the urgent need to discuss it, then it can be included. Do not ever include AOB in the agenda, because participants should use it as a rare exception and not a rule.

Determining who should be invited

If you are inviting people to a regular meeting of a standing committee, then the cast list will change little between meetings. If it is a one-off meeting it becomes a little trickier. Sometimes we invite too many people for fear of causing offence if we don't invite them. If in doubt, take advice about who should be invited. Too many participants make discussions long and decision-making difficult. If you invite too few, they or others may complain that certain interests are not represented and so the meeting has no real authority to make an informed decision. Try to find people representing each key interest, argument or viewpoint for the major topics being discussed. See who has attended similar meetings in the past, ask the Chairs of other meetings for their recommendations and ask those whom you know should attend if there is anyone vital missing from the list.

The invitation to the meeting

Nowadays we tend to e-mail rather than post meeting agendas, unless there are hard copies of background reading to be included. The agenda is often an attachment to an e-mail inviting participants to attend. Your invitations should:

1 Reiterate the subject, date, time and venue of the meeting. Typically, where budget allows, you would invite participants for coffee around 30 minutes before the official start of the meeting. In most cultures, the social chat before the meeting is important.
2 Make clear what background reading participants must do before attending. Attach the reading where possible.
3 Ask participants to take note of who is expected to address which topics.
4 Mention dress code if this is important or not known/obvious to participants.
5 Provide travel and parking arrangements. Use online mapping services to embed a map, directions and details of parking and public transport links within your invitations.
6 Give contact details, including an emergency number to phone if you have difficulty getting to the meeting on the day.
7 Ask about special dietary requirements if you intend to feed the participants.
8 Ask participants who intend to use slides or other supporting materials to send them before the meeting so that they can be copied for other participants. If it's important that the other participants read them before the event, then ask that the materials be circulated a working week before the meeting.
9 Ask participants to confirm their attendance by a set date, giving your contact details for their reply. This is important, if only for catering purposes!

> There is a certain wisdom in the idea that the further
> someone has to travel, the earlier they will arrive
> and vice-versa. If half of your meeting participants
> have travelled some distance to a venue and
> the other half are local, it's likely that the locals
> will arrive later.
>
> I recently attended a meeting in a large government
> building. The participants were all from one team,
> based in another part of the same building. Many of the
> participants arrived late, explaining that they had never
> been in this part of the building before and couldn't find
> their way around. I had travelled more than 250 km to
> attend the meeting and arrived half an hour before the
> first in-house participant.

Choosing a venue

In practice, you will select a venue before completing the
agenda and sending out the invitations. Here are some things
you may want to consider in choosing a venue:

1 familiarity
   – Have you/the participants used the venue before?
2 location
   – Is the location onsite or offsite? Onsite is familiar
     and easy. Everyone knows where everything is and
     you have access to telephones, copiers and in-house
     expertise. It's also easier to gain access to the in-
     house computer network. However, participants may
     find the proximity of colleagues distracting and, if the
     meeting is on the participants' own office premises,
     you'll find that getting them back to the meeting after
     breaks is difficult because 'I'll just go and check my
     e-mails' leads to people disappearing from the meeting
     ('to sort out an urgent issue') and either not returning
     or missing important parts of the meeting. Meeting
     offsite may give participants a greater sense of the
     importance or seriousness of a meeting because they

can see the investment in it. External catering may offer a refreshing change. Because it's more difficult for participants to check e-mails and disappear to their desks, you may find they get more involved. However, it will inevitably be more expensive than running a meeting in-house. Most organizations don't pay their employees' travel costs from home to work but do pay for travel to external venues. Check that you have sufficient budget to cover all the costs of an outside venue.
- How close is it to the base locations of the invited participants? Are you asking participants to travel further to the venue than they would to work? Early starts and bad traffic or unpleasant public transport breed tiredness and bad feeling, and ideally you want to start any meeting with participants who are wide awake and in good spirits
- How easy is it to find?
- Is it close to public transport links?

3 space required
- How many people need to be accommodated? Is the room sufficiently large? Is there space between and behind the chairs? If the meeting is likely to be long, are the chairs (too) comfortable?

4 equipment
- If projectors and/or sound equipment are required, can the venue provide them or should you bring your own? Can they supply four-block power supplies so that you can plug in equipment? Can they supply rubber masking or duct tape to ensure that you have no trailing wires? Can they provide flipcharts and pens? Insist on dark-coloured flipchart markers – whiteboard markers are useless on paper and red and green ink is difficult to read at any distance from the flipchart.

5 catering arrangements
- Do not over-cater. People work better hungry than full!
- Ensure that the caterers are able to meet any special dietary requirements.

6 seating arrangements
- Can you arrange the seating so that the appropriate people sit together/apart according to office politics, relationships and other sensitivities?
7 ease of access based on participants' base locations
8 ease and cost of parking
- Check your budgets. Many city-based car parks charge punitive amounts for a few hours' parking.

Tell the venue administrators the name of your meeting and organization, who is attending and the room number. Ask them to put up signage showing your participants how to get to the room.

Check on the security arrangements. Do participants need passes to move between sections of the building? There is little more aggravating (and, for some, embarrassing) than having to ask someone resident in a building to accompany them to the toilet because the toilet area is behind a door requiring an electronic security pass. Plead the case for temporary security passes for your participants and they will have a more comfortable day.

Timing and sequencing of a meeting

If you plan to start the meeting late in the morning, consider whether or not you will need to arrange a working lunch in the middle or whether it is appropriate to break off for lunch.

If you plan an afternoon meeting, will you provide lunch first? Will the meeting finish in time to allow those travelling some distance to get home at a reasonable hour?

People tend to work better before a meal than after. Thus, you may want to sequence the agenda topics so that the more difficult discussions take place before lunch.

Accommodation

If people have to stay overnight before or after a meeting, ensure that you/they have the budget to do so. It is courteous if you are the owner or organizer of a meeting to book overnight accommodation on behalf of your participants. If you do so, make sure that they are aware of the payment arrangements – have you paid in advance, or guaranteed the room for them to settle the bill on arrival or departure? Your organization may have an agreed lower rate in certain hotels and an upper spending limit for accommodation and meals.

Check:

- the proximity of the accommodation to the venue
- the cost of the room
- which meals, if any, are included in the room rate
- whether WiFi is available (and, more importantly, whether it is free). Increasingly people want to work in hotels and easy and free access to WiFi within their bedrooms rather than in public areas makes their stay more comfortable (and productive).

Send participants a map showing both the meeting venue and the overnight accommodation, indicating the distance between the two and how to get from one to the other.

Preparing participants for the meeting

It may be useful to talk to participants who are expected to present at the meeting to ensure that they understand the purpose of the meeting and the reason why they should present. Reiterate the timing of their topic – both the start time and the duration – and check that they are comfortable about what they have been asked to do.

Summary

Every meeting should have a clear purpose which is known and understood by the participants. The agenda should combine scene-setting information and a running order and should exclude 'Any other business'. Send invitations only to those who can make a valid contribution to the meeting's purpose, and, in writing the invitation, consider the question 'What would I want to know if I were being invited to this meeting?' Use the checklist in this chapter to ensure that the venue is fit for purpose and think carefully about the timing and sequencing of the meeting. Remember that some participants may need overnight accommodation before or after the meeting, and remember to brief anyone who is expected to present at the meeting.

Fact-check (answers at the back)

1. The starting point in preparing for a meeting is:
   a) Determining the purpose of the meeting ❏
   b) Sending out invitations ❏
   c) Deciding who should come ❏
   d) Writing the agenda ❏

2. Any other business (AOB):
   a) Should usually be included in an agenda ❏
   b) Should always be included in an agenda ❏
   c) Should be an optional extra in an agenda ❏
   d) Should generally be excluded from an agenda ❏

3. People tend to work better:
   a) Before lunch ❏
   b) After lunch ❏
   c) Over a working lunch ❏
   d) Without lunch ❏

4. The role of the meeting recorder is:
   a) To record the meeting so those not attending can hear what happened ❏
   b) To make notes of significant points arising from the meeting ❏
   c) To write down everything that is said, verbatim ❏
   d) To collect evidence which may be used against meeting participants ❏

5. It can be useful to hold meetings away from the workplace because:
   a) It reduces distractions, like e-mail and interruptions from colleagues ❏
   b) It is cheaper ❏
   c) It's nice to get away for the day ❏
   d) Hotels and conference centres have better meeting rooms ❏

6. It is useful to brief participants who are going to address a topic at the meeting because:
   a) They need to know that you will be on their side in the meeting ❏
   b) They need to know the politics surrounding the issue ❏
   c) It gives them the option to decline the invitation to the meeting ❏
   d) They need to understand the purpose and timing ❏

7. You should inform the administrators at an external venue of the name of your meeting, your organization and your participants so that:
   a) They can meet, greet and guide people to the meeting room ❏
   b) They can boast in their marketing literature that your organization is their client ❏
   c) They can have coffee and croissants ready for your arrival ❏
   d) They can prepare name badges in advance of the meeting ❏

8. Check on the corporate spending limits for meals and accommodation so that:
a) Participants can make sure they spend up to the limit ❑
b) Participants can make sure that they don't overspend ❑
c) Participants feel guilty that you are spending money on them ❑
d) You can catch participants out if their expense claims are too high ❑

9. When you send an invitation to a meeting:
a) Simply include an address – people should be able to find their own way to the venue ❑
b) Tell people to ask directions when they get close to the venue, because it may be tricky to find ❑
c) Just give them a postcode so they can use satellite navigation to find the venue ❑
d) Include a map and directions to help people to find the venue ❑

10. When determining who should be invited to a meeting:
a) Err on the side of inviting too many, because that way you won't offend anyone by missing them off the list ❑
b) Err on the side of 'less is more' and invite the smallest number possible to keep the meeting short ❑
c) Take advice if you are unsure about who can best contribute ❑
d) Invite the people who can tell a good story and will entertain the others ❑

CHAPTER 23

Participating in a meeting

As a participant in a meeting you have rather more to do than simply turn up!

If you attend a meeting and say nothing, then you have contributed nothing to the meeting's success.

If you dominate the meeting, whether or not you have more of use to offer than some of the other participants, then the meeting served little point other than as a platform for you to air your views, and others will question their own attendance and may resent you.

You may be nervous about contributing, feeling that others have more experience, more seniority or more useful things to offer than you.

You may be bored by the meeting and subconsciously display signs of your boredom to others.

In this chapter we'll look at the skills you need to get the best out of a meeting and to contribute most effectively to its success. We'll start with a self- assessment and use it as the basis for much of what follows. Answer each question honestly – answering quickly will yield a more truthful view than answering slowly. When you have completed the assessment, read the analysis below to see what your score signifies.

While the assessment carries no scientific rigour, it will indicate the areas in which some development would yield rewards for you.

Your participant skills	1 Never	2 Occasionally	3 Frequently	4 Always
I am comfortable in meetings, greetings and social talk before a meeting begins				
I am a good listener and genuinely interested in the answers others give to my questions				
I allow others to finish making their point before I speak				
I am confident when making a point or stating my views				
I am concise and articulate in stating my case in a meeting				
I'm good at reading and understanding others' body language				
I'm aware of my own body language and how others may interpret it				
My body language suggests engagement and self-confidence				
I am able to assert myself when I have something useful to say				
I am able to concede when I am wrong				
I can control the tone of my voice when I feel nervous or anxious				
I dress appropriately for each meeting I attend				
I listen carefully to what other people are saying in a meeting				
I am thoroughly prepared for every meeting I attend				
I know what my objectives are before I attend a meeting				
I always do the background reading required of me before a meeting				
I carefully review the notes of the previous meeting				
I research in advance the views of the other participants at a meeting				
I share a common purpose with the other participants at a meeting				
If a meeting is not relevant to me, I will not attend				
Totals				

Analysis	
20–39	You have a lot of work to do to develop your participant skills. Make sure that you understand what is expected of you when you accept an invitation to a meeting, do the background preparation and make sure that you contribute actively and appropriately
40–59	You have the basic participant skills and now it's time to hone them so that you can contribute even more effectively
60–80	Your meeting skills are good. Now it's time to turn them from good to excellent

Before the meeting

Do your homework:

1 Discover why the meeting is taking place – what is its purpose?
2 Find out who owns it.
3 Do the background reading.
4 Pick up on topics which are of particular interest or relevance to you and decide whether there are particular contributions you want to make to them.
5 Check how to get to the venue and how long it will take you.
6 Double-check the timing.
7 Check the dress code.

The social aspect of a meeting

Meetings, greetings and business cards

You arrive 20 minutes before the start of a meeting. Other participants are starting to congregate. Some are familiar and some are new to you. It's time to introduce yourself.

Do not underestimate meetings and greetings. We form impressions of others within 5–7 seconds of meeting them and, whether or not they are accurate, others will treat us as though their impression of us is true. Did you ever meet someone whom you disliked at first and then grew to like? Or perhaps you liked someone at first and then grew to dislike them? Either way, your first impressions were wrong. Unfortunately, most of us will act as though they are right, rather than suspending our judgement until we get to know someone a little better. The way in which you meet and greet someone counts enormously towards their perception of your credibility. If they like you on first meeting they are more likely to be sympathetic towards the views you express. If they dislike you, they are more likely to attack your views or, at best, not take you very seriously.

Let's start with handshakes. When you shake someone's hand, grasp their hand in yours with a flat palm and a firm grip, and shake their hand up and down two or three times. Do not offer your hand to be shaken – a handshake is an active greeting, not a passive display of submission. Equally, do not offer your fingers – there is little more unpleasant to someone with a good, firm handshake than to be offered a set of fingers to waggle.

A weak handshake sends out the wrong signals. It puts you on the back foot with a domineering or aggressive person, who, whether consciously or subconsciously, will see you as a person they can dominate or bully.

As you shake hands, smile at the other person, look them in the eyes and make sure that your eyebrows are momentarily raised and lowered. Socially functional people (and chimpanzees) flash their eyebrows in a fraction of a second on greeting others. Socially dysfunctional people (and chimps) keep their eyebrows still.

As you smile and flash your eyebrows, give your name – twice! For example, I would say 'Hello, I'm David – David Cotton'. When people meet for the first time, they are often focused inwards, worrying about how they appear to others. For this reason, they tend not to hear others' names properly on introduction. If you say your first name, then your entire name, it will sound entirely natural and double the chances that they will remember who you are. It's then easier, and less embarrassing, for them when they come to introduce you to others, to remember your name and introduce you without having to say 'I'm sorry, I didn't catch your name'.

Listen to other people's names and repeat a name as you hear it, to help you to remember it. For example, if someone says 'Hi, I'm Pat', say 'Hello, Pat, it's nice to meet you'.

Many people claim to be poor at remembering others' names on first meeting. In reality, many of us are so focused on ourselves and the impression that we are creating that we don't listen well when others tell us their names.

Try this. When someone introduces themselves, tell them it's nice to meet them and use their name – 'It's very nice to meet you, Ahmed'. Then mentally repeat their name to yourself several times as you look at them and listen to them talking. As you meet the next person, do the same again, then glance back at the first person and ensure that you still remember their name. This simple repetition of the name, once out loud and several times silently, with a few checks back to each person you have met, will help you remember many names.

When the meeting starts, if you are able to address people by name, your credibility will rise. Remembering someone's name first time sends a message that they were important enough to you to merit you remembering them, which is very flattering to them.

Here's an interesting quirk for you. When two men meet socially or in a business setting, they should always stand slightly angled to each other. If a man greets another face on, it feels as though they are 'squaring up' to each other and gives the impression of being confrontational. When a man and a woman meet, they should stand facing each other. If a man angles himself towards a woman it will feel as though he is 'sidling up' and has another agenda. Two woman are generally comfortable either angled or face to face and will often stand closer to each other, even on first greeting, than two men or a man and woman. These little things make a big difference to others' level of comfort with you. And from that comfort comes credibility.

If you exchange business cards after the initial greetings, make sure you know something of the culture of the people you are meeting. In Japan, for example, business cards are generally offered and received with two hands, studied and then left on the table in front of the recipient during a meeting. In Western society, cards tend to be offered and received one-handed, briefly studied and then pocketed.

Seating

Ask the Chair if there is a seating plan. If there is none, sit where you can catch the eye of the Chair easily, so you can indicate clearly when you want to speak. Be tidy, putting your briefcase or computer bag out of the way and ensuring that you have all the paperwork, pens and other equipment you need in front of you when the meeting starts.

Presence

Switch off all your toys – mobile phones, BlackBerrys, computers, iPods, iPads and anything else which has an off switch – and put them out of sight. If you are serious about attending this meeting, then you should demonstrate that you are present. A communications device on the table in front of you will simply distract you, which is discourteous to other participants, suggesting that your work is more important than the meeting in hand.

Knowing who's who

If there are several people around the table who are unfamiliar to you, it's worth sketching a table plan and noting their names. Knowing others' names will give you more confidence to address them.

Listening

Now the meeting has started, it's time to listen. Are you a good listener? Are you hearing what is actually being said or what you expect someone to say?

Scribble some brief notes as you listen to others speaking, so you can address directly what they said rather than something half-remembered or misattributed.

Reading people

William Glasser,5 an eminent psychiatrist, says that from around puberty until death we will have, hard-wired into our brains, certain drivers of behaviour and we will seek out those things which meet the needs of our drivers. If we find them, we will tend to be happy and contented. If we do not, we will tend towards unhappiness and discontent.

There are five drivers:

- love and belonging
- power and status
- freedom
- fun
- survival.

Most of us will have one as a primary driver of our behaviour and another as a secondary driver. The other drivers will be less important to us. While we may have a temporary shift to a different driver according to situation, most of us will seek to fulfil our primary and secondary drivers throughout our lives.

The five drivers are relatively easy to spot in others and, once we know them, we can treat them like 'hot buttons' to press in order to get the best out of them and out of our relationships with them.

Let's look at the characteristics of these drivers:

1 *Love and belonging*. People with this driver tend to be drawn towards teamwork, seeking out the camaraderie of others and feeling uncomfortable and isolated if they cannot work in a team. In meetings, you will see them seeking consensus and wanting to be sure that others agree and approve of any ideas that they put forward.

2 *Power and status*. People with this driver want recognition. They want to stand out from the crowd. In meetings you'll see them airing views contrary to those expressed by others because immediate agreement may suggest that they don't know their own mind and would bring them down to the same level as the other participants. Don't be subservient to them, but openly acknowledge their ideas. If you have

a good idea, even if you are certain that it is right, suggest that this is something you wanted to bounce off the others and then look at the person driven by power and status and ask them directly '[Name], what do you think?' They will find something to change, but are more likely to accept your idea because you flattered them by asking them first.

3 *Freedom*. People driven by freedom want autonomy. They feel constrained by rules and are uncomfortable with processes. Give them the space to create ideas and be careful in the language you use to address them, avoiding statements like 'you must' and 'the rules state…'. Do not expect them to be 'teamy', but tap into their potential for great creativity. If you can engage them and get them on your side, they can provide a wealth of new ideas unconstrained by 'the way we do things around here'.

4 *Fun*. People driven by fun may seem the most difficult to work with because their primary driving force is enjoyment and others may take a meeting extremely seriously. Fun people will make jokes, appear to deviate from the subject under discussion and give the impression of not taking anything seriously. In reality, they are listening very closely to what others say – they have to in order to find the fun in it. Like the traditional Shakespearean 'fool', they are able to see through pomposity and starchiness and get to the nub of an issue very quickly. Fun and humour are creative and, if you channel their creativity, you'll see that they have a lot to contribute to a meeting.

5 *Survival*. At its basic level, you are unlikely to meet people at work with survival as their primary driver, because it's about not knowing where your next meal will come from or whether you will have a roof over your head tonight. However, each of us can switch to another driver temporarily as our life circumstances change, and you may well meet people who feel concerned for their livelihood, threatened in their jobs or generally uncomfortable with their current position who will display the behaviours of someone driven by survival. Treat them kindly, but not patronisingly. Be factual without being harsh.

Knowing when to speak and asserting yourself

When you first join a committee or working group, or find yourself in a corporate meeting, it's easy to think that everyone else knows more than you, has more experience and therefore has more valid contributions to make. Step back from this for a moment: you were invited to the meeting, and so you have a right to be there. If you sit in silence you may learn a great deal but you will have contributed nothing and may not get a repeat invitation. Most people around the meeting table are happy to accept you as a valid member of the group with something to say. You have a right to speak and a right to be heard.

One of the best ways of speaking at a meeting if you are a little nervous is to ask a question. Don't worry about sounding silly or naïve. When someone else speaks, say, for example, 'Tell me a little more about that' or 'I'm not familiar with that – would you mind expanding on it?'. Generally the person you address will be pleased to say more, and you will have made your first contribution.

Knowing when to speak can be difficult. In formal meetings, contributions are made through the Chair and people motion to the Chair that they wish to speak. An astute Chair should be looking for non-verbal signs that people want to contribute and invite comments if they know that you have expertise in a particular area. In less formal meetings, it's usually a free for all in which you get to speak by jumping in at an opportune moment. In the early stages, notice how other people successfully indicate that they want to speak and then follow their lead.

Be bold when you speak. Avoid apologies and do not play the 'I'm the new kid on the block' game for too long because this will annoy seasoned meeting-goers. Clearly and audibly say what you have to say. Stick to the point. If you want to make a bold assertion, it can be useful to start it with 'In my own experience...'. Your own experience is incontrovertible – whether or not others agree with your point, they cannot argue with your experience!

Presenting within a meeting

Sometimes you will be asked to make a short presentation within a meeting. Be concise and argue your case or make your key points very clearly. If you have the chance to prepare beforehand, it's useful to have a structure for your presentation.

Presentations have a beginning ('Tell them what you're going to tell them'), a middle ('Tell them') and an end ('Tell them what you told them'. Do not introduce more than two or three key themes and do not overrun. Nobody will mind if your presentation is shorter than the allocated time.

There's a useful mnemonic to help you structure the introduction to a presentation. Although designed for longer presentations, it can be adapted for a shorter presentation. Remember 'INTRO':
Interest/impact
Needs
Timing
Range
Objectives

Interest/impact: grab people's attention right at the beginning with an interesting statement or, better still, a question that makes them sit up and listen. Avoid telling them your name and saying 'I'm here to talk about xyz' – be interesting!

Needs: a simple statement which indicates why they should need to listen to you.

Timing: how long you plan to speak.
Range: the themes you will cover.

Objectives: what the participants will take away with them at the end.

Here's an example. Imagine you lead a team that sells widgets and are addressing the sales team at their regular meeting:

(Interest/impact) 'Welcome! Last week we bid for one of the biggest contracts in our history. It would have netted us 15 million euros. Our sales manager, George Brown – alas no longer with us as of Friday – led the bid. (Need) Had George understood that the tendering company wanted both widgets and wodgets, he might have been here today to share his success. Unfortunately, George had immersed himself in the wonderful world of widgets and knew little about our company's other offerings, and so was unable to cross-sell them. (Timing) Over the next 20 minutes, (Range) I'm going to introduce you to the humble wodget, how it's made, what it looks like and our pricing structure so that (Objective) you will feel rather more comfortable than our friend George in cross- selling our products and be able to come back and share your triumphs with us.'

Many of us will feel reasonably confident sitting down but less so standing up. Our brain sends out a rush of adrenaline as a protective mechanism, and this adrenaline allows us to fight or run away from the thing which frightens us (the 'fight or flight' syndrome). Because we can neither beat up the other meeting participants nor run away from them, we are left with the side-effects of undissipated adrenaline, which may include a dry mouth, butterflies in the stomach and shaky hands and legs. You can reduce your nerves through good preparation, rehearsal, a little deep breathing, making notes of keywords and breathing deeply before you start. Do not have a cold drink because it tends to tighten your vocal cords and your voice will sound strained. A warm drink is better. The more practice you have, the easier it becomes.

Summary

You have a right to attend a meeting and you are expected to contribute. If you know the purpose of a meeting, you can make a reasonable guess about why your experience is relevant and therefore what is expected of you at the meeting.

Do all the background reading and ensure that you have taken all the actions assigned to you at an earlier meeting.

Rather than go along with prepared speeches, think about the points you would like to make and, when the chance comes, indicate that you want to talk and make your points. There is nothing worse than thinking after a meeting 'I wish I had said something at that point'.

Meet and greet with confidence, listening to and repeating others' names and giving your own clearly, twice.

When the meeting starts, listen and observe. Notice the level of formality or informality and act at that level. See what drives others' behaviour and use that in responding to them so that they can see that you understand them, even if you don't agree with them. Be free from distractions.

Above all, remember that you have a right to contribute and your contributions are as valid and valuable as anyone else's.

Fact-check (answers at the back)

1. When meeting and greeting:
a) We form impressions of others in around a minute ❑
b) We form impressions of others in around 30 seconds ❑
c) We form impressions of others in 5–7 seconds ❑
d) We form impressions in around 2 seconds ❑

2. Our first impressions:
a) May be wrong ❑
b) Are invariably right ❑
c) Are always wrong ❑
d) Don't matter ❑

3. Having your phone on during a meeting:
a) Is perfectly acceptable. As a professional, you are expected to multitask ❑
b) Sends out a signal that you have more important business to attend to than the meeting ❑
c) Sends out a signal that you are important and boosts your credibility among the meeting participants ❑
d) Relieves the tedium of the meeting ❑

4. Sketching a table plan:
a) Will help you to remember where you were sitting when you return from a break ❑
b) Is a useful distraction during a boring meeting ❑
c) Is generally a waste of time ❑
d) Helps you to know who's who so you can address them with more confidence ❑

5. Glasser's five behavioural drivers are:
a) Love and belonging, power and status, freedom, fun and survival ❑
b) Love and belonging, money, freedom, fun and survival ❑
c) Love and belonging, power and status, recognition, fun and survival ❑
d) Love and belonging, power and achievement, reward, fun and survival ❑

6. One of the best ways to talk for the first time in a meeting is:
a) To make a bold assertion ❑
b) To ask a question ❑
c) To interrupt the most vocal participant ❑
d) To ask the other participants if they would mind you speaking ❑

7. When you speak for the first time at a meeting:
a) Apologize ❑
b) Start by saying that you really don't know much about the topic ❑
c) Be relatively aggressive to establish your right to speak ❑
d) Do not apologize ❑

8. In the INTRO mnemonic, which helps you to introduce a presentation, 'I' stands for:
a) Instruction/information ❑
b) Information/interest ❑
c) Interest/impact ❑
d) Instruction/impact ❑

9. If you are nervous about speaking:
a) Have a drink of cold water ☐
b) Have a warm drink ☐
c) Do not drink anything ☐
d) Drink a small amount of alcohol before the meeting ☐

10. When you go into the meeting room:
a) Check whether there is a seating plan ☐
b) Sit wherever you are most comfortable ☐
c) As a courtesy, let everyone else sit down first and take the remaining seat ☐
d) Sit nearest to the door so that you can leave early if the meeting is boring ☐

CHAPTER 24

Chairing a meeting

Without a Chair to maintain some level of control, many meetings would descend into disorder. The Chair plays a crucial role in ensuring that a meeting meets its objectives. The role brings with it a certain degree of power and good deal of responsibility.

Many organizations rotate the chairing of a regular meeting, and so, even if you are relatively junior within an organization, you may be expected to chair a meeting. This chapter sets out the skills, tools and techniques which are needed for effective chairing. Let's start with the Chair's Charter – a checklist of the things which a good Chair will do, and which will set a benchmark for you as you develop your chairing experience.

We worked with a board of directors who were obsessive mobile phone users. We ran a three-day event for them and confiscated their phones, giving them to a temporary secretary who was hired to take their calls and pass on messages during breaks, when they were allowed to use their phones again.

On day one, the directors were nervous and twitchy, missing their fix.

On day two they were visibly calmer.

By day three they said that they felt like a burden had been lifted from them, and they were experiencing a new-found sense of freedom.

We heard afterwards that it became common practice in their own organization to ban phones from meeting rooms.

The Chair's Charter

- I demonstrate the behaviours that I expect from participants
- I check before the meeting that everyone has been notified of it
- I do all the appropriate background reading before a meeting
- I schedule regular meetings of the same group one year ahead
- I compile the agenda, either alone or with someone else who will be attending the meeting
- I allocate time slots to agenda items based on how critical they are, how divisive I believe the discussion will be and how many items we must cover during the meeting
- I check the action points from the last agenda and note which ones I need to deal with under 'action points from last agenda'
- I am not tolerant of failure to complete the actions agreed at the last meeting – I expect that those who agree to actions will take those actions
- I check that the air temperature in the meeting room is comfortable and that there is reasonable ventilation
- I do not sacrifice humour for the sake of seriousness, but I do expect us to work through the agenda

- I sit in a position where as many participants as possible can see me
- I start meetings absolutely on time
- I set out the purpose of the meeting at the outset and check that everyone understands it
- I check the base level of understanding of a topic before we discuss it in detail
- I do not deviate (nor allow deviation) from the meeting agenda
- I am impartial in all matters discussed in the meeting
- I listen to what is said and ask clarifying questions to ensure that everyone understands the points being expressed
- I allow everyone to be heard, whether or not I agree with their viewpoint
- I use other facilitative techniques to stimulate discussion
- I do not allow anyone to dominate the meeting, regardless of their seniority or perceived importance
- I do not allow subgroup conversations during the meeting
- I ask all participants to switch off telephones, BlackBerrys, computers and other equipment before the meeting starts
- If someone chooses to use a telephone or BlackBerry during the meeting, I stop the meeting and ask them to switch it off
- I handle disruptions calmly and patiently and will not let them spoil the meeting
- I summarize what has been said and check that I have done so fairly
- I observe participants closely and use their body language as a gauge of the pace and atmosphere of a meeting
- I ensure that agreements and action points are recorded
- I encourage quiet participants if I believe that they can make a useful contribution
- I check that everyone knows the actions they must take following the meeting
- I finish every meeting exactly on time – I have a reputation for working to time

It's a long list and some of the elements require considerable skill and diplomacy.

Let's look at some of these in more detail:

Demonstrating what I expect from others

The Chair's role is a leadership role and, in any leadership position, what you do and say gives permission for everyone else to do and say the same things. You must be a role model for good conduct at all stages before, during and after the meeting.

Checking action points from the last meeting

One of the early agenda items is 'actions from the last meeting'. If people do not undertake the agreed actions, then there was no point to the meeting. Meetings are undertaken to produce results of some kind, and you should politely indicate that you are not tolerant of failure to take those actions. Even less forgivable is a failure to notify you or others before the meeting of the reasons why you have not undertaken those actions.

Starting on time

A meeting is said to be 'quorate' when an agreed minimum number of people have arrived at the allotted start time and 'inquorate' when they have not. If you are chairing a fairly regular meeting, find out what number makes the meeting quorate and, if you have the required minimum at the start time, then begin. You have no obligation to help late arrivals catch up. As a role model you should demonstrate and encourage punctuality.

Purpose and understanding

At the start of the meeting, welcome everyone and state the reason for the meeting. At the start of each new agenda topic, check that everyone understands the topic, its importance and the background to it. Very often a small number of people will debate something hotly and, when the Chair asks for other contributions, someone will shyly admit that they did not really understand what was being discussed.

Make sure that you have done all the necessary background reading before the meeting. Put someone on the spot, asking them for their comments on a background paper. This will demonstrate what you expect of others when you chair the meeting. If they are embarrassed because they have not done the background reading, that's their problem!

Keeping on track

It's easy to get side-tracked in a meeting. A chance remark can lead everyone away from the topic and the meeting loses its way. One of your jobs as Chair is to bring everything back on track. Do it gently (at least at first), suggesting 'We seem to have drifted away from the topic in hand', and use it as an opportunity to summarize the discussions up to that point. Then invite someone to continue.

Ensure, too, that you stick to the agenda throughout.

Impartiality

You must remain impartial during a meeting even if everything inside you is screaming out that the opinions you are hearing are wrong. If you show bias towards a particular side in an argument then it will seriously damage your credibility.

Allow everyone an equal opportunity to speak even if you disagree fundamentally with their viewpoint.

Facilitation skills

If a meeting is designed to create new ideas, then it's useful to have some facilitation skills to draw on rather than addressing every agenda item by discussion and debate only.

> A colleague and I once facilitated a meeting of directors and senior managers in a major organization to determine their ten-year IT strategy. We told them that a ten-year IT strategy was not feasible, but they insisted that they had sufficient knowledge and background to achieve it.
>
> We were instructed to facilitate only and to offer no other contributions.

> During the meeting, the participants determined that their organizations would not introduce the internet nor embrace e-mail because each was a passing fad and would go away. True to our word we ventured no opinions. The Chair's job can sometimes be frustrating!

In traditional brainstorming, the facilitator describes the issue and the participants call out ideas for a given time period to resolve it. Each is recorded and when time is up the items are discussed and their merits are debated. This method is somewhat flawed. We solve problems best by stepping back, putting them on the backburner and engaging in other things. During this time, our subconscious continues to work on them. The answers tend to come to us when we are thinking of something unrelated to the problem in hand. Traditional brainstorming does not allow our subconscious to get to work. Brain-friendly brainstorming resolves this problem:

● Brainstorm for two minutes.
● Stop for two minutes and discuss something unrelated to the issue.
● Brainstorm for another two minutes.

You'll notice that we generate ideas for a very short time. The break in the middle allows our subconscious to continue to work on the issue, and we tend to generate more creative ideas after the break than before it.

Now we have a long list of ideas and need to debate each one to see whether it is worthwhile. Not only is this time-consuming, but people tend to be proprietorial about their own ideas, defending them even when others can see they have little merit. To quickly sift the worthwhile ideas, use 'PMI' (plus, minus, interesting). 'Plus' items are worth further consideration; 'minus' ideas are not worth further discussion; 'interesting' ideas may be useful at another time but are not strictly relevant to the current issue.

Call out each idea in turn from the list that the group has generated. Ask for a show of hands for each one. How many think that the idea is a 'plus'/a 'minus'/an 'interesting' idea.

Go with the majority and mark the ideas in green for plus, red for minus and a neutral colour like black or blue for interesting. In just minutes you have created a list of ideas which are worthy of further discussion without having to control more senior or vocal people who will make more noise in support of their own ideas. In this version, democracy rules!

Force-field analyses

If you are planning a project or a change, then the force-field analysis is useful in helping you to see what may help the project/change to succeed and what may hinder it. It's a structured form of brainstorming.

Write a brief description of the central issue down the centre of a flipchart sheet, and head two columns either side as 'Helpers' and 'Blockers'. Ask participants to call out or write directly on the sheet everything they think will help the project/change to succeed and everything they believe may hinder it. Ask them to assign scores to each idea on a scale of 1–10 according to its importance. Alternatively, ask them whether each idea is a big, medium or small issue and draw arrows whose length corresponds to their rating (long, medium and small). You might like to use green for helpers and red for blockers for greater visual impact. The idea is to use this as the basis for discussion of the major stumbling blocks which need to be reduced or removed and the helpers which you may be able to capitalize on to remove some of the blockers. It's a simple and useful visual tool for sparking discussion.

Helpers	Statement of the issue	Blockers

Difficult people and situations

The meeting hog is an attention-seeker who addresses every topic and replies to every question. Hogs stop others from having their say, and when they do say something worthwhile, it's often taken less seriously because it's seen as part of their general chatter. Because hogs want attention, one way to deal with them is to *give* them attention. When Fred is about to speak for the fifth time, say 'Come on everyone, don't make Fred do all the work!' Fred will be delighted because you have given him the attention he craves, suggesting that he is the hardest worker there. He is the only one in the room who does not realize that he has just been told to be quiet. If subtle tactics don't work, tell the hog either openly in front of the whole meeting or quietly in a break that, while you appreciate his or her level of contribution, it's really important that others have an equal say and ask him or her politely to give others a chance.

Inevitably you will encounter conflict in meetings. Two people who disagree publicly often become more heated than they would privately because they do not want to lose face.

Conflict tends to come from three main sources – professional disagreement, power struggles and personality issues. If you already have a reputation for running tightly controlled meetings, there is a reduced chance that the conflict will become serious. If you do not, then it's time to toughen up, insisting that:

● people speak only after raising a hand
● only one person may speak at once
● everyone will be given an opportunity to contribute.

Depersonalize the conflict: if one participant says something derogatory about another, instruct them that personal comments are not appropriate. Get people to focus on 'what' they have a problem with and not 'who'.

Ask objective questions of those in conflict. Ask them what solution would make something acceptable to them.

If it's appropriate and you have the authority (and courage), it is worth talking individually to the warring factions after the meeting to get to the bottom of their issues and try to prevent a repeat of the conflict.

Summarizing

Every so often, pause the discussion and summarize.
Summarizing:

- shows participants what they have achieved
- creates a natural break which may lead people to feel that the discussion has run its course
- helps participants to take stock of all the views they have heard and so make more reasoned judgements or counter-arguments.

To summarize well you have to listen well, sometimes asking clarifying questions to check your own understanding and to help others who may be reluctant to admit a lack of understanding. Make brief notes of key points rather than writing verbatim what people have said so that you can spend more time observing the group.

Observing body language

A major myth about body language is that single gestures have universal meaning. For example, many books will tell you that someone sitting with arms folded and legs crossed is feeling defensive and shutting others out. This may be true. Equally, they may be cold, or perhaps they always sit like that! What is true is that we are generally consistent in our personal use of body language, just are we are consistent in accent, dialect and word choice in our spoken language, but we will still sound different from everyone else.

Body language can tell you a lot about how people are feeling, but it's best to observe *changes* rather than continued *similarities* in body language. If someone is happy, cheerful and contributing well, with arms folded and legs crossed, then you can reasonably assume that this is just a comfortable way for them to sit. If they suddenly change their posture for reasons other than physical comfort, then you can guess that their emotional or psychological state just changed, and it's these changes that you should begin to notice. If you meet the same people regularly, pay careful attention to the words they use, their voice tone and their body language and start to notice how each aligns with the others as their moods change.

In a meeting, observe these same signs and you'll start to notice when someone wants to speak, dislikes what they are hearing, dislikes another person, or agrees or disagrees with someone else. Use these subtle clues to bring different people into the discussion at the most appropriate time, gently silence the person who is aggravating others and offer a chance to speak to someone who is reluctant to assert themselves.

Recording the meeting

One of your jobs as Chair is to ensure that significant outcomes are recorded. Ask someone before the meeting to act as recorder and tell them what you would like them to note.

Traditionally, 'minutes', a blow-by-blow record of proceedings, were taken, and in some government circles and organizations where an audit trail or public record is needed, this is still commonplace. For the most part, people find minutes boring and simply skim through them, looking for their own name or agreed actions.

In most organizations, only action points are recorded. Action points are the specific actions which people are to take as a result of the meeting and should exclude opinions, interpretations (unless agreed by all) and anything judgemental.

The recorder should note:

1 the agreed action
2 who has agreed to take the action
3 when they have agreed to do (or at least begin) it
4 anyone else whose involvement is needed to make the action possible.

At the end of the meeting, the Chair should ask the recorder to read back the actions and check that they are a fair summary of what has been agreed.

Ensure that action points are distributed within four days of the meeting.

Drawing out quiet participants

If you sense that someone has something useful to say but is reluctant to speak, make a point of smiling and nodding in their direction as someone else is talking, both to show that you are aware of them and to hint that you are about to invite them to speak. Say, for example, 'Linda – I think you have something to add here...?' Always thank new members of a group or reluctant speakers for their contributions to let them know that what they have said is fine and to encourage them to contribute more.

Closing a meeting

At the end of a meeting, you may choose to ask people to evaluate the meeting (more of this in Chapter 26). Ask the recorder to read back the agreed actions and amend them if necessary. Agree the date of the next meeting if appropriate. Thank people for attending and contributing and tell them you look forward to seeing them again.

Summary

The Chair has a vital role in making meetings work. As Chair, you are owner, organizer, facilitator, mediator and the only impartial person at the meeting. You set the tone for the meeting and dictate and demonstrate the commitment and professionalism you expect from others. If you play your role well, people will feel that their presence and contributions are valued and the meeting will be a motivating experience.

From the outset, imagine that you have just been invited to a meeting. What would make it work for you? Think through the participants' experience right from the start – from receiving an invitation, through the meeting itself to follow-up after the meeting. What are the big things that must be right? What are the little niceties that could make it a more pleasant experience? What can you do which, if you get it right, people may not even notice but if you get it wrong they will? What can you do which, if you get it right, people will notice with pleasure?

Set out to create a model which others will copy. Get it right first time and your credibility will soar.

Fact-check (answers at the back)

1. As Chair, I have the right to:
   a) Expect that people will carry out agreed actions if they have time ❑
   b) Expect that people will carry out agreed actions ❑
   c) Expect that people will carry out agreed actions if they find them sufficiently interesting ❑
   d) Expect that people will carry out agreed actions if, on reflection, they believe that they are appropriate ❑

2. In chairing a meeting:
   a) I believe that anyone attending should already understand the basics of any topic on the agenda ❑
   b) I assume that nobody understands the basics of a topic before we discuss it, so I explain them first ❑
   c) I am not worried about whether or not participants understand a topic before discussion – they will pick it up as they go along ❑
   d) I check that everyone understands the basics of a topic before we discuss it ❑

3. In chairing a meeting, if I do not agree with a participant:
   a) I offer an opposing viewpoint ❑
   b) I have a right to tell them that their viewpoint is wrong ❑
   c) I allow them to have their say anyway ❑
   d) I ask them to be quiet ❑

4. In chairing a meeting:
   a) I allow the most senior people to dominate ❑
   b) I ensure that everyone has an equal opportunity to express their views ❑
   c) I dominate the meeting, because my role is the most important ❑
   d) I make sure that the quietest people get to speak more than the usually vocal people would ❑

5. In chairing a meeting:
   a) I draw out quiet participants where it appears that they can make a useful contribution ❑
   b) I force quiet people to speak so that they don't waste our time by coming to a meeting but contributing nothing ❑
   c) I make no effort to draw out quiet people, because they are making no effort to speak ❑
   d) I prefer that quiet people don't speak because they often embarrass themselves and other participants ❑

6. In chairing a meeting:
   a) I start on time as long as the meeting is quorate ❑
   b) I wait until everyone has arrived before starting ❑
   c) I start on time whether or not we are quorate ❑
   d) I don't pay much attention to timekeeping ❑

7. In chairing a meeting:
a) It doesn't matter whether or not we keep to the agenda ❏
b) It is important that we keep to the agenda ❏
c) It's fine to change the agenda midway if people are not finding the original agenda very interesting ❏
d) I don't usually work from an agenda ❏

8. PMI stands for:
a) Plus, minus, interesting ❏
b) Plus, minus, inconsequential ❏
c) Positive, minus, interesting ❏
d) Plus, minus, inconsistent ❏

9. To resolve conflict:
a) Tell people that you will send them away if they continue to fight ❏
b) Allow them to argue their point and hope that the conflict will burn itself out ❏
c) Toughen up by insisting, for example, that people speak only after raising a hand and that only one person may speak at once ❏
d) Shout at the offending participants ❏

10. It is important that we record:
a) Minutes of the meeting – a verbatim account of the discussions ❏
b) Things which the recorder thought were interesting enough to note ❏
c) Nothing – a record is unimportant ❏
d) Action points – the agreed actions that participants will take after the meeting ❏

CHAPTER 25

Virtual and other types of meeting

We've focused so far on a fairly traditional style of meeting – bringing people together in small groups to talk to each other face to face. While this remains the most common form of meeting, there are many alternatives.

Increasingly, organizations use technology to cut costs and lower their carbon footprint. It may be considered unethical for participants to travel vast distances when they could as easily talk online or use other technology. Travelling time is expensive and may be unproductive. If you can meet others without leaving the office – indeed, without leaving home – you have a longer day in which to do something useful.

Technology brings its own rewards and challenges, and each form of technology-supported meeting is very different.

A large conference-style meeting has a very different feel to a small group meeting.

Audio meetings are cheap and can be very effective, but don't allow you to see the other participants.

Stand-up meetings – some organizations insist that meeting rooms have no seats!

And let's not forget the humble one-to-one meeting, the mainstay of the appraisal and objective process and one of the most common forms of meeting in working life.

This chapter is all about alternative types of meeting, how they differ from the traditional small group face-to-face meeting and the techniques and skills needed to make them work.

> I was once invited from the UK to New York to attend a meeting to discuss a project on which I had been working. I was told that the meeting would last around 45 minutes. As much as I love New York, it would effectively take three working days – travel to New York, attend the meeting, wait for the return flight, fly overnight and return in the early hours of the morning too tired to work effectively.
>
> I asked if the organization had a video conferencing kit. They said they did and I told them that I had it within view of where I was sitting.
>
> They still insisted that I went to see them in person. I asked why and they said 'Because we need a warm body!'.

Audio conferences

Psychology professor Albert Mehrabian has stated that, in face-to-face communication, we only have three ways to communicate – words, voice and non-verbal communication (body language) – and each affects the extent to which we are liked by others: words: 7 per cent; voice: 38 per cent; non-verbal communication: 55 per cent. In audio conferences we lose the ability to see each other and thus the dynamics change. Because we cannot pick up on others' body language, we have to rely more on tone and word choices to create an impression of each other. Some keys to effective participation are to use rich language, modulate your voice, speak as fluently and clearly as you can and listen!

Audio conferences, which require people to dial into a central number and type in a PIN on their telephone, are:

- relatively cheap (compared with face-to-face meetings)
- quick to set up (many organizations have an account with a telecoms company which offers an audio conference service)
- effective for relatively small groups (I once trained 40 people via audio conference, but for a meeting a group of seven to eight people is fine).

We'll assume here that you have called the meeting. To set up an audio conference, call the telecoms service provider to ask for the dial-in number, a PIN code for you as the facilitator and a separate PIN code for the participants. The meeting will typically be shorter than a face-to-face meeting, because people have a lower threshold of concentration when they have only one channel of communication. Your agenda, however, will look very much like the standard agenda which we have already seen. E-mail the agenda and invitation in good time for people to plan to attend, and request confirmations of attendance.

Make sure that you dial in first – ideally a couple of minutes before the meeting starts. It's annoying for participants to be invited to a meeting only to discover that the Chair is not there. As with a face-to-face meeting, start on time to show that you mean business.

It's quite tricky to chair a meeting when you cannot see people. Participants in audio conferences are often side-tracked by e-mails and other distractions, and you need to keep the meeting sharp and snappy and involve participants by name. The audio conference is no place for long speeches.

Take a roll call to check who is on the line (some audio conference facilities announce the names of each person as they join), thank people for attending and state the purpose of the meeting. Reiterate the duration of the meeting, and stay within that time.

You may want to distribute a set of slides or other supporting materials to participants and refer to these during the meeting. This tends to increase engagement, because it gives participants something to look at and something to do with their hands – all of which reduce the likelihood of them losing focus.

Video conferences

Top tips for video conferences:

Test the equipment at each end before the participants arrive – arrange with a colleague in the other location to arrive early and check that the picture and sound are working.

Position chairs so that everyone can be seen. Sit in each seat in turn and ask your colleague to do the same in the other location.

Check that each can see the other in every position and note whether some people will be obscured by others.

Test the sound from different parts of the room. Most video conferencing kits use a flat, circular table-top microphone which should be able to pick up sound from all corners of the room.

Choose a well-lit, well-ventilated room. If you can switch off air conditioning, this will reduce the background noise picked up by the microphone.

Have a facilitator in each location. Their job is to marshal conversation and ensure that only one person at a time is speaking.

Have everyone introduce themselves, location by location.

Ask people to remain relatively still unless they are taking deliberate actions which they intend others to see. Too much movement may become distorted on screen.

Keep the meeting relatively short – an hour is probably long enough.

Ensure that you have the number of the technical support department on hand.

Web meetings

Web meetings are growing in popularity. Broadband internet costs are lower than ever, bandwidth has increased and most working people have internet access at home as well as in the workplace. There are many commercial platforms for web meetings, such as Sametime, Webex and LiveMeeting, which offer a similar set of tools, including desktop sharing, video, a virtual whiteboard, question and answer features, the ability to raise a virtual hand to alert the facilitator, breakout facilities and online chat.

Some organizations find that sound and video drain their internet resources and prefer that only the facilitator (or Chair) be visible through video and that participants speak to each other through standard audio conferencing.

Because you will typically see only the facilitator and not the other participants, you have to be self-disciplined in a web meeting, using the hand-raise tool to tell the facilitator when you want to speak rather than simply talking. If you are using the in-built sound tools, most web-meeting software allows the facilitator to mute everyone and then virtually hand the microphone to participants one at a time.

A big problem with web meetings is that participants, because they cannot see each other, tend to mentally drift off and do other things while the meeting is taking place. Some software shows the facilitator when a participant is doing something else on their computer, and a good facilitator will use the chat facility to send a private message to the offending participant to nudge them back into the meeting. Many facilitators will use the display capabilities to show slides or other visuals to try to engage the participants.

Some golden rules for web meetings:

1 Keep web meetings short – shorter than a face-to-face meeting.
2 Allow a little small talk at the beginning, as you would in a traditional meeting.
3 Set out a clear purpose for the meeting at the outset.
4 Do things in ten-minute bursts with breakouts and variety of presentation to constantly re-engage participants.
5 Make the meetings as interactive as possible – ask opinions, stimulate debate and use the survey/question tool to pose questions.
6 Use video if your infrastructure will stand it.
7 Treat web meetings as seriously as you would any other meeting.

Stand-up meetings (no seats allowed...)

A big complaint about meetings is that they take too long. A simple solution is to remove the seats! The average stand-up meeting takes around 20 minutes, which seems to be the longest that anyone can comfortably stand. Often a high bar-style round table is used for paperwork and to give people a writing surface. Sometimes, participants simply stand.

The benefits:

- speed
- people stick to the point
- decisions are made quickly.

The disadvantages:

- decisions may be made too quickly with insufficient debate
- people become aggressive when others wander away from the point
- some constantly complain that they do not like standing up.

Do not dismiss stand-up meetings before first trying them. In some organizations, they have become the norm.

> One of my clients held all of its meetings standing up.
> They had other rules, too:
>
> Agendas must be posted out at least three days before a meeting.
>
> A maximum of two items could appear on the agenda.
>
> A meeting must last no more than 20 minutes.
>
> Topic owners have 2–3 minutes to speak on their topic and 2–3 minutes' discussion time afterwards.
>
> Action points are recorded and must be e-mailed to participants within 20 minutes of the end of the meeting.
>
> They were (and remain) a remarkably efficient and profitable organization.

Large conference-style meetings

The sheer scale of conference-style meetings demands a level of project management that is unnecessary in a straightforward round-the-table meeting. We'll assume for these purposes that you have been asked to attend one, either as a delegate or as a speaker.

Let's focus here on a few highlights for you as a speaker:

Equipment

- Rather than operate any equipment yourself, you may need a sound technician. The best technicians set sound levels, adjust them a little when participants arrive (because acoustics are different in empty and full rooms) and then leave them alone. They are on hand constantly to monitor and fix any problems as they arise and are otherwise unobtrusive. The worst technicians are obsessive knob-twiddlers, never content with the sound balance and playing with it incessantly to the detriment of the event.
- If you are speaking at the event, check all the equipment before you start.
  - Check whether you will have a collar (lapel) microphone, a microphone taped to your face, a handheld 'lollipop'

mike or a fixed mike on a stand or behind a podium. The style of microphone affects your performance. If you are nervous at speaking in front of a large group, go for the lapel mike so you can move around and rid yourself of excess adrenaline, or the lollipop, which allows movement and gives you something to do with your hands, but note that juggling the lollipop and your speaker notes can be tricky!

- If you are using slides, check how to change them. Some technicians give you a signalling device to tell them when to change or blank a slide. Some give you a remote control allowing you to change the slides yourself. If you are using the former, work through the slides with the technician, showing them which are build slides, for which a single click simply makes the next bullet or image appear. Be aware of sleepy and distracted technicians who miss your signals. If using the remote device, note that you can point it towards the audience and it will still work, rather than pointing at the screen, which means that you have your back to the audience.

Now let's assume that you are a delegate.

Speaking from the floor

If you speak from the floor at a large event, you need to be heard. Usually, someone will hand you a lollipop-style hand-held microphone. You may have witnessed people tapping the end, blowing into them and shouting '1–2–3, testing', which makes them look amateurish. At a well-organized event, the microphone is switched on, the sound level has been checked and the technician has adjusted the volume for the mike you are holding. Most hand-held mikes are directional, so hold them angled just a little down, so people can still see your face as you talk, rather than underneath your chin.

Do not shout – the mike will pick up a normal speaking voice. Speak a little slower than usual because microphones tend to pick up the lower voice tones, and if you speak quickly they have the effect of making you sound as though you are mumbling. Do not gesticulate with your mike hand, because it will move the mike away from your mouth and nobody will be able to hear you.

Ideally, stand up to talk so that people can see you. If you choose not to, for the first few moments after you begin to talk the other participants will be looking around trying to see where your voice is coming from and may miss the first things you say. Be inclusive as you speak, looking around the room and making eye contact with as many people as possible. Be concise, sit down and hand the mike back to whoever gave it to you. Do not switch it off!

Managing a large group

If you are chairing a large meeting, be aware that some people will be nervous at speaking to a large group. It's useful to ask questions of the whole group which demand a show of hands or give participants a red and green card and ask them to show approval or disapproval of an idea by raising their card.

Arrange lots of table group breakout activities. Give table groups flipchart paper and ask them to brainstorm and present back their ideas. Set up competitions between table groups. Introduce variety and interactivity to stimulate the participants and make them feel actively involved.

One-to-one meetings

One-to-one meetings are, by their nature, very personal. When you are arranging a one-to-one meeting, consider the following:

- What is its purpose?
  - For example, appraisal, objective setting, disciplinary, personal development planning, counselling, coaching, mentoring.
- What is the most appropriate location?
  - People feel more comfortable on home ground, so it's a nice concession to go to them rather than have them come to you. Alternatively, you may choose to meet on neutral ground, even out of the workplace.

- How sensitive is the issue?
- How much does the other person need to know in order to prepare for the meeting?
- Stick to the timing you have agreed and do not cancel.
  - This is really important if you are dealing with a sensitive issue. Last-minute cancellation or re-arrangement can be very upsetting for someone who has steeled themselves to come to the meeting.

Partial attendance meetings

Have you ever agreed to attend a meeting because there was one significant agenda item and then found yourself dutifully sitting through irrelevant items, trying not to look bored and desperately wishing you could be somewhere else? People who have no particular vested interest in a subject can bring a fresh perspective to a discussion. Most of us, however, are distracted by the thought of the work piling up in our absences and do not consider these meetings a great use of our time.

If all the invited participants are based in the meeting location, then partial attendance is a useful way to manage your own and others' time. Time slots are allocated to each agenda item and the Chair ensures that the group adheres strictly to those times. A five-minute 'turnaround' break is scheduled between agenda items. During the short break, participants for whom the next topic is irrelevant leave and are replaced by others for whom it is relevant. It's a good way to ensure that the meeting is focused and that the best people are there for each discussion.

There is a danger that if the timings are not accurate then either the core group in the meeting finds it has a lot of spare time on its hands because an item finishes early and the next participants are not yet due, or there is a domino effect on waiting participants if an item overruns from which it may be difficult to recover. Partial attendance meetings rely on good planning and strong chairing.

Summary

Think carefully about the purpose of a meeting, the available budgets and equipment, the locations of the intended participants and the time needed for the meeting, and choose the meeting type accordingly.

This table may help you to decide, assuming that you have access to the relevant equipment. One-to-one meetings are exceptional and have been excluded.

	Traditional face-to-face and partial attendance meetings	Stand-up	Web	Audio	Video	Large conference style
Large number of topics	Y	N	N	N	N	Y
Small number of topics	Y	Y	Y	Y	Y	N
Long meeting	Y	N	N	N	N	Y
Small number of participants	Y	Y	Y	Y	Y	N
Large number of participants	N	N	Y	Y	Y	Y
Low budget	N	Y	Y	Y	Y	N

We have assumed here that stand-up meetings take place between people in the same location (it could be considered rude to invite people to travel some distance to a meeting and then not offer them a seat). You'll notice that web, audio and video all follow the same patterns – low budget, able to accommodate both small and large numbers of participants, and useful when there is a small number of topics and the meeting is designed to be relatively short.

In an organization steeped in tradition, it may be difficult at first to persuade people to break away from the standard face-to-face meeting. Use cost–benefit analysis to persuade people to try other forms of meeting and to use technology. And good luck with the stand-up meetings!

Fact-check (answers at the back)

1. We should consider using technology as an alternative to traditional meetings because:
a) The technology is there, so we may as well use it ❏
b) It may cut costs and lower carbon footprints ❏
c) It's a bit of a novelty ❏
d) It's more fun than a real meeting ❏

2. Albert Mehrabian says that in face-to-face conversation, likeability is based on:
a) Words: 38 per cent, voice: 7 per cent and non-verbal communication: 55 per cent ❏
b) Words: 55 per cent, voice: 38 per cent and non-verbal communication: 7 per cent ❏
c) Words: 7 per cent, voice: 38 per cent and non-verbal communication: 55 per cent ❏
d) Words: 10 per cent, voice: 10 per cent and non-verbal communication: 80 per cent ❏

3. In running an audio conference, I can engage participants by:
a) Distributing slides or other supporting materials for use during the meeting ❏
b) Cracking jokes to amuse them ❏
c) Presenting to them and inviting questions afterwards ❏
d) Asking them to tell funny stories ❏

4. In running a video conference:
a) It's best to have no facilitator ❏
b) It's best to have just one facilitator ❏
c) It's best to rotate the faciliation of the conference ❏
d) It's best to have a facilitator in each location ❏

5. In running a web meeting:
a) The facilitator should leave all microphones on so people can contribute when they wish ❏
b) The facilitator should mute all microphones and hand the virtual microphone to someone who has raised their hand ❏
c) The facilitator should mute all microphones except those belonging to people who can make a real contribution to the meeting ❏
d) The faciliator should not allow anyone else but him/ herself to speak ❏

6. Stand-up meetings:
a) Are useful when there are a lot of topics to discuss ❏
b) Are designed to punish unruly participants ❏
c) Are never useful ❏
d) Keep the participants sharply focused ❏

7. In large conference-style meetings:
a) It's best to sit down when speaking from the floor ❏
b) It's best to stand up when speaking from the floor ❏
c) It's best not to contribute from the floor ❏
d) It's best to walk to the front before contributing ❏

8. In a one-to-one meeting:
a) The location is unimportant ❏
b) The location is very important ❏
c) The location is not relevant ❏
d) The location is the most important consideration ❏

9. Partial attendance meetings:
a) Ensure that people only spend time in the sections of the meeting which are relevant to them ❏
b) Effectively put people's expertise on trial ❏
c) Ensure that people do not interfere in areas which do not concern them ❏
d) Have no purpose at all ❏

10. It's important to use alternative types of meeting because:
a) Kids these days are used to technology and so expect to use it for meetings when they first start working ❏
b) Traditional meetings have been shown repeatedly to be useless ❏
c) They may be a better match for the group, the meeting type and the budget ❏
d) We should always try new things ❏

CHAPTER 26

After the meeting

Purposeful meetings are an integral part of a working process. Just as a meeting must be well prepared, so it should be followed up effectively and quickly to ensure that people have completed delegated action points, are working in the ways they agreed during the meeting, are prepared for the next meeting and are happy with the way that the meeting was conducted.

Think of it a little like training. If a group of people attend a training course and afterwards return to their workplace and assume the same old routines, then the training course serves little purpose. If the training is part of a broader programme and the learning from the training is immediately applied in the workplace, then both individuals and the organization will see some benefit from it. If a meeting is seen as an interruption to work and when people return to the workplace nothing changes, then the meeting has served no purpose. Action-based meetings and good follow-up prove the worth of the meeting.

In this chapter we'll look at the things you should do after a meeting, either as a participant or as the Chair of the meeting.

The first follow-up action, a debrief, may actually be taken at the end of the meeting.

Meeting debrief

The most successful organizations are constantly looking for ways to improve. Meeting debriefs are one such method of improvement.

At the end of a meeting, it is useful to discover:

- what worked well and should be continued, either as it stands or with some tweaking
- what could be changed, and how to make future meetings better.

Normally, the Chair leads this discussion. If that's you, you must be sufficiently resilient to take implied or direct criticism. If the meeting didn't work well, some of the reasons may be attributable to you. We looked earlier at single-loop and double-loop learning. The meeting debrief should be an example of double-loop learning, in which we look at the underlying causes of a problem and change our methods so that we do not see the problem again.

Here's some typical feedback that you may hear in a meeting debrief, along with some responses or suggestions for improvement:

- 'I did not feel that people listened to me.'
  - Be cautious here. It may be that the person was boring or what they said was irrelevant. There may be other factions who disagreed with them. Children often claim that nobody is listening to them when what they mean is that nobody agrees with them. Adults sometimes act like children...
- 'I did not get much of a chance to speak.'
  - Be sure that you give people both an equal opportunity to speak and the same air time. If on reflection you did not do this, accept it quietly and tell people that you will make doubly sure next time that people have equal opportunities to speak.
- 'One or two people seemed to dominate the meeting. The rest of us couldn't get a word in edgeways.'
  - As above.

- 'I do not feel we spent enough time on XYZ, which was an important issue.'
  - Explain that timings were given on the agenda, which was distributed some time before the meeting. If participants believe that timings are inaccurate for future meetings, adjust them accordingly.
- 'We spent too much time talking about XYZ and there were more important issues which did not get sufficient air time.'
  - As above.
- 'The meeting was too long.'
  - Ask for a general view on the ideal length for such a meeting. Go with the majority view.
- 'The meeting was too short.'
  - As above.

Action points

As a meeting participant, you will probably have agreed to take certain actions after the meeting. If you do them while the meeting is still fresh in your mind, it's likely that you will do them with more enthusiasm than if you leave them for later. Have you been to a meeting and felt fired up by the discussions and keen to follow up on your agreed actions, but then you go to a different meeting, with a new cast of characters, and suddenly the newer actions you've agreed to undertake seem more interesting?

If we do not act while the memory of a meeting is still fresh, there's a danger we will not complete the actions we committed to at all. When you accept a meeting invitation, schedule time in your diary for the next day to do the follow-up work. Do it immediately and you will associate it with the meeting, and next time you meet the same group it will be easier to remember the actions you took in relation to that meeting.

As the Chair, your responsibilities include distributing action points and following up on them. Ideally, distribute action points within 24 hours of the meeting, so they are still fresh in everyone's minds.
Check the due dates assigned along with the action points, give people one or two days' leeway, and then call them to ask

them about their progress. Be positive and encouraging but do not tolerate poor excuses for inaction. If someone tells you that they have not yet started, ask them when they will and say you will call them again the day after their revised starting date to see how they are getting on. If they have not begun the next time you call, you need to probe a little deeper.

Common reasons why people do not do the actions assigned to them:

1 *They were unclear on what they agreed to, but were embarrassed to say so.* Gently help them to understand, without being patronizing or judgemental, so that they feel able to undertake the agreed action with more confidence. Do not make any reference to their embarrassment at the next meeting; treat their now completed action as you would any other.

2 *They are not competent to take the action.* Do not berate them for agreeing because they may have done so in good faith, believing that they were capable and possibly wanting the experience of doing something which later proved too difficult. Ask them what help they need and put them in touch with others who can help them. With luck, the assistance they receive will help them to be self-sufficient next time.

3 *They have other priorities.* So does everyone else the moment they leave a meeting. At the time of the meeting, everything seems terribly important and possibly urgent. After the meeting, we go back to our everyday work and our routine kicks in again.

4 *They claim not to have time.* Be careful of this one. Claims of being busy are not well tolerated in some organizations. In 1938, C. Northcote Parkinson published *Parkinson's Law*,6 which states that 'Work expands so as to fill the time available for its completion'. No matter what we have to do and how long we have to do it, it will take the time available for that amount of work. When people claim not to have had the time to complete an action, it may be true or it may be that it was simply not a high priority for them. Ask them if they need help from someone else who attended the

meeting or if there are any particular obstacles or concerns which make completion difficult.

5 *Organizational politics*. Someone agrees to an action but then falls foul of organizational politics, discovering that the action will arouse political or other sensitivities. You may not be close enough to the politics (nor inclined to get involved) to be able to deal with it. Just try to understand the situation, offer support or encouragement in any way which seems appropriate and hope that the situation can be resolved.

Follow up with people you met for the first time at the meeting

Sometimes you will go to a meeting and meet someone you find inspiring, funny or useful and you'll want to stay in touch with them. You've exchanged business cards or contact details. Now what?

Every contact could some day be useful. You never know when:

- you will need someone else's specialist knowledge
- you will find yourself in a strange town and realize you actually know someone there
- you will want a new job.

It used to be said that six degrees separate any two human beings: we can connect ourselves to anyone else through our own connections, their connections and their connections' connections, etc. The internet-savvy world may have reduced the number to four or five degrees of separation. Even if the person you have just met does not appear to be useful to your career progression now, they may be in future or they may have a network which could be helpful to you.

After a meeting, send a short e-mail to your new contact telling them that it was nice to meet them and commenting on something interesting they said at the meeting. Ask if they would mind you contacting them when you are next in their area. If they agree, do it sooner rather than later to

427

keep the relationship warm. Many people are sloppy e-mail housekeepers and once you have sent them an e-mail, it's likely to remain in their account for a long time. An e-mail is a cheap way to get your name in front of them!

Alternatively, send them an invitation to connect through one of the online business networking services like Plaxo, Ecademy or LinkedIn. The default invitation is not enough – personalize the invitation and follow up when they accept.

If they look really interesting, send them an invitation to a work-related event which you think they may find interesting.

Private resolution of public conflict

Sometimes meetings degenerate into verbal fights. Two opposing parties start to snipe at each other and before long are engaged in a full-blown argument. As Chair, you have a duty to stop the fight. We looked at how you might do this in Chapter 24. The danger is that next time the two meet, the fight will resume. Have a quiet conversation with each of them after the meeting to see what the underlying causes of the conflict are and find some way to resolve them.

If emotions are running high at the end of the meeting, it may be difficult to have a rational conversation with either person, so wait a few days before making contact.

Talk to them individually (e-mail is too impersonal). Say that you had observed the friction between them and ask if it was purely related to the discussion topic or whether there is more to it. If the topic inflamed their passions, check that they are happy with the outcome. If it was the person, indicate (gently) that it's important to keep meetings as objective as possible and ask them to try and depersonalize any future arguments.

Preparing the agenda for the next meeting

If you have checked on completed action points, nudged defaulters, talked sagely to those who came close to blows and evaluated the meeting (either at the end or as a separate exercise), then you are in prime position to prepare for the next meeting.

You may want to include:

- a short section on the evaluation of the meeting
- a section on actions taken since the last meeting.

This nicely creates a sense of continuity from one meeting to the next.

Summary

After a meeting, reflect on:

- what you discussed and the impact and importance of the discussions for you, your colleagues and your area of work

- the actions that you have agreed to take and the ways in which you will tackle them

- whether or not the meeting:

  - met your personal objectives

  - met its overall objectives.

- how the meeting was conducted:

  - what you can learn from that, as either participant or Chair

  - what you would do differently in future meetings

  - who you met and wish to maintain contact with and how you will do so.

- who appears to have personality clashes:

  - are you able to do something about it?

Now plan your actions. If you were well organized, you would have allocated time for your action points the day after the meeting.

If you were not, now is the time to do this. Schedule time in your diary for the day after your next meeting for follow-up activities. Now prioritize your actions. Tackle the urgent and important ones first, then the important but not urgent ones. If they are neither urgent nor important, there was probably little point in agreeing to them, because nobody will notice whether you do them or not!

Fact-check (answers at the back)

1. It's useful to schedule time in your diary for the day after an important meeting so that:
   a) You can put off going back to your day job ❏
   b) You can take time off because the meeting was exhausting ❏
   c) You can call round the other participants and ask them what they thought of the meeting ❏
   d) You can undertake the actions to which you agreed ❏

2. A meeting debrief is designed to:
   a) Focus on things that went wrong so they can be fixed ❏
   b) Assess what worked well and what can be done better ❏
   c) Focus on things that went well so they can be done again ❏
   d) Assess who was a nuisance so they can be blamed or disciplined ❏

3. If someone claims that they did not have a chance to speak in a meeting, as the Chair you should:
   a) Dismiss the statement as nonsense ❏
   b) Consider whether this was, in fact, the case ❏
   c) Tell them they should speak up a bit ❏
   d) Not invite them to future meetings ❏

4. If someone claims that too much time was given to a single agenda item at the expense of the others:
   a) Dismiss the statement as nonsense ❏
   b) Tell them that they can have their turn to speak on a favourite topic at the next meeting ❏
   c) Explain that the timings appeared on the agenda which was circulated before the meeting ❏
   d) Tell them that you are in charge of timing but they have the right to question it ❏

5. It's best to take action immediately after a meeting because:
   a) It gets it out of the way so we can get back to our everyday work ❏
   b) We work better when the issues are fresh in our mind ❏
   c) It will keep the Chair happy, which is what it's all about ❏
   d) It's generally more interesting than our real work ❏

6. A common reason why people do not undertake their assigned actions is:
   a) They never intended to take the actions ❏
   b) They agreed to the action to appear to be doing something useful ❏
   c) They were not clear on the action, but embarrassed to admit it ❏
   d) They are too lazy ❏

7. In following up with new contacts after a meeting:
a) It's useful to send a personalized invitation to connect through an online networking service ❏
b) It's useful to send the default invitation to connect through an online networking service, because you do not want to appear overfamiliar ❏
c) It's best to wait for them to contact you ❏
d) It's useful to wait a few weeks to test whether or not they still remember you ❏

8. If two people argue fiercely during a meeting:
a) It's best to berate them publicly during the meeting ❏
b) It's best to talk to them individually a few days after the meeting ❏
c) It's best never to mention it again ❏
d) It's best to talk to them together a few days after the meeting ❏

9. In preparing the agenda for the next meeting:
a) It's useful to include items which suggest continuity between meetings ❏
b) It's best to avoid apparent continuity so that the approach is completely fresh each time ❏
c) It doesn't matter whether or not there is any sense of continuity between meetings ❏
d) It's useful to reverse the order of the last agenda to keep participants on their toes ❏

10. Parkinson's law states:
a) 'Work contracts so as to fill the time available for its completion' ❏
b) 'Work contracts so as to allow it to be completed within the allotted time' ❏
c) 'Work expands so as to fill the time available for its completion' ❏
d) 'Work expands so as to take more time than is available for its completion' ❏

CHAPTER 27

The perfect meeting

In this chapter we'll bring together everything you have learned in the form of a short story.

We'll meet two fairly junior members of an organization who have been asked to set up and run an important in-house meeting. Although they have attended many meetings, they have no experience of running one themselves. We'll see through their mistakes and the solutions they find how to set up, run and follow up after the perfect meeting. Along the way, they note what they would do differently next time. You may find their notes helpful in planning and running your own perfect meetings.

Meet the characters

Bob and Pat are junior managers in a large service industry. Each had an internship with the company the summer before their final year at university, and they started together at the company three years ago on a graduate induction programme. They are bright, ambitious and always seeking development opportunities. Bob is cautious and concerned about what others think about him. Pat throws caution to the wind and sometimes takes actions without considering the consequences. She is often frustrated by Bob's conservatism. He is scared that she will do something which casts them both in a bad light. Despite this, they are close colleagues, often working together, and they socialize with the same group outside work.

An instruction from above

Their director, Alison, sees running a meeting as a relatively high-profile development opportunity for them. She has given them an outline of the purpose of the meeting, a list of participants to be invited and told them that, because she is tied up in a project over the next couple of weeks, they should do everything they can to arrange the meeting, one of them should chair it and they should talk to her only if they encounter any issues which they cannot resolve.

Determining the purpose

Bob and Pat study the outline for the meeting.

'It's a bit vague, isn't it?', says Bob. 'It says it's a meeting of the regional directors to plan staff training and development and associated budgets over the next two years.'

'Seems clear enough to me', says Pat. 'What more do you need?'

Bob is unhappy at the lack of detail. He doesn't know many directors, knows little about current staff training and development plans, and doesn't know where to start with the agenda.

Pat scans the list of participants and sees that the HR Director, who is responsible for staff development, will be attending the meeting. She picks up the phone to call him. Bob stops her, saying that they should first decide what they need to know to get the best from the call. Between them they agree that they should find out about:

1 current training and development plans
2 significant planned and expected events in the organization which may have an effect on training and development
3 current training development budgets
4 attitudes of the directors towards training and development.

Pat makes the call. The HR Director, although pleasant, is busy. He offers to e-mail them the current plans and budget details but says that he is not in the best position to talk about planned and expected events. They should speak to someone else about this – he is vague about who could help them. He feels he would be speaking out of turn if he commented on other directors' attitudes, and this is something best gauged during the meeting. Bob is concerned that he sounds offended at the question. Pat is unconcerned.

They debate whether or not to call Alison and decide not to bother her just yet. They think they have enough to start creating an agenda. Pat makes a mental note:

> **Always determine the purpose of a meeting and discover as much as you can about it before attending**

Setting the agenda

Bob has checked back through the files and discovered that the regional directors usually use a standard agenda for their meetings. He talks to Alison's secretary, who provides a copy and remarks that this agenda is for their quarterly meetings, but that this is an additional, exceptional meeting called before the budgets are finalized because it could result in a big spend. She is unsure whether the standard agenda will work.

The standard agenda says:

- Action points from last meeting
- Director's report: Northern region
- Director's report: Southern region
- Director's report: Midlands region
- Review of action points
- Next steps and date of next meeting

'Doesn't tell us much', says Pat. 'Let's write our own.'

Bob is worried that any deviation from the standard agenda will annoy the directors, but Pat reminds him that this is an extraordinary meeting with a specific purpose and so the standard agenda is not relevant. Bob notes:

> **Create an agenda which is relevant to the purpose of the meeting**

They agree that they should talk through everything they know about the meeting and logically think through what will help them to get to the desired outcome – planning training and development over the next two years and creating a high-level budget for it.

Participants, they decide, will need to know where they stand now and where they anticipate the company is going – the current level of spending on training and development, the current breadth and depth of training and development offered throughout the company, any planned major projects which may generate a training spend and any forecast changes to the business which may in turn create training needs.

'Some of this we can provide as background reading', says Bob. 'We have the current plans and budget details. If people read this in advance they will be better prepared for discussion. I imagine each of the directors, if they are interested in people's development, will come up with ideas of how they would like to develop their own staff, and between them they should have some good ideas about things which may affect the plans and the spend.'

Pat is impressed. She jots a note to herself:

> It doesn't all have to be done in the meeting. Pre-reading can cut down on tedious discussion!

They begin to sketch out an agenda and assign names to specific topics:

Meeting subject: Determine the staff training plans and high-level budgets for the next two years from 1 May

Meeting objectives: Agree on the major requirements for training and development for all staff in the next two-year period, and estimate the costs of the training for budgetary purposes

Meeting organizers: Bob Jenkins and Pat Wilson

Meeting recorder: Vanessa Barton (they assume that Alison's PA will record the meeting)

Names of invited participants: Alison Meads, James Law, Selma Goode, Frank Abbott, Delia Mays

Venue, date and time: Meeting Room 14, HQ, 7 April, 09:45 am

Pre-meeting reading: Current year training plans and training budget (attached)

Apologies for absence

09:30	Coffee
09:45	Welcome and purpose
10:00	Review of current training plans and budget (Frank Abbott, HR Director)
10:30	Training requirements for Northern region (Selma Goode, Regional Director North)
10:45	Training requirements for Southern region (James Law, Regional Director South)
11:00	Training requirements for Midlands region (Delia Mays, Regional Director Midlands)
11:15	Anticipated business changes which will create training and development needs (all)
11:45	Proposed high-level budget requirements (all)
12:30	Summary of action points
12:45	Close

Happy that this covers everything, Bob insists that they ask Alison to review it before sending it out. A wise move, because she raises a number of issues in her e-mail back to them:

Bob, Pat

A nice start, but a few changes needed before sending it. Subject and purpose are fine. Best to ask me before commandeering Vanessa for half a day. She's far too busy and I can't spare her. While one of you is chairing, the other could record the meeting.

You've left the Ops Director, Bill Jones, off the list. He'll be mad if he doesn't get an invite and he always has something to contribute. If we start at 09:30, those travelling some way will have to come down the night before. You'll need to book hotels for them. Don't have the meeting in-house – you'll never get them to stay in the meeting room for two consecutive minutes. Take it offsite and don't spend more than the agreed limits. You're expecting people to have the bladder of a camel – no break for nearly four hours? I don't think so! You'll need to stretch the session on budgets a bit – always leads to an argument, so lunch will be needed. Could you please revamp it – I don't need to see it again before you send it.

Alison

The pair revise the agenda:

09:30	Coffee
09:45	Welcome and purpose
10:00	Review of current training plans and budget (Frank Abbott, HR Director)
10:30	Training requirements for Northern region (Selma Goode, Regional Director North)
10:45	Training requirements for Southern region (James Law, Regional Director South)
11:00	Break
11:15	Training requirements for Midlands region (Delia Mays, Regional Director Midlands)
11:30	Anticipated business changes which will create training and development needs (all)
12:00	Proposed high-level budget requirements (all)
13:00	Summary of action points
13:15	Close

The venue

Bob and Pat are uneasy about choosing an offsite venue and remember that the training manager, Jean Philips, uses a number of outside locations for training. She recommends a local hotel which provides sizeable meeting rooms and a good service at a reasonable delegate rate. They call, ascertain that a room is free on their required date and book it.

Preparing for the meeting

Pat sends out the agendas with an e-mail cover note and the background reading attached. Its subject is 'Training meeting' and the body of the note simply says 'Meeting agenda attached. Please respond asap.'

A week before the event, Pat has heard from nobody and Bob suggests they call each participant to check that they are coming. They are surprised when several directors deny receiving anything and, on searching for the e-mail, find it and say they had no idea what it was about so filed it for later reading. Some are angry because they had made other plans for the meeting day. They ask where the meeting is taking place and what it's about. Pat is tempted to tell them that all the detail is in the attachment, but holds back, sensing that they are already sufficiently annoyed. Ultimately, all agree to come.

Pat jots another note to herself:

> Next time I send out an agenda, spell out in the cover note what it's about, when it is and who people should respond to

Bob calls the hotel to finalize the arrangements. He has arranged the catering, asked that the room be set up in boardroom style, and requested a flipchart, pens, and a projector and screen. He has also arranged for those staying overnight before the meeting to stay at the same venue. He intends to provide his own laptop for the directors to show their slides.

The day of the meeting

Bob and Pat arrive an hour and a half before the meeting is due to start. Immediately, they encounter problems:

- The room is difficult to find and badly signposted.
- The power cable from the projector is trailing dangerously across the floor to the wall socket.
- The venue has provided whiteboard markers instead of flipchart markers.
- There is almost no space between and behind chairs.
- The room is small and claustrophobic and the air conditioning is noisy.

Bob talks to the conference administrator who, although happy to move the group to another room, says that the only other available room is a good deal bigger and there will be an additional charge for it. They have no flipchart markers ('Nobody ever complained before') and they promise to put up signs and tape down the cables. By 08:30, they have moved to a lighter, airier room with more space and good ventilation.

At 08:30 Alison arrives, a little flustered: 'I arrived at reception and nobody know who I was. When I told them which meeting I was coming to they directed me to the room number you gave on the agenda but there was nobody there. It's taken me five minutes to find you here.'

Pat explains that they have moved and the reasons why, and rushes to reception to tell them who's coming and where to direct people. Finally, the administrator puts up signs directing the participants to the appropriate room.

Alison asks where the agendas and other paperwork are. Bob says that he assumed people would bring it with them. Alison laughs and tells him to go and make copies.

Bob makes a mental note:

> Be explicit about what you need in the meeting room.
>
> Check out the room and equipment before the day of the meeting.
>
> Make additional copies of any required paperwork before the meeting begins.

> **Ensure that receptionists know who to expect and where to send them.**

Participants start to arrive, but by 09:45 two who are driving to the meeting from out of the area are still missing. Pat is keen that the meeting start, but Alison tells her that for this particular meeting they need everyone there from the beginning. Finally, at 10:00, the two other directors arrive. They say that they spent 15 minutes circling, trying to find parking and, unfamiliar with the area, had to spend another 15 minutes walking from the car park to the venue.

Pat makes another note:

> **Always send out a map, directions and details of nearby parking.**

Alison tells them to start. Pat is chairing and Bob is recording. The meeting starts well, and everyone is engaged and interested. Before James begins his report he asks Pat where his slides are. Bewildered, she says she hasn't got them. James insists that his secretary e-mailed them this morning. She explains that she came straight from home to the venue and didn't know that she should have expected the slides. James is annoyed but has the good grace to realize that she was not told in advance to expect the slides. Bob asks if he has them on a USB memory stick – luckily he does, and Bob sets them up for him quickly and the moment passes.

Bob and Pat both make a mental note:

> **Ask for supporting materials before the event.**

Everything continues smoothly until the discussion of expected business changes. Bill Jones mentions that one of the best call centre team leaders is leaving and Frank is furious, asking why he hadn't been told. Before long, they are having a full-blown row and Pat does not know what to do. Finally, she calls out 'Gentlemen, it's important that we stick to the agenda. Could you please continue this discussion after the meeting?

For now, we need to continue our discussions. Could I ask you please to remain objective in your discussions, rather than letting them become personal.' Bill and Frank hang their heads like naughty schoolchildren and out of the corner of her eye Pat sees Alison give her an almost imperceptible wink. The rest of the meeting is uneventful.

At the end, Bob reads back the action points. Because Bob is so fastidious that they are an accurate and uncontested record of what was agreed.

Lunch

The sandwich lunch has arrived and participants seem to be tucking in happily. All except Delia, who asks where the vegetarian sandwiches are. Bob says he wasn't aware that she had requested any and Delia says she assumed that any self-respecting venue would provide them without being asked. Bob says he will see what he can do and, on discovering that it will take at least 30 minutes for the venue's caterers to produce anything else, hurries to a local shop, where he buys a selection of vegetarian sandwiches, borrows a plate from a sandwich trolley outside a neighbouring meeting room and brings in the sandwiches. Delia appears very happy with them.

After the meeting

Bob and Pat meet Alison on the afternoon of the meeting to discuss what happened and what they learnt. Above all, they say, it's about attention to detail – walking through every stage as though you are a delegate, anticipating problems and not making assumptions. Alison tells them that, all in all, they have done a good job for a first attempt and that the other directors commented on how well the meeting ran.

'Now', says Alison, 'who's going to chase up the actions, and who's going to bang Bill and Frank's silly heads together?'

Summary

In the end the meeting was a success.

There were no major disasters and things which could have gone wrong were spotted early and remedial action was taken. Bob and Pat learnt a good deal from their experience and summarized well what they would do next time – walk through each element from the participants' point of view and avoid making assumptions.

Let's look at the truth behind those assumptions:

The assumption	The truth
People will read the invitation to a meeting	Only if it's absolutely clear that they are being invited to something. Be absolutely explicit
Unbidden, participants will send you slides and other supporting materials before the meeting	No they will not. You will need to ask for them
Participants will bring agendas and other supporting materials with them	Some will and some will not. Print additional copies for the defaulters
They will find the venue without difficulty	No they will not! Unless you send explicit directions, someone will struggle to find it
They will find a parking space	No they will not. Send them a map showing the local parking, the venue and the distance between the two
They will find their way from the car park to the venue	No they will not. Send them a map and directions from one to the other
Meeting rooms will meet high health and safety standards	They will not, because they are not designed by a Health and Safety Officer. Inspect the room for possible hazards before a meeting
Venues will automatically cater for special dietary requirements	Sometimes they will. Often they will not. Tell them in advance exactly what you want
Signage at meeting venues is generally good	It can vary enormously from completely absent to very detailed
Receptionists will know that your meeting is taking place, the correct room number and the names of people who will be attending	Only if you tell them. Take a list of participants to a venue and give it to the receptionist along with your mobile number to call if there are any problems

Fact-check (answers at the back)

1. Immediately after Alison's briefing, Bob and Pat:
   a) Had sufficient information to create the agenda ❑
   b) Had insufficient information to create the agenda ❑
   c) Had insufficient information to create a good agenda, but it didn't matter ❑
   d) Had far too much information to create the agenda, which just proved confusing ❑

2. The biggest problems which Bob and Pat faced arose because:
   a) What can go wrong will go wrong ❑
   b) The directors deliberately made things difficult for them ❑
   c) They lacked the experience to do anything properly ❑
   d) They made assumptions and did not walk through the plans step by step ❑

3. Was Pat correct in saying that much of the information about plans and budgets could be sent out as pre-reading?
   a) No, because the information should be read out during the meeting ❑
   b) No, because nobody would read it ❑
   c) Yes – it freed up time in the meeting for informed discussion ❑
   d) Yes, to test whether anyone actually does the pre-reading ❑

4. Were Bob and Pat safe to take a recommendation for a venue without checking it out for themselves?
   a) Yes, they should trust other people ❑
   b) It was risky – they were lucky this time ❑
   c) Yes. A venue is a venue. They are all pretty much the same ❑
   d) Absolutely not – they were very misguided ❑

5. Was it reasonable to assume that the venue would signpost the meeting room without a request to do so from Bob and Pat?
   a) No – it's best to set out precisely what you need ❑
   b) Yes – a venue should do these things automatically ❑
   c) It doesn't matter either way. People should be able to find their way to the meeting room without help ❑
   d) No – they should have made and taken their own signs ❑

6. Should a venue ensure that cables are taped down so that nobody trips over them?
a) No, it should be the responsibility of the meeting organizer ❑
b) No, people should have the sense to notice and step over loose cables ❑
c) Yes they should. Any professional venue should do this as a matter of course, especially when they provided the equipment ❑
d) Yes, and we should be prepared to sue any venue which fails to do so ❑

7. Was it safe for Bob and Pat to assume that people would bring agendas and other paperwork with them?
a) Yes, it's reasonable to assume that people will bring everything they need ❑
b) No – people cannot be relied on to do anything properly ❑
c) Yes. It would be unusual for professional people to forget anything ❑
d) Sadly not. People are forgetful and it's best to accommodate their forgetfulness ❑

8. Should Bob and Pat have sent out maps and directions?
a) Yes – it's a courtesy when people are coming to an unfamiliar area ❑
b) No – people should be able to find their own way ❑
c) They should not have chosen a venue which was hard to find ❑
d) No – they should simply have sent the address and the postcode ❑

9. Was Pat right to handle the dispute in the way she did?
a) Absolutely not. What she said was rude and made it worse because she was junior to the other people in the meeting ❑
b) It's a tricky one – maybe she was, maybe she wasn't ❑
c) Absolutely. In a formal meeting, the Chair outranks everyone else and has the right to be assertive in keeping order and getting the meeting back on track ❑
d) No, because she should not have been allowed to chair the meeting in the first place ❑

10. Is it reasonable to assume that a venue will cater for special dietary requirements without being asked to do so?
a) No, but they should be able to produce something appropriate on the day, whatever the requirements ❑
b) Yes – they should know that people have different dietary needs ❑
c) People should not be so fussy – they should eat what they are given ❑
d) No – it's best to tell them what you want ❑

7 × 7

1 Seven key ideas

- Meetings must have a purpose. A day of the week is not a purpose, so question why you need a 'Monday meeting'.
- Everyone else suffers the same level of meeting fatigue as you do. Do you really need a meeting, or could you resolve an issue by other means?
- Is 'information sharing' a valid purpose for a meeting? Haven't you got technology for just that? And if people are not using the technology, isn't that an education or management issue?
- Consider using collaborative problem-solving and decision-making techniques to enliven the meetings and re-energize them: brain-friendly brainstorming, reverse brainstorming, random word technique, World Café, PMI, Six Thinking Hats – the internet is awash with creative techniques which will bring a spark back to your meetings and generate new ideas.
- Only invite people with something useful to contribute to your meeting. Never invite people simply out of politeness. The larger the group (within reason) the slower and less effective the meeting will be.
- Remember, when planning or attending meetings, that time is the most valuable commodity of all.
- Give feedback to the Chairs or organizers of badly run or unsuccessful meetings. If they don't hear what participants think, they will continue to run time-wasting meetings.

2 Seven things to do

- **Ensure that your meeting has a purpose**. If you are the meeting owner, ensure that its purpose is clear - whether that be making a decision, agreeing actions or averting a crisis. Meetings are expensive: consider whether other channels would be more appropriate.

- **Turn off your phone before the meeting**. If your phone is on, you are not truly present in the meeting.
- **Read the agenda and prepare**. If you are unprepared, others have to waste meeting time explaining things to you that you should have known had you prepared properly.
- **Plan gaps between meetings**. If you have one meeting finishing at 10.30 and another starting at 10.30 you'll either have to leave one early, or join one late, neither of which is acceptable. Equally, you won't have time to get into the right mindset, find the right paperwork etc. for the second meeting. So plan a gap between meetings. If you have so many meetings back to back, you might question whether they are all of real value anyway...
- **Contribute**. If you choose to say nothing during a meeting, others may question why you have attended.
- **Give others space to talk**. Extroverts often speak in order to know what they think – they crystallize their thoughts by articulating them. Introverts tend to reflect before speaking – they crystallize their thoughts before articulating them. It is easy for the extroverts to dominate, allowing no space for their introverted colleagues. Be sensitive to your more introverted colleagues and invite them to speak.
- **Note the actions you have agreed to take**. And take them!

3 Seven things to avoid

- **Being late**. If you arrive on time, you're late. If you arrive early, you're on time. If a meeting is scheduled to start at 9.30 then arrive at 9.20 so that the meeting can begin on time.
- **Any other business**. This has no place in a well-designed agenda. In general, if it's not on the agenda, it shouldn't be discussed (unless it's an emergency, in which case, question whether it is a meeting topic at all).
- **Running over time**. Nobody will be upset if a meeting finishes earlier than scheduled.

- **Interrupting**. The greatest sign of respect you can show someone is to listen. Of course, if they simply won't shut up, have a quiet word with the Chair about keeping more control...
- **Arriving unprepared**. It's a discourtesy to others, it prolongs the meeting and is likely to make the meeting less effective.
- **Doing other work during the meeting**. It would be better to leave the meeting during agenda items which are not relevant to you than to do other work because you have nothing to contribute.
- **Attending irrelevant meetings**. As a rule of thumb, if you can't contribute something to the meeting nor learn from it, it's a waste of your time. Politely decline the invitation. If you are in a meeting in which a meeting is taking place, you may want to prime the Chair to invite you in only for the agenda items which are relevant to you.

4 Seven tips for online meetings

- **Test your microphone**. Research the best audio settings in an application. If you can't be heard clearly, you can't contribute.
- **Check your lighting**. If the light is behind you, it throws your face into shadow. Others want to see you. Remember that what you see on screen is what other participants see: if you can't see yourself clearly on screen, they can't see you clearly either.
- **Blur your background or buy a green screen**. Typically, you wouldn't invite your colleagues or clients into your home for a meeting, and virtual meetings can feel a little intrusive if you are working from home. Many virtual platforms (such as Zoom and Webex) allow you to blur the background so that others don't get that glimpse into your home.
- **Tell your housemates you are going to be in a meeting**. It can be embarrassing when others from your household wander behind you when you are conducting a serious meeting. Warn them, if your living circumstances allow, that you will be in a meeting, and that they should avoid a starring role in your meeting!

- **Arrive a few minutes early**. This way you can check your connection before the meeting officially starts.
- **Keep your camera on**. You wouldn't hide behind a black screen in a face-to-face meeting, and you have no reason to hide in a virtual meeting. You damage trust and credibility if you have your camera off. We have been using online platforms for so long now that 'my WiFi signal is not very good' is becoming a lame excuse!
- **Observe others closely**. Virtual meetings offer a unique perspective – you see everyone else's face from the front, where in some face-to-face meetings you may not see them clearly at all around a table. This gives an opportunity to see their changing emotions (albeit in two dimensions) and gauge, for example, those who support or are not convinced by what you are proposing.

5 Seven great quotes

- 'If you had to identify, in one word, the reason why the human race has not achieved, and never will achieve, its full potential, that word would be 'meetings.' Dave Barry
- 'Meetings should have as few people as possible, but all the right people.' Charles W. Scarf
- 'As a leader, you must consistently drive effective communication. Meetings must be deliberate and intentional – your organizational rhythm should value purpose over habit and effectiveness over efficiency.' Chris Fussell
- 'Meetings are at the heart of an effective organization, and each meeting is an opportunity to clarify issues, set new directions, sharpen focus, create alignment, and move objectives forward.' Paul Axtell
- 'The longer the meeting, the less is accomplished.' Tim Cook
- 'Meetings are a symptom of bad organization. The fewer meetings the better.' Peter Drucker
- 'You have a meeting to make a decision, not to decide on the question.' Bill Gates

6 Seven things that will enliven your meetings

- Rotate the Chairing of the meetings. A new Chair brings a fresh perspective.
- Change the venue regularly.
- Incorporate breakout sessions.
- Use the full features of your virtual platform (breakouts, whiteboards, polls, reactions etc.).
- Start the meeting at an 'odd' time. Who says it must start on the hour or half hour? Whatever time you choose, start it at exactly that time.
- Assign a role to each person before the meeting so that they are actively involved even when not speaking. Roles could include recording each time the meeting strays off topic; recording how often participants interrupt each other; recording the number of times people look at their phones during the meeting. Each person reports back at the end of the meeting, without naming and shaming, and the net effect is to improve the way everyone participates in meetings.
- Have stand-up meetings. Remove the seats from the meeting room (being sensitive to those who are unable to stand up during the meeting). Extend this idea to virtual meetings, asking participants to stand up throughout. The result is shorter, more focused meetings.

7 Seven tips for team meetings

- **'Tuned in'**: Each participant has a piece of paper with 'Tuned in' written on it. When the Chair or a speaker feels that people are not listening, they hold up their 'Tuned in' sheet. All other participants must hold up theirs, too. The last one to hold up their sheet must pay a forfeit of some kind. Make sure that it is nothing too embarrassing!
- **Interruption donations**: Each time someone's phone rings during a meeting, they must make a donation to a charity.

- **My passion**: Include a regular slot on your team meeting agenda for someone to talk about a personal passion, which should have nothing to do with their work.
- **Regular polls**: Use polls to gauge the team's mood or feelings about work-related issues. Constant, well-placed temperature checks can help the team to feel that the organisation is listening.
- **Monitor energy levels**: Monitor your own and others' energy levels. If you notice them dipping, acknowledge it, ask others how they are feeling, suggest a break, a different activity, a stretch - anything which changes the mood.
- **Prioritise collaboration, not announcements**: Use collaborative tools such as Slack to gather and disseminate information and use your team meetings to work together on problem-solving, decision-making and planning.
- **Ask more than tell**: Pose questions to stimulate discussion. Questions open doors, where statements close them. Well-formed questions open up debate and fresh thinking.

Answers

Part 1: Your Business Communication Masterclass

Chapter 1: 1c; 2d; 3c; 4a; 5b; 6b; 7a; 8b; 9c; 10d

Chapter 2: 1c; 2d; 3b; 4a; 5b; 6c; 7d; 8c; 9c; 10a

Chapter 3: 1b; 2c; 3d; 4a; 5d; 6d; 7c; 8b; 9a; 10b

Chapter 4: 1d; 2d; 3b; 4a; 5c; 6b; 7a; 8d; 9c; 10c

Chapter 5: 1a; 2d; 3b; 4b; 5a; 6c; 7d; 8d; 9a; 10c

Chapter 6: 1b; 2c; 3d; 4d; 5a; 6c; 7b; 8b; 9a; 10d

Chapter 7: 1c; 2a; 3d; 4b; 5b; 6a; 7c; 8a; 9d; 10c

Part 2: Your Persuasion and Influence Masterclass

Chapter 8: 1b; 2a; 3d; 4b; 5a; 6b; 7a; 8c; 9b; 10a

Chapter 9: 1c; 2a; 3d; 4b; 5a; 6a; 7a; 8b; 9c; 10a

Chapter 10: 1c; 2a; 3d; 4a; 5a; 6d; 7c; 8b; 9b; 10b

Chapter 11: 1a; 2d; 3c; 4a; 5d; 6a; 7b; 8c; 9a; 10c

Chapter 12: 1c; 2c; 3a; 4b; 5a; 6b; 7b; 8d; 9c; 10a

Chapter 13: 1c; 2a; 3d; 4a; 5a; 6b; 7d; 8c; 9b; 10b

Part 3: Your Public Speaking Masterclass

Chapter 14: 1b; 2d; 3d; 4b; 5a; 6b; 7c; 8c; 9d; 10a

Chapter 15: 1c; 2a; 3a; 4b; 5c; 6a; 7b; 8c; 9d; 10b

Chapter 16: 1d; 2a; 3c; 4b; 5c; 6d; 7b; 8c; 9d; 10b

Chapter 17: 1a; 2b; 3c; 4a; 5b; 6d; 7b; 8a; 9c; 10a

Chapter 18: 1b; 2b; 3c; 4d; 5b; 6a; 7b; 8a; 9c; 10c

Chapter 19: 1c; 2b; 3c; 4d; 5b; 6b; 7c; 8a; 9d; 10c

Chapter 20: 1b; 2a; 3c; 4d; 5b; 6b; 7c; 8a; 9c; 10b

Part 4: Your Successful Meetings Masterclass

Chapter 21: 1b; 2c; 3a; 4b; 5c; 6d; 7d; 8a; 9c; 10b

Chapter 22: 1a; 2d; 3a; 4b; 5a; 6d; 7a; 8b; 9d; 10c

Chapter 23: 1c; 2a; 3b; 4d; 5a; 6b; 7d; 8c; 9b; 10a

Chapter 24: 1b; 2d; 3c; 4b; 5a; 6a; 7b; 8a; 9c; 10d

Chapter 25: 1b; 2c; 3a; 4d; 5b; 6d; 7b; 8b; 9a; 10c

Chapter 26: 1d; 2b; 3b; 4c; 5b; 6c; 7a; 8b; 9a; 10c

Chapter 27: 1b; 2d; 3c; 4b; 5a; 6c; 7d; 8a; 9c; 10d

Notes